# Raymond Aron's Philosophy of Political Responsibility

# RAYMOND ARON'S PHILOSOPHY OF POLITICAL RESPONSIBILITY

## *Freedom, Democracy, and National Identity*

CHRISTOPHER ADAIR-TOTEFF

EDINBURGH
University Press

Edinburgh University Press is one of the leading university presses in the UK. We publish academic books and journals in our selected subject areas across the humanities and social sciences, combining cutting-edge scholarship with high editorial and production values to produce academic works of lasting importance. For more information visit our website: edinburghuniversitypress.com



Edinburgh University Press Ltd
The Tun – Holyrood Road, 12(2f) Jackson's Entry, Edinburgh EH8 8PJ

First published in hardback by Edinburgh University Press 2019

Typeset in 10.5/12.5 pt Sabon by
Servis Filmsetting Ltd, Stockport, Cheshire
and printed and bound by CPI Group (UK) Ltd,
Croydon, CR0 4YY

A CIP record for this book is available from the British Library

ISBN 978 1 4744 4708 9 (hardback)
ISBN 978 1 4744 4709 6 (paperback)
ISBN 978 1 4744 4710 2 (webready PDF)
ISBN 978 1 4744 4711 9 (epub)

# Contents

# *Raymond Aron: An Introduction*

"'What would you do?'"
Raymond Aron[1]

Raymond Aron was one of the most respected and admired intellectuals of the twentieth century, but he was also one of the most influential critics of those same twentieth-century intellectuals. This combination of being part of one group yet being critical of it was typical of Raymond Aron. It meant that he was often regarded as an "outsider": someone who counseled prudence and responsibility, and who combined theory with facts. He was born a French citizen and remained a French patriot all of his life, but his inclination to things French was largely overshadowed by the influence of German, English, and American thinkers. In addition, Aron combined political realism with philosophical rigor and emphasized the importance of the individual but never at the cost to society. He was a philosopher, a sociologist, and a historian but, above all, he was a political thinker. He had the ability to see a political issue in its various manifestations, to diagnose it as a political problem, and then to provide the proper solution for it. He rejected accounts if they were too simplistic, but he did not embrace complex ones merely because they appeared more philosophical. Rather, he thoughtfully appraised the situation and then offered a proper solution. In essence, Aron was never content to be just a *thinker*; he was a *doer* as well. Thoughts and results mattered equally to him. Aron valued truth and honesty over collegiality and even friendship – his break with many of his left-leaning friends was a testimony to that. Like many of them, Aron was often driven by his convictions, but unlike most of them, he always possessed a strong sense of responsibility. In his memoir about Raymond Aron, Edward Shils set out to describe his fellow political thinker, sociologist, and friend. Shils wrote of Aron's "respect for truth" and "his devotion to freedom", his "tenacious courage" and his "lucidity of outlook." Shils alluded to the fact that these qualities were rare and set Aron apart from many of their contemporaries; however, Shils believed that Aron had one quality that was even rarer. In Max Weber's term, it was the "Verantwortungsethik," meaning the "ethics of responsibility" (Shils 1985: 1–3). This type of ethics will be discussed in the chapter on Weber, and like Weber, Aron was convinced that the genuine political actor needed to consider the possible outcomes of his actions. Later in his life, Aron would write that Weber had taught him the importance of responsibility and the need to value consequences more than convictions (Aron 1990: 53). Aron was one of the most astute diagnosticians of political problems but he was also one of the most realistic of those political thinkers who tried to find genuine solutions to those problems. As I began writing this book, I began to realize how important thought and action were for Aron's political philosophy. However, after a short time, I realized that there was another theme in his thinking: one that was less visible but more important. This is the idea of political responsibility. It is a major notion in Max Weber's political work and it is found in Carl von Clausewitz's military writings, but it is central to Raymond Aron's thoughts about politics and policy. It is the focus on responsibility in this book that separates it from other books on Raymond Aron's political thinking. Other scholars have chosen to highlight other themes in Aron's work. Daniel J. Mahoney chose liberalism in his *The Liberal Political Science of Raymond Aron*. Brian C. Anderson opted for politics in *Raymond Aron: The Recovery of the Political*. Reed M. Davis emphasized understanding in *A Politics of Understanding: The International Thought of Raymond Aron*. These are fine and informative books and they ought to be read by anyone who is interested in Aron's political philosophy. However, none of these scholars considered how critical the sense of responsibility was to Aron. The term responsibility is missing from the indexes of all three books. Nor is the sense of responsibility found in any of the chapters in José Colen and Élisabeth Dutartre-Michaut's *The Companion to Raymond Aron*. Yet, it seems to me that it is one of the most crucial notions, if not *the* most crucial one, in Aron's thinking. The fact that other scholars have not accorded much importance to it is one of the reasons why I do not spend much time discussing their books. Another is that I did not want to spend time exploring their interpretations but instead prefer to try to explain what Aron thought about various people and ideas because, like Davis, Mahoney, Reed, and others, I am convinced that Raymond Aron was one of the greatest political philosophers of the twentieth century and one whose concepts, ideas, and interests continue to resonate into the twenty-first century.

## THE LIFE OF RAYMOND ARON

There are many aspects of Aron's life and work that will be omitted in this book. He was a highly respected journalist and a well-regarded columnist, who wrote thousands of pages for various French journals, newspapers, and periodicals, but all of those would be of interest mostly to scholars of French history and politics. He was actively engaged in editorial work and was politically active, but that part of his life will also be absent from these pages. Thus, this book is neither a basic introduction to Raymond Aron nor is it a general treatise on his politics. Instead, I will concentrate on his philosophy of history, his appreciation for Max Weber and Carl von Clausewitz, and his explorations of war, peace, ideology, and liberty. And I intend to demonstrate the importance that the concept of responsibility plays in his political philosophy.

There are two biographies of Raymond Aron: one in English and one in French. Robert Colquhoun published his two-volume work first in 1986. Volume one covered the years 1905–55 and had the subtitle *The Philosopher in History*, while volume two covered the years from 1955 until Aron's death in 1983; its subtitle was *The Sociologist in Society*. Nicolas Baverez published *Raymond Aron: Un Moraliste au temps des idéologies* in 1993. Both biographies are rich in details and are extremely helpful in understanding Aron's life and works. Unfortunately, Baverez's book has not been translated into English. However, Baverez provides a brief but informative overview in his "Life and Works: Raymond Aron, Philosopher and Freedom Fighter." This essay is the first chapter in the recently published *Companion to Raymond Aron*. Then there are Aron's own memoirs: the French original appeared in 1983 while the English translation was published in 1990. While the biographies by Baverez and Colquhoun are scholarly masterpieces, Aron's memoirs are more reflective of both his politics and his wit.

Raymond Aron was born on March 14, 1905 in an apartment on the Rue Notre-Dame-des Champs in Paris. He was the fourth child born to Gustave and Suzanne Aron. Their first child had died at birth, Adrien was born in 1902, and Robert the following year. Raymond wrote that he remembered nothing of the apartment but that is because the Aron family soon moved to an apartment on the Boulevard Montparnasse. He was tutored at home until he was eight and then went to the Lycée Hoche. He then could have gone to the Lycée Louis-le-Grand but chose instead to attend the Lycée Condorcet because it was closer. It was there that he took a course in philosophy; it not only affected Aron in terms of philosophy but steered him to the left politically. In 1924 he entered the prestigious École Normale Supérieure, where he continued to study philosophy and formed friendships with a small group of others who were interested in philosophy, including Jean-Paul Sartre. The study of philosophy was primarily limited to epistemology and the history of philosophy; the professors who taught there were not very interested in the philosophers who followed after Kant. There was almost nothing on Hegel or Marx, and there was virtually no political philosophy. Aron's favorite philosopher was Kant and he wrote a 40,000–word essay on Kantian philosophy that was lost for many years. According to Colquhoun, Aron never reread it but always remembered the importance that philosophy had for him. Colquhoun also noted that, while at the École Normale Supérieure, Aron was also greatly interested in politics; thus, he was already combining philosophical thinking with political action (Colquhoun 1986a: 30, 33). Aron's favorite professor there was Léon Brunschvicg, who, Aron wrote, was "a mandarin among mandarins" and who "philosophized" more than the others. Aron respected him and he appreciated Brunschvicg's attempts to combine philosophy and science (Aron 1990: 26).

In his memoirs, Aron passes over the eighteen months that he was in military service and in 1930 he obtained a position at the university in Cologne, Germany. It was there that he began to read Marx but admitted that he did not know enough economics to judge *Das Kapital* competently. And it was there that he fell in love with German culture and recognized the "elective affinity" ("Wahlverwandschaft") that he had with Max Weber (Aron 1990: 40–1, 43). But it was there that he witnessed the final years of the Weimar Republic and Hitler's rise to power, and it was in 1932 that he met Suzanne Gauchon, who became his wife the following year (Aron 1990: 51–2). Their first daughter, Dominique, was born in 1934. In 1935, he became a part-time lecturer at two different schools in France. In March of 1938, he defended his doctoral theses and was appointed as a lecturer at Toulouse. Between 1935 and 1938, Aron wrote three books, one on sociology and two on the philosophy of history. He had little positive to say about the philosophy books, later asserting that *Introduction to the Philosophy of History* was too symmetrical. In contrast, he thought that his *Contemporary German Sociology* had considerable merit because it drew French people's attention to the German sociologists. While some knew the name of Max Weber, few French people recognized names such as Werner Sombart or Karl Mannheim (Aron 1990: 78–9).

When World War Two broke out, Aron was assigned to the weather service in Charleville in the northern part of France, but he spent most of his time reading and writing. The long-anticipated German offensive occurred during the early part of May 1940; as a result, Aron was forced to move further south and was able to meet with his wife in Toulouse. They discussed whether Aron should leave for Great Britain, which he did, arriving there on June 26 (Colquhoun 1986a: 214). Aron wrote that he had joined a tank outfit but that he was directed to do accounting work. However, several people persuaded him to give that up and to write articles for the newly established journal, *La France libre*. Aron was rather proud of his articles because they reflected his understanding of the war and what the meaning of the war was to the people of France. More importantly, he believed that he was defending democracy without resorting to propaganda (Aron 1990: 119, 121–2). Aron also indicated that he had learned English and moved in some English circles. None the less, he lived primarily among the French and he later wrote that there was never any question in his mind that, once it was possible, he would return to France: "I would never change my country. I would be French or I would have no country" (Aron 1990: 133).

Suzanne was able to join Aron in July 1943 and their daughter Emmanuelle was born June 18 of the following year. Those were not the only changes in Aron's life. In his memoirs, he wrote how he had grown indifferent to the epistemological issues that he had found so interesting before the war. And he suggested that, although he had written for *La France libre* for years, he did not consider himself a journalist until he began to write for *Combat* in March of 1946 (Aron 1990: 140–1, 149–50). Unfortunately, *Combat* soon failed and in 1947 Aron started writing for *Le Figaro*, which he would continue to do for the next thirty years (Aron 1990: 157). He considered the years between 1945 and 1955 the decade that he was a journalist. Yet he admitted that he never had the journalist's love of the new and he was not always comfortable with his colleagues (Aron 1990: 178).

The period 1946 to 1955 was an eventful one for Aron. There was the birth of their third daughter, Laurence, in July of 1950 and the death of Emmanuelle of leukemia in December of that same year. Aron wrote that he was overcome by sorrow and sought relief in work (Aron 1990: 229–30). He continued writing for *Le Figaro* but gave lectures in Frankfurt in 1946 and 1950, and was a visiting professor at Tübingen in 1953. In the spring of 1955, he published *The Opium of the Intellectuals* and shortly after that became a professor of sociology at the Sorbonne. Colquhoun wrote that Aron's failure to obtain a professorship in 1948 was largely due to factors that were beyond his control but he also suggested that Aron had not had the right degree of deference to those who were in charge of making the decision. Colquhoun indicated that when the opportunity arose again in 1955, Aron had changed his attitude and that he really wanted to return to the university (Colquhoun 1986b: 3–4). Aron wrote that giving lectures in French, English, and German kept him in shape, and when he moved to the Sorbonne after a twenty-seven-year absence, he found that nothing had changed. However, Aron admitted that he departed from tradition and chose topics that were not typical, addressing the subject in an objective manner. His first course was on industrial society and he discussed the five-year plans, collective agriculture, and the show trials. He justified this because the Soviet Union was considered the ideal type of regime and he believed that it was one of the tasks of sociology to help students break free from their prejudices. He confessed that his lecture hall was not packed but the number of students increased each year. However, he attributed that more to the increase in the number of students admitted rather than to any increase in interest (Aron 1990: 232, 235). Aron turned his lectures on industrial society into a book, which was then translated into English as *Eighteen Lectures on Industrial Society*. Aron would often turn his lectures into books and many of them were translated into English.[2] He seemed aloof; as a result, students rarely sought him out. He seemed rigorous; consequently, students often thought him cruel (Aron 1990: 235–7). It seemed that Aron was bothered not only by the students but also by the whole issue of higher education in France. Colquhoun listed a number of points that Aron was critical of: the almost total autonomy of the professor; the indifference that most French professors felt towards their colleagues' work; the too high degree of difficulty of the final examination at the end of secondary education and its inadequacy for determining entrance into the university; and finally, the fact there was no proper preparation for either teaching or research (Colquhoun 1986b: 327–8).

The year 1968 was a watershed one for France and for much of the Western world. It was the year of student unrest in the United States and in many European countries. It was also a year of significant unrest in France. It proved to be a crucial time for Aron in several ways. In January, Aron resigned from the Sorbonne but that did not mean that all of his ties to the university were cut. He followed the May disturbances with a growing sense of dismay. While he agreed with many of the students' complaints, he was wary of their demands. He was particularly concerned about the students with working-class backgrounds because he knew that they were suffering general hardships. In contrast, he had little respect for the better-off students. Aron thought that they were play-acting as revolutionaries and he believed that no one could reason with them. Aron was scheduled to travel to the United States, where he was to give three lectures, but was so alarmed by what was happening in France that he cut his visit short. Because of the airline strikes, he had to fly to Brussels and then make his way back to Paris. He published a number of articles in which he was quite critical of both the students and the authorities. As a result, he was criticized by many but one of the most vicious attacks came from Sartre. Sartre insisted that Aron had never challenged himself and had no right to be a professor. Aron later wrote that he was not angered and he did not respond. He left it up to his friends if they wanted to defend him. As for himself, he said that he was always challenged by his students and by himself; not to be so meant that one was probably stagnating. Aron was somewhat sympathetic towards some of the professors who capitulated to the students because he understood their fear of being ostracized (Aron 1990: 313–26; Colquhoun 1986b: 327–45).

Colquhoun wrote that many students followed Aron when he started teaching at the École Pratique des Hautes Études and they enrolled in his Friday seminar. He gave that every year from 1968 until 1977 and Colquhoun quotes from Alain Besançon, who was a participant in the seminar. Besançon wrote that a person presented his or her paper and then Aron reformulated the student's thesis before making his critique. He noted that everyone who presented a paper felt trepidation, even a student in his early fifties who knew his subject well and had evidently seen combat. Even he was reduced to a stammer (Colquhoun 1986b: 366–8). Aron's students were not his disciples because he had no doctrine, but they respected him greatly. He also joined the faculty at the Collège de France and gave twelve courses, turning three of them into books. In his opinion, the others were not good enough to warrant publication. The three were the lectures from 1970–1, which formed *The Imperial Republic*; those from 1971–1972, which became *Clausewitz*; and those from 1975–6, which made up *The Decline of the West*. Colquhoun adds that Aron held seminars in the early part of 1978 and was made emeritus in the fall of 1981.

During the latter part of his life, Aron taught and did research at numerous institutions around the world. He lectured at Harvard and at the London School of Economics. He gave the Jefferson Lectures at the University of California at Berkeley and the Gifford Lectures at the University of Aberdeen. He was honored by many institutions – he was awarded honorary degrees from Brandeis, Cambridge, Chicago,

Harvard, Hebrew University of Jerusalem, Louvain, Oxford, Seoul, and Southampton. After his death, *The Times* published an obituary in which it noted that "he collected Honorary Doctorates as other men collect postage stamps" (quoted in Colquhoun 1986b: 595). In honor of his sixty-fifth birthday, he was presented with a two-volume "Festschrift," which contained fifty essays. The contributors included Edward Shils, Michael Polanyi, and Daniel Bell. Aron was also awarded the André Arnoux Prize, the Paul Valéry Prize, and the first Alexis de Tocqueville Prize (Colquhoun 1986b: 370).

In April 1977, Aron suffered a stroke, which left him paralyzed; it took him months to regain his speech and mobility, and he realized that he would likely never recover fully. Colquhoun wrote that Aron was able to give his thirteen lectures for a course at the Collège de France but they were to be his last. He was able to travel to give some lectures but he read them in French, English, and German (Colquhoun 1986b: 521–3). He became Chairman of the Editorial Committee for *Le Figaro* but resigned shortly after and moved to *L'Express*, where he continued to write until resigning in 1981. That same year, he became emeritus professor at the Collège de France. The number of publications between 1977 and 1982 dropped significantly but he still managed to publish eleven works in 1977; fifteen in 1978; ten in 1979; eight in 1980; ten in 1981; and eight in 1982. Some of these works were reprints or updated editions of older writings and some were short contributions to journals. None the less, it was an impressive number from someone who had suffered a stroke and was in his seventies.

In 1983, Aron offered to testify in a libel suit. He had reviewed a book written by Zeev Sternhell, in which the Israeli historian suggested that Bertrand de Jouvenel was a "fellow traveler" in the 1930s. Aron indicated his displeasure about Sternhell's charge that Jouvenel was a collaborator during the Nazi Occupation of France. Jouvenel decided to sue both Sternhell and his publisher for libel and Aron offered to testify on his behalf. Aron testified on October 17 and, after doing so, he left the courtroom and climbed into a car that was waiting to take him to the offices of *L'Express*. According to Colquhoun, he died almost immediately from a massive heart attack. Baverez indicated that, after watching the suffering that his brother Robert had gone through, as well as Sartre's decline, Aron would have preferred a sudden death to their long illnesses (Bavarez 1993: 504). Aron had uttered his last words just minutes before getting into the car. Referring to his testimony, Aron remarked, "I think I said what needed saying." Colquhoun suggested that that sentence could serve as Aron's epitaph (Colquhoun 1986b: 591).

Raymond Aron published forty books and the three most famous of these are *The Opium of the Intellectuals, Peace and War,* and *Clausewitz.* Aron maintained that people's reactions to *The Opium of the Intellectuals* were divided according to their politics, with right-wing types approving of it and left-wing types disliking it. But many people appeared to misunderstand what Aron was attempting to convey (Aron 1990: 223–34). Aron had thought about writing a book on international relations for a decade and *Peace and War* was the result. When it appeared, Aron thought it "significant" but later admitted that he "probably exaggerated its value." Henry Kissinger thought Aron's book brilliant but difficult; however, Aron did not think the latter was applicable. Leo Strauss thought it was the best book on the subject (Aron 1990: 302–3). By 1972, Aron was ready to write another large book and ended up working on Clausewitz. Aron did not appear to offer much of an evaluation of his book but he noted that the Napoleonic Wars seemed civilized, compared to the wars of the twentieth century (Aron 1990: 409–11).

Aron wrote thousands of columns, articles, and essays. In his biography of Aron, Colquhoun has two bibliographies. That in volume one is eighteen pages long while the other in volume two covers twenty-nine pages (Colquhoun 1986a: 501–19; Colquhoun 1986b: 615–44).[3] Colquhoun's biography of Aron is also massive – it totals more than 1,200 pages and Baverez's biography is 542 pages long, so my account here has only touched on some of the important points in Aron's life. And this book can only provide an account of some of the critical issues that Aron wrote about and leaves many others untouched. This book is an attempt to provide Aron's answers to the question "what would you do?"

## THE CHAPTERS

This book is composed of eight chapters; seven of these are approximately the same length while the eighth is rather brief. Five are on ideas whereas two are on individuals, and one short chapter is devoted to Aron's legacy. The chapters can be read as independent essays, yet there is a chronological order to them and together they provide an account of Aron's political philosophy.

Chapter One is "On History" and covers both Aron's early philosophy of history and his understanding of, and appreciation for, history. For Aron, history was both an object of study in its own right as well as the instrument that was necessary for responsible politics. His interest, if not fascination, with history can be divided into two groups: his interest in the philosophy of history from his pre-war years and his understanding of how history can inform politics from his post-war years. The early philosophy of history is Neo-Kantian in origin and reflects the ideas of German thinkers such as Heinrich Rickert and Max Weber but also of Aron's own French philosophers. His writings are not easy to understand and have been regarded as less than successful; however, his training as a philosopher and his theories regarding history are crucial for grasping his approach to political theory and political action. This is evident by his treatment of causality and his discussion about reality. It is also important for his understanding of international relations and the causes of war. Finally, it is crucial for his notion of intelligibility. History cannot offer us a guarantee of how the future will be, but it can provide us with an idea of what might happen. Similarly, we cannot look at the past and insist that it had to have happened as it did. However, we can consider what might have happened if other choices had been made. We lack the certainty that is found in the natural sciences but we do possess a type of probabilistic thinking. And it is the study of historical examples that can help us in making our choices about the future.

Chapter Two is "On Weber" and it is reflective of Aron's own use of Weber's theoretical and political thinking. This chapter builds upon the previous one by considering how Weber's sociological thinking differed from Rickert's philosophy of history but it also moves in a new direction by considering the impact that Weber's political philosophy had on Aron's own political thinking. While Aron did focus more on Weber's sociology in his early writings, his concern with Weber's politics is clearly evident. Yet it is in Aron's later writings that his preoccupation with Weberian political thinking becomes really pronounced. And Aron's most definitive discussion of Weber's politics is found in his lecture at the 1964 conference of the Deutsche Gesellschaft für Soziologie. In that lecture, Aron both explained Weber's national politics and defended his political realism. Aron may have always been inclined towards a politics of prudence but Weber certainly contributed to his politics of responsibility. There is no doubt that there were many individuals who helped form Aron's thinking, but there is also little question that Max Weber was one of the most important influences, if not the major one.

Chapter Three is "On Clausewitz" and it reveals both the depth and the breadth of Aron's understanding of the great German general's writings on war. Aron intended to understand Clausewitz's views and not substitute his own. Furthermore, he was willing to challenge some of the accepted opinions and showed that they were often based upon an erroneous reading of Clausewitz's writings. Aron admitted that he borrowed from his predecessors in developing his account of Clausewitz's theories regarding war, yet he went far beyond them in the second volume when he showed how relevant Clausewitz is in the atomic age. Aron's book on Clausewitz is a masterful exposition of some difficult material and a contentious topic. While it never achieved the popularity of *The Opium of the Intellectuals*, Aron's *Clausewitz* is a superb book that deserves reading.

Chapter Four is "On War." If one assumes, as Aron did, that conflict is inevitable between nations and that there is no institution that can resolve these conflicts peaceably, then war is inevitable at some point. Aron devoted much of his life to the study of conflict by reading Weber for political conflicts and by studying Clausewitz for war. Aron agreed with them about the need to be realistic and recognized that many factors contributed to quarrels between states. However, Aron disagreed with many other scholars because, in his estimation, they paid far too much attention to economic factors and neglected the political ones. Furthermore, his studies of war showed that, as much as war has been historically disastrous, they were showing him that a modern nuclear war would be devastating. That is why he wrote about the century of war and about total war; it was necessary to understand what had happened during previous wars in order to develop a better sense of what would likely occur in a war with atomic bombs. He argued that one should not be naïve and expect peace, but one should anticipate war; the realistic approach was far more likely to forestall a nuclear conflict. Aron did not live to see the end of the Cold War but it is likely that he would warn us against complacency. He understood human nature better than many scholars and recognized that history was often cyclical; just because we are in a time of peace does not mean that a time of war will not come in the future.

Chapter Five is "On Peace" but it could have been entitled "On International Relations" because it contains Aron's theory of international relations. Although the title of Aron's book is a play on Tolstoy's *War and Peace*, it is a serious examination of the causes of war and the realistic hopes for peace. And, while Aron places himself firmly in the Realism category, his account also includes morality. Thus, it is a combination of politics and ethics, and is seemingly at odds with Weber's theory of politics, which excludes questions of morality. However, this is only an apparent contradiction because Weber endorses the "ethics of responsibility." Aron follows Weber in this, particularly in the section on "Conviction and Responsibility." Like Weber, Aron knows that force is part of politics and its use is often justified, but he insists that force must be used responsibly. Thus there are tensions in international relations: between power and ethics, between idealism and realism, and between peace and war. It is Aron's attempt to set out these tensions and to offer a reasonable way to balance them. As in other cases, he recognizes the damage that comes with failure so emphasizes that states should adopt a posture in the international arena that is reasonable, prudent, and responsible.

Chapter Six is "On Ideology and Totalitarianism"; it does not just focus on these two ideas but incorporates ideas from several other people. Aron began his life-long study of ideology by reading Karl Mannheim. Like his friend Edward Shils, Aron was at first rather impressed by Mannheim's examination of the concept of ideology, but also like Shils, Aron grew dissatisfied with Mannheim's rather Marxist-leaning account. In 1955, Aron published *L'Opium des intellectuels*, his most famous book, which has been translated into numerous languages. The English translation did not prompt the same amount of disruption that the original French version had, but it still was strongly criticized by leftists in the United States. Aron's major topic was Communist ideology but he also included the ideology of the Nazis. Thus there is an association between ideology and totalitarianism. As Shils was Aron's "companion" regarding ideology, one can consider Hannah Arendt as Aron's "companion" in respect to totalitarianism. And, while he shared many of the same criticisms of the nature and effects of totalitarianism, it seems that his approach was slightly more understanding of its causes. In other words, his approach was not quite as dogmatic as Arendt's in that he understood better why people were drawn to its power. In this sense, his understanding of ideology was similar to that regarding totalitarianism. He was heavily critical of both and denounced them for their pernicious effects, but he realized why people were attracted to them. Finally, he was never as certain as some others that people had reached the "end of ideology": that is why he appended the question mark to it.

Chapter Seven is "On Freedom." However, Aron places his analysis of what it means to be free in three different contexts. One is his contrast between the historical accounts of freedom: specifically, the one offered by de Tocqueville and the one given by the young Marx. Another is Aron's comments on and criticisms of F. A. Hayek's account of individualistic freedom, and while he finds much that is attractive in Hayek's view, he ultimately determines that it is based too much on economic philosophy and does not consider how far the individual is also part of a group. Aron's third context is placing his account of freedom within the confines of modern industrial technology. While many innovations have made life easier, he is concerned that they also end up isolating individuals and detracting from our roles within the political process. The focus of this chapter is not purely analytical; it also attempts to emphasize the passion that Aron felt for freedom and the importance politics had for him. Yet politics is more than a realm where force operates; it is also a forum for reason, prudence, and responsibility. Even when Aron is championing freedom, he does so with moderation and respect.

The final chapter is Chapter Eight and it is devoted to the legacy of Raymond Aron. It is divided into three sections. The first is an account of his legacy from the time of his death until the present. The second is my own assessment of Aron's legacy while the third is an attempt to look into the future. Accordingly, the first section is the most objective, the second is the most subjective, and the third is the most provisional. One would hope that Aron would have no quarrel with any of these three approaches because they each mirror his own approaches to people and ideas. Aron was a believer in historical truth and factual accuracy: hence scholarship is an "objective" science. Yet he recognized that time and place influenced one's outlook: hence there is a subjective element in any analysis. Finally, he understood that history could only be a guide to what is known, and while the future cannot be foretold with any degree of certainty, we are naturally inclined to speculate about it.

The first seven chapters are intended to explain Aron's approaches to people and concepts and to show the importance of thought and action in his political thinking. Above all, they are intended to help catalogue how much he believed that the concept of responsibility must play in any reasonable and prudent political philosophy. The final chapter is designed to address Aron's continuing relevance and to demonstrate that his insistence on being responsible should resonate today.

## NOTES

1. The sentence is: "what would you do if you were in his place?" It was the question that Joseph Pagnon, an undersecretary in the Foreign Ministry, posed to Aron in 1932. Aron had returned from Germany and had talked at length about the dangers of Hitler and the Nazis. The reference to the other person was to Édouard Herriot, who was the head of the Foreign Ministry (Aron 1990: 40). It seems that Aron learned much from this exchange and he never forgot the lesson of "what would you do?" "Mais vous qui m'avez si bien parlé de l'Allemagne et des perils qui lèvent à l'horizon, que feriez-vous si vous étiez à sa place?" (Aron 1983b: 59).

2. Colquhoun provides a list of Aron's lectures that he gave at the Sorbonne during the thirteen years that he taught there (1955–68). Colquhoun also notes which ones were made into books and which ones were translated into English (Colquhoun 1986b: 7–8).
3. There is a complete bibliography of Aron's writings online at <http: raymond-aron.ehess.fr> (last accessed 30 August 2018).

# CHAPTER ONE

# On history

"Men of learning have discovered the secret of fire but not that
of history."
Raymond Aron[1]

Raymond Aron was always interested in many different things but the
two that stand out clearly are *politics* and *history*. Aron believed that
it was necessary to have a good understanding of history in order to
inform one's politics. That is also why he thought Miriam Bernheim
Conant's choice of title for her collection of his writings, *Politics and
History*, was clearly appropriate. It was so because it was an accurate
reflection of his twin concerns. The placement of "politics" before "history" in the title might seem to indicate the importance of the former
over the latter; however, Aron believed that the study of history should
precede the action of politics because one must have understanding in
order to act wisely and responsibly. This emphasis on the temporal
primacy of history is evident in the chronology of Aron's own writings.
Thus his work on the philosophy of history comes before his writings
on the politics of responsibility, but it is also obvious because of his
conviction that historical thought should guide responsible political
action.

The focus of this chapter is Aron's interest in history, or to put it
more accurately, his fascination with history. His fascination encompassed actual histories as well as the philosophy of history. And, as
he never seemed to tire of saying, actual histories and the philosophy
of history are closely connected (see Aron 1961: 13). Yet, his major
focus was on understanding what history was: that is, a philosophy of
history. This is apparent in the description that he gave: "intelligible
history," which means that Aron did not subscribe to the older notion
of history "as it happened" but believed that the historian selected

certain events and attempted to explain how they occurred and why they mattered. Aron did not use the phrase "intelligible history" until rather late in his life but this idea of understanding is found throughout his writings about history. Given his life-long preoccupation with history, it is rather remarkable that scholars have not examined his various notions of history in more detail.[2] The focus here is to trace Aron's conceptions of history and his philosophy of history from his earliest historical writings to his later ones. His writings can be broken down into two major periods, with the Second World War as the major division between them. The first, rather brief, period is his "pure philosophy" and the second, much longer, period is his "applied philosophy."[3] As much as Aron was always preoccupied with history, he was not especially interested in history for history's sake. Rather, his concern was how the political philosopher can, and *should*, learn from history. The goal here is to show what Aron understood history to be and how his appreciation for it influenced his political thinking. Rather than being an account of a dry philosophical study, this chapter helps to explain one of the key points of reference for Aron's philosophy of responsible politics. Accordingly, this account of Aron's philosophy of history helps set the stage for each of the following chapters.

## ARON'S PRE-WAR WRITINGS ON THE PHILOSOPHY OF HISTORY

In his "Introduction" to Miriam Bernheim Conant's collection of his writings, Aron downplays the importance of his pre-war work on the philosophy of history. While he noted that the criticisms of his dissertation were excessive, he admitted that they were rather justified.[4] This was especially true of his first attempt at writing a dissertation, but Aron apparently thought that his successfully defended second one was not much better. Aron argued in his "Introduction" that, while readers may understand a work better than its author, he insisted that the author understands his own intentions better than any reader (Aron 1978b: xvii). Aron's claim may be debatable but it is certainly true that his two early writings on the philosophy of history suffer from some significant defects. Therefore, they will be treated rather briefly in this chapter while the major focus will be on his later writings on history.

According to Aron's biographer, Robert Colquhoun, Aron's first attempt at writing his dissertation was a failure. That it would likely be considered a failure is suggested by its title: *Essai sur la théorie dans l'Allemagne contemporaine: La Philosophie critique de l'histoire* and that was because it promised far more than its young author could possibly deliver.[5] Colquhoun explained that Aron's dissertation director, Léon Brunschvicg, thought it insufficient but Aron himself later regarded that as "severe criticism." Later, Aron explained that Brunschvicg's "severe criticism" was probably warranted in large part because Aron had concentrated on Wilhelm Dilthey, Georg Simmel, Heinrich Rickert, and Max Weber. Aron added that Brunschvicg had suggested that Aron should not provide an account of four rather unknown (in France, at least) thinkers, but should offer his own theoretical account. But, as Colquhoun noted, Aron's first attempt at writing his dissertation is "an essential preliminary" to Aron's second, and successful, dissertation (Colquhoun 1986a: 119–20). It may not be essential but it is difficult to understand. Part of this is because of its subject and part of it is because of its language. As Colquhoun noted, it was written in a rather Germanic style but the major obstacle to comprehension was the sheer scope of Aron's book (Colquhoun 1986a: 120). While Aron did not offer a complete survey of modern philosophies of history, he did provide extensive chapters on four its major representatives: Dilthey and Simmel on the "psychological" point of departure and Rickert and Weber on the "logical" view. Any one of these thinkers would be challenging enough, but to attempt to explain all four was a task that was undoubtedly doomed to failure.[6]

Aron pointed out Dilthey's similarities to Kant: just as Kant had sought to discover the sources and limits of understanding in his *Kritik der reinen Vernunft*, Dilthey sought to find the origins and the limits of historical reason in his *Einleitung in die Geisteswissenschaften* (Aron 1950a: 24–5; Aron 1983b: 110). Yet it seemed as if Aron did not think that highly of Dilthey's attempt because he suggested that it was made up from many sources: Kant, Hegel, and Nietzsche, to name three (Aron 1950a: 25, 109–10). Furthermore, it seemed that Dilthey was not able even to present the problems correctly, much less offer an answer. In contrast, Aron appeared to have thought better of Simmel, although he noted that Simmel appeared to follow some of Dilthey's ideas such as the emphasis on life and the importance of ethics (Aron 1950a: 166, 169). What Aron appeared to have valued in Simmel's writings was Simmel's progressive thinking. That is probably why Aron continuously noted the variations in the successive editions of Simmel's writings and why he juxtaposed Simmel's "Lebensphilosophie" ("philosophy of life") with his notion of historical laws. This is supported by Aron's emphasis on the changes in Simmel's *Die Probleme der Geschichtsphilosophie* from the first edition (1892) to the second (1905) to the third (1907) (Aron 1950a: 165, 167, 186–7, 189). It is also supported by Aron's choice of title for his first section on Simmel: "Philosophie de la vie et logique de l'histoire" ("Philosophy of Life and the Logic of History") (Aron

1950a: 159). This underscores the dual aspects of Simmel's thought: his emphasis on both the subjective and the objective – that is, internal inspection and external knowledge (Aron 1950a: 165). Aron, though, not only points out that these two are opposites, but also questions whether there are historical laws (Aron 1950a: 189). However, Aron suggested that the point of natural science is to try to predict the future and it uses laws to do so, but that the point of historical science is to understand the past (Aron 1950a: 189–91). Aron insisted that as much as Simmel contributed to developing a philosophy of history, he was never a historian in the proper sense of the word (Aron 1950a: 203). Instead, Simmel was a philosopher and a sociologist, and there was an epistemological tension between his earlier sociological writings and his later metaphysical "Lebensphilosophie." None the less, Aron contended that Simmel was always concerned with the philosophy of culture and still had much to say to us (Aron 1950a: 206–9). In particular, Aron praised Simmel for showing us that culture should be regarded not as a fixed thing but instead as a continuing process (Aron 1950a: 209, 213). This emphasis on process and change reveals the influence of Schopenhauer and Nietzsche on Simmel's philosophy in general and particularly on his philosophy of history (Aron 1950a: 218).

Heinrich Rickert was rather dismissive of "Lebensphilosophie" in its various forms and mostly objected to Schopenhauer's and Nietzsche's influence in philosophy. That is because he insisted that philosophy had to be rigorous and not subjective or psychological. Aron correctly identified Rickert's major focus, which was the formation of concepts, and also correctly emphasized Rickert's overall concern with values (Aron 1950a: 115–17). He also carefully explained that Rickert held that the historical sciences had different concept formations than the natural sciences: the former were interested in particular concepts for individual events whereas the latter generated universal laws for general theories (Aron 1950a: 118–23). Before turning to his criticism of Rickert, Aron noted that Rickert had just died and that he was already being forgotten (Aron 1950a: 141). Since Dilthey and Simmel were still regarded as offering important ideas on the philosophy of history, Aron hinted that it was sad that the same was not thought about Rickert. After all, Aron praised Rickert for having correctly identified the problem of how to develop historical concepts. None the less, Rickert unfortunately failed to establish a reliable method for employing them (Aron 1950a: 154–7).

How much Max Weber borrowed from Rickert is still a matter of dispute, but Aron believed that Weber had learned considerably from his friend and colleague. Aron was of the opinion that Weber adapted the notion of selection from Rickert and the emphasis on values. However, as Colquhoun maintained, Aron had "almost unreserved admiration" for Weber and that was because Weber alone came closest to "clarifying the problems posed by the critical history of philosophy" (Colquhoun 1986a: 124). Aron maintained that one of Weber's most valuable contributions to the discussion of history was his invention of the "ideal type." It was valuable because of its epistemological utility. It was "an instrument of investigation"; it was a heuristic device (Aron 1950a: 228, 234–5). According to Aron, Weber's second valuable contribution was his notion of historical causality. Aron noted that Weber regarded it as regressive and he mentioned how this was similar to causal explanation in law. The historian selects what was the likely cause of the historical event just as the lawyer selects what was the likely cause of the accident (Aron 1950a: 239). Weber's third contribution was his emphasis on the notion of choice. Unlike the Marxist account of historical determinism, Weber believed that humans were at liberty to choose. Weber did not mean that one's choices were unlimited and Aron noted that Weber often believed the choices were often limited. Furthermore, Aron noted that in selecting from a limited number of options, the historian acts similarly to the politician. In Aron's opinion, Max Weber was equally a political actor and an academic thinker (Aron 1950a: 219, 265).

Aron's first dissertation was not a success and not only because of its style and its scope. It was not successful because Aron did not offer a reasonable answer to the question about critical history: that is, what are the limits regarding an historical object. Aron may not have been able to provide an answer because he was too preoccupied with setting out and critiquing the philosophies of histories of Dilthey, Simmel, Rickert, and Weber, and, it may have been because he had not yet come close to formulating any plausible alternative. In contrast, Aron's second dissertation differed from the first in two respects: it was less critical and slightly more positive. This may be why the second dissertation was considerably more successful than the first one.

The notion of "successful", however, is a matter of interpretation. There is no doubt that the *Introduction to the Philosophy of History* was submitted and successfully defended, and there is little question that it became a somewhat influential work. However, it did not appear to achieve what Aron had intended to accomplish, which had been relatively minimal. As Aron noted in the "Introduction," this work should not be regarded as one belonging to the great idealist tradition; nor should it be considered as providing a definitive answer to the question regarding objectivity. Like many of the Neo-Kantians, Aron rejected Hegel's attempt to construct a complete account of history, replete with purposes and goals. And, like them, Aron rejected Ranke's attempt to offer an account of history "as it really happened." Like the Neo-Kantians in general and Max Weber in particular, Aron sought to provide an account of the limits of objectivity in history. By "objective," neither Aron nor Weber meant "impartial," but rather "universal" (Aron 1961: 9–12). But, even here, the term "universal" is rather misleading because, as Rickert and Weber had both shown, history is never simply a discussion about something "universal" in the sense of a "totality" or a "generality." Instead, history is always a particular process of selection – one that determines which past occurrences are worthy of being investigated.

Aron defined history in both a narrow sense and a wide sense: the former refers to the specific knowledge of the actual past while the latter refers to the general knowledge of the past (Aron 1961: 15). Aron began by insisting on the importance of the individual before moving on to general knowledge and that is why he placed so much emphasis on individual consciousness and individual memories. The past is remembered either as personal stories or as an impersonal history. A story is like a poem and it may play with words; history is more like a science so it must employ concepts. A story may have a point or it may simply be for entertainment; history should have a point because it is intended to educate. In this regard, history is similar to natural science; however, Aron argues that history utilizes concepts about individuals but that natural science employs concepts about generalities (Aron 1961: 29–30; Aron 1948: 31–2). The natural sciences can be regarded as constructive and logical; historical science must be considered to be descriptive and phenomenological. Unlike a natural science, history can never achieve a validity that would likely be universally accepted (Aron 1961: 44; Aron 1948: 45).

Historical knowledge is both objective and subjective because it is *about* us and it is *by* us. As such, our knowledge is the "most incontestable" as well as the most "mysterious" (Aron 1961: 49; Aron 1948: 53). While there is no question regarding the subjectivity of historical knowledge because it is a person's recalling the past, there may be some doubt in calling history "objective." That is because history is not simply about one's self, but also about others (Aron 1961: 55–9; Aron 1948: 57–64). Thus recollection is both subjective and objective, but as Aron points out, not every recollection is historical knowledge. Instead, he provisionally defines historical knowledge as the grasp of the past that is both spiritual and social (Aron 1961: 79; Aron 1948: 82).

Slightly later, Aron discusses what counts as historical knowledge. He notes that one can never succeed in divorcing a "historical atom" from its historical context; nor can history be regarded as reproducing events. The first is because no individual acts completely alone and the second because the historian reconstructs. The result is a "conceptual translation" and as such it is ideal (Aron 1961: 112–13; Aron 1948: 114–15). The process of "conceptual translation" proceeds in three steps: first, *recapitulation* of the idea; second, *construction* of the fact based upon the experiences of those who lived them; and third, *organization* of the consciousnesses. The first two steps seem understandable whereas the third does not. What Aron appears to mean is that the historian considers the idea, checks it through various sources, and then organizes it into a *"constructed fact."* However, he cautions against regarding this as objectively "given"; instead, it is merely conceptually given (Aron 1961: 119; Aron 1948: 120). Thus, the element of choice is present in the historian's account; and while it may seem to be liberating, it is also anarchical (Aron 1961: 144–9; Aron 1948: 147–50). The historian still bases his selection upon his attempt to tell a complete story; the historian is an "interpreter of all men" (Aron 1961: 154–5; Aron 1948: 155–6).[7]

The concept of cause is one of the two primary themes of the Third Section,[8] entitled "Historical Determinism and Causal Thought." Marx is the first theme and Weber is the second. Leaving aside historical determinism and Marx for the time being, Aron's appropriation of Weber's notion of causality is intriguing. Like Weber, Aron contended that the historian cannot definitively state that what happened had to happen; rather, the historian has to consider why it happened in the way that it did, as well as how it might have otherwise turned out. The natural scientist relies on laws and certainties, but the historian must deal with individual occurrences and probabilities. Here, Aron's debt to Weber is quite evident: he uses Weber's notions of "objective possibility" and "adequate cause."[9] What Weber meant by "adequate cause" was that something could be regarded as causing something to happen if it was likely to have been the cause of that happening. Turner and Factor point out that this is true in history and in law, but that the level of intent is more important for law than it is for history (Turner and Factor 1981: 7–8). By "objective possibility," Weber meant that a thing "makes sense" (Turner and Factor 1981: 5). Aron uses these phrases in discussing the possibility that the Persians had won at the battle of Marathon; if they had, then there would have been a theocratic government in Greece and Greek culture would have suffered (Aron 1961: 160–1). Thus it seems as if the distinction between the natural sciences and history is that the former operate under laws while the latter operates under "rules." These are general guidelines and are

21

said to apply to "normal cases." However, history is not composed of "normal cases" but of individual events – thus "singular causality" (Aron 1961: 163, 167). Aron changes Weber's theory of historical causality by adding the notion of responsibility. The historian wishes to assign responsibility and that implies determining intentions, similar to the lawyer. Unlike the lawyer, the historian does not seek someone to blame and that is because the historian's job is to understand and not to judge. The judge or moralist starts with the "offense" and then determines which party is guilty, followed by the determination of how much guilt is appropriate. In terms of war, the judge can determine who was responsible for starting the war and then assign the appropriate amount of blame. In contrast, the historian does not regard the war as a crime (Aron 1961: 170). This is mostly because the historian's approach to history differs from that of the lawyer (or judge) to a crime. The lawyer intends to prove that the accused did, in fact, commit this act and thus is responsible for the crime. There is a high degree of certainty that accompanies the lawyer's proof. In contrast, the historian is uninterested in proof since that is impossible. Rather, the historian is concerned with retrospective probability (Aron 1961: 172–3; Aron 1948: 175).[10] The historian can choose his or her degree of probability based upon the choice of "level." By that, Aron meant the choice to focus on something small and particular or something larger and more general. The first approach is microscopic and the second approach is macroscopic. Regardless of which approach is chosen, the historian is hindered to some degree and that is because the historian can never know for certain what would have happened if something had *not* occurred. Aron illustrated this by indicating that we will never know what would have happened if Archduke Ferdinand had *not* been assassinated in 1914 (Aron 1961: 181; Aron 1948: 185).

Aron indicates that there are different types of causes. Causes can be geographical: thus mountains, forests, rivers, and seas can influence historical events. Causes can be social: thus marriages, birth rates, death rates, and population density can influence historical occurrences (Aron 1961: 188–98; Aron 1948: 192–200). Aron concludes that, despite being general, natural causes never imply necessary effects because they are indifferent to human institutions. Furthermore, social causes do not imply necessary effects because they are singular and they tend to be regarded as being more or less adequate (Aron 1961: 224; Aron 1948: 227).

Aron raises three questions regarding cause: first, can we identify a primary cause? Second, can we enumerate all of the causes? Third, can we show the relations between typical causes? He answers no to each of these and suggests that part of our inclination to answer them in the affirmative is partly because of our inclination to compare history to science and partly because of our inclination to certain ideological principles. Both inclinations are predicated on assuming the power of reason: in the first, to see history as determined like nature, and in the second, to see it determined by economics and classes. Aron concludes that there are no laws in history and that history is not determined (Aron 1961: 245–64; Aron 1948: 246–64).

In the final section, Aron stresses the importance of plurality in history: that different people in different times and different places regard things differently. This plurality of views has led to historicism, which Aron believes is a combination of skepticism and irrationalism (Aron 1961: 291–7; Aron 1948: 295–300). He contends that historicism cannot be defeated by any absolutist approach, be it idealistic and theological like that of Ernst Troeltsch or materialist and economic like that of Karl Marx (Aron 1961: 291–3, 306–11; Aron 1948: 297–8, 309–15). Instead, history is composed of choices and that is why Aron links choice and action. Man is in history, both as a unique individual and as a part of a general environment. One is influenced by society but one also influences it. One transfigures the past in the way that one considers it. Aron concludes that life is always active and is an unending struggle: "Human life is dialectic."[11]

At the conclusion of the first section of *Introduction to the Philosophy of History*, Aron referred to "another book," meaning his first dissertation. He acknowledged that his results were negative and that the attempts by Dilthey, Simmel, and Rickert failed. Even Max Weber failed to offer a theory of historical knowledge (Aron 1961: 44; Aron 1948: 45). *Introduction to the Philosophy of History* also failed and not just because he failed like Dilthey, Simmel, Rickert, and Weber. It also failed like his first dissertation because the second one was also too abstract and too metaphysical, and lacked a focus on specific historical and even political problems. And Aron observed in the final footnote that he had not provided a conclusion and that this omission was deliberate. In order to offer a conclusion he would have to write another book (Aron 1961: 347, note 1; Aron 1948: 350, note 1). However, he felt that he had no time to write that book. As it was, Aron admitted that he wrote *The Introduction to the Philosophy of History* rather hurriedly because he was worried that a war was rapidly approaching. The impact of the war was no doubt a tragedy for the world, for France, and for Aron himself, but it did have the considerable benefit of making Aron's writings on history less abstract and less philosophical and more specific and more political. Finally, it can be regarded as successful in another way: Aron succeeded in prompting the French to become interested in the philosophy of history by showing that it should no longer be regarded as being discredited.[12]

## ARON'S POST-WAR WRITINGS ON HISTORY

During and after the war, Aron was involved in writing for various journals. It was not until the end of the 1940s that he returned to the topic of the philosophy of history. In 1949, he wrote "History and Politics" but the discussion of it will be postponed until the end of this chapter. Around 1949, Aron was asked to contribute an entry on the philosophy of history for a new edition of Chambers *Encyclopedia*, which was published in 1950. While the *Encyclopedia* continued to reflect its British and Scottish roots, it was also considerably more international than previous editions. That is because the editor of the 1950 edition had enlisted writers from around the world, including Aron. The entry was titled "The Philosophy of History," and while it owed much to his pre-war philosophical investigations, it is a clearer and more insightful account of the notoriously difficult topic. Aron begins as he had in his second dissertation by distinguishing between reality and knowledge of reality, and while history wants to know the whole of reality, in fact, it cannot (Aron 1978c: 5). This is the problem with Ranke's wish to show history as it happened ("wie es geschehen ist") (Aron 1978c: 6). This was the first of Aron's five classifications regarding philosophies of history. The second classification is made up of specialists and Aron dismisses this rapidly. While the specialists may have succeeded in understanding certain small components of history, they have failed in understanding history as a whole and they lack critical understanding. This leads to the third classification, which has two divisions: Nietzsche for one and the Neo-Kantians for the other. Nietzsche regarded history as being "monumental" and thus providing examples for life. However, this may lead to the diminishing of the importance of learning and truth (Aron 1978c: 6–7). This fault is not possible for the followers of Kant because they believe in historical knowledge just as scientists believe in natural knowledge. Both types of knowledge are reconstructions but they differ in their approaches to knowledge: "Natural sciences search for law, history for particulars" (Aron 1978c: 8). Both natural science and historical science cannot know "total reality"; thus, both the scientist and the historian employ a process of selection. Aron focuses on Weber's process of selection, which was based upon values. Something is historically relevant if it has value for us. However, as Aron points out, what is valuable to historians in one period may not be valuable to those in another, thus leading to historical relativism. And, as much as Weber believed that the historian could have "hypothetical objectivity" based upon finding causal connections, he was wrong. That is because his process of selection is too simple and rather misleading. It is not "objective" in the sense of being "universal" because its "total reconstruction" may be fruitful but still represents the values of that particular historian (Aron 1978c: 8–10).

Aron was not as dismissive of this type of historical relativism as he had been about the earlier positivist approach to history or Nietzsche's belief in "monumental" history. That is because the historians understand that their approach is relative and multiple relative values yield the "richness of life." By "richness of life," Aron means the acceptance of the dialectical movement of history that never ends and the realization that history cannot be regarded as universal because none of its events are universal (Aron 1978c: 10). For Aron, history is the attempt to uncover an actor's intentions. This is by no means easy because no one can be sure what one's own intentions are and the historian can only base his assumptions about an actor's intentions upon many complex and often conflicting circumstances. But he was convinced that an account of the whole can be partially achieved when the historian uncovers or assigns meaning (Aron 1978c: 12–13). The notion of meaning brings Aron back to the fundamental tension between history as a science and history as a philosophy – the first as reality and the second as an epistemological account of it. It is one thing to offer a unitary philosophy of history, like Augustine's, but it is another to offer a comparative philosophy of history, like the contemporary historians. This presents further difficulties, depending on whether one takes an approach like Spengler, and talks about different cultures, or one takes an approach like Hegel, and talks about the unity of history (Aron 1978c: 15–16). The problem with Spengler's approach is that, by claiming that cultures are incapable of understanding other cultures, it raises the question of how it is then possible for Spengler to understand them. A different problem confronts the Hegelian, and by extension, the Marxist. While the Marxist philosophy of history may seem promising because it attempts to find the meaning of the whole, it is not feasible because of its optimistic belief in progress. By this, Aron suggests a connection between the belief in the science of the Enlightenment and the belief in the class struggle of Marxism. However, Aron insists both are outdated and both belong to the past. As he put it, we can no longer put our faith in progress or history, but we still need to develop a philosophy of history. That is because our soul and our existence are dependent upon it (Aron 1978c: 17–19).

Aron's conclusion to "The Philosophy of History" is a clear indication that he did not believe that he could offer one at that time and that his account was primarily an account of the failures of previous attempts. He would continue to write more on other historians before returning to the examination of what a philosophy of "universal history" might look like.

In 1960, Aron was invited to give a lecture at the Hebrew University in Jerusalem and he chose to title it "The Dawn of Universal History." Aron begins by offering a word of caution – that the title was not his and it did not reflect what he intended to do. Rather, it was his publisher's idea for a history book that would cover the period from 1914 to about 1960. Aron objected that no serious historian would agree to take on such a task because the events were too isolated and it was too soon. Furthermore, Aron pointed out that he was not a historian but was a philosopher or sociologist. Accordingly, he replied to the publisher that while he could not write that book on that history, he could write one on what he called "universal history." This was the subject of his lecture but he cautioned his audience that he could not provide a full account, although he could offer a number of comments on what a universal history might be like (Aron 1978g: 212).

Aron observed that, beginning with the advent of the nineteenth century, each European generation believed it was unique. Comte believed he was living in the new industrial society, de Tocqueville in democratic society, and Marx in capitalistic society. Aron begins with Comte, who believed that labor has replaced war as constituting the supreme good and that free labor meant that the need for colonial conquests was finished. Aron noted that people were justified in ridiculing Comte for this belief but the future would have likely turned out more along the line of his predictions if history had "developed in accordance with the wisdom of men of good will" (Aron 1978g: 215). Comte was wrong to think that Europe was the "center of the universe" but he was right that its industrialization could serve an example to the world. Because gold and silver no longer constituted wealth, war was no longer necessary. Instead, wealth consisted of labor that was rationally organized. Aron turned to Marx: like Comte he was dogmatic but the difference was that Marx explained everything by conflict. However much Marx may have been right in the short term, Aron insists that in the long term he was wrong because workers are largely satisfied with the peaceful increase in their standards of living (Aron 1978g: 216–17). But both Comte and Marx underestimated the importance of politics and both seemed to have overlooked the dual factors of modern history. On one hand, history is progressive and Aron points to the radical changes that occurred in the nineteenth and twentieth centuries. He particularly cited the change in the amount of petroleum use – from a few tons at the beginning of the twentieth century to billions of tons around 1960 and increasing at the rate of 10 percent per year (Aron 1978g: 217–18). On the other hand, history is traditional, and by that Aron meant the type of history that wondered what might have happened if a different person was acting at a certain time or if the same person was acting under different circumstances. He wondered what might have happened in Great Britain if Churchill was not there in 1940 or what might have happened if Hitler had chosen not to invade Russia in 1941. Traditional history is governed in large measure by chance but it always seems to have its share of grandeur as well as cruelty. Aron insisted that the two types of history need to be combined: history "as it usually is" along with history as the "rapid change of industrialization."

Aron returns to Thucydides because it was he who first showed how war breaks out when the equilibrium is upset: Sparta regarded Athens's growing power as a threat and acted accordingly. The same thing basically occurred at the start of the "thirty-year war" (1914–45) when the Western and the Eastern powers perceived the challenges presented by each other. But there were virtually no changes in warfare during the Peloponnesian War; in contrast, the rifles used in 1945 were replaced by machine guns, tanks, and ultimately the atomic bomb (Aron 1978g: 221–3). Thus, the war between industrial societies was largely determined by the quantity and especially the quality of weapons (Aron 1978g: 224).

Aron points to the contrast in the approaches to modernization taken by China and by Japan. Japan attempted to blend tradition with industrial modernization whereas China simply adopted a new ideology. Aron wonders what might have happened if the process of industrialization would have continued under the Czar or even under Alexander Kerensky; instead, we know what happened under Lenin's and Stalin's ideology (Aron 1978g: 226). Yet, in the second half of the twentieth century, the Soviet Union embraced a form of modernization and at the time that Aron gave this lecture the Soviet Union and the United States were facing each other in a Cold War with the possibility of mutual nuclear annihilation.

This time is the moment of the "dawn of universal history," and while Aron insisted that he could not give a full account of it, he did offer two points. First, there was unification within the "diplomatic sphere." What Aron means is that each nation's actions impact many, if not all, of the other states. Furthermore, there is increasing homogenization; Aron notes the similarities between airports and factories, regardless of whether they are in Tokyo, Paris, Peking, or Rio de Janeiro (Aron 1978g: 228–9). However, despite the universality, there is a fundamental opposition between capitalist society and communist society, so universal history has yet to become actual.

Aron concludes by observing that there are two types of philosophies of history. One is optimistic and the other pessimistic. Optimists, whether liberal or Marxist, believe that the future will be better; pessimists, like Spengler, hold that there will continue to be a clash of cultures. In Aron's opinion, both make the mistake in thinking that the current age is decadent and he offers two reasons why this belief should be rejected. European countries can and should help developing countries and both sides have many reasons why they should not slaughter each other. Aron is cautiously optimistic that the peaceful time of universal history may arrive (Aron 1978g: 231–3).

Around the same time that Aron presented "The Dawn of Universal History", he also published "Thucydides and the Historical Narrative." From this title one would think that it is rather specific and that it has nothing to do with "universal history," yet a close reading of this essay shows that that impression is not quite reflective of its contents. As its title indicates, the subject is Thucydides and yet it is not just the spirit of Thucydides that is present in this essay but the spirit of Max Weber as well. Weber is specifically identified eight different times and is implicitly referenced in a ninth. Weber's spirit helps Aron to clarify his own developing notion of history.

Aron begins by observing that "the history of wars has gone out of fashion" and that war has been replaced by economics as the subject of historical interest. He also observes that this lack of apparent interest in war does not seem to fit the current age, which is the age of war. He further asserts that historians are not warmongers but seek to understand history, and in Aron's view, one of the most important subjects in history is war. Finally, he contends that the best history of war was Thucydides' account of the Peloponnesian War. War is important because it deals with the struggle of men against men, and Thucydides' account of the Peloponnesian War is a masterful account in ancient history because of his approach. Thucydides was a spectator whose distance to his subjects made his account of them just. It lacked the ideologies present in contemporary historians, regardless of whether they are American or Russian (Aron 1978d: 20–1). In addition, Thucydides' account operates on two different levels: the narrative and the philosophical interpretation. That is, he describes the events and indicates their significance. Finally, Thucydides offers a sense of human destiny coupled with human failings: the Athenians were doomed to defeat because they allowed themselves to be carried away by pride and the will to power. Aron suggests that Thucydides thought that if the Athenians had been reasonable, they would have been victorious. Aron notes that history is selective and it chooses to remember those who deserve to be remembered; these individuals have a particular quality. This quality is primarily political and the most political action there is, is war. Aron adds that modern politics is sometimes taken for policy but this is a mistake. It is a mistake because policy is also part of business and has little, if nothing, to do with politics. Politics is a dialectic: a dialogue between two who recognize each other. War is no longer a dialogue but an action, an action between two who continue to recognize each other but wish to dominate each other. War is both the completion and the negation of politics (Aron 1978d: 22–3). Man is similarly an apparent contradiction: he is both rational and passionate. Politics is reason and peace but war is its opposite. The most "perfect" war for Thucydides was the Peloponnesian War – not in the sense of "best" but "ideal." It is "ideal" in Weber's sense of exemplifying the traits that make up the object. In other words, it is ideal in the conceptual sense rather than in any moral quality. Aron clarifies this by pointing to Thucydides' tendency to stylize his account. Modern commentators have trouble with this because they employ concepts that are too vague whereas Thucydides' account is something between anecdotal and general. Aron maintains that an analysis inspired by Weber helps explain Thucydides' apparent paradoxical account (Aron 1978d: 25). Weber wrote of actions that are "Zweckrational": that is, actions in which means are chosen in order to achieve a particular end. And it is this type of explanation that Thucydides employed. Aron repeats his claim that Thucydides' account of the Peloponnesian War is stylized: that it was "ideal" in that Athens and Sparta were presented as being almost Weberian "pure types" (Aron 1978d: 28–9).

Aron shifts his focus to modern historians to seek to explain history on the basis of economics. He sets out three ways in which this might apply: to engage in war because of, first, economic needs; second, economic objectives; or third, economic alliances. Aron argues that none of these three applies to the Peloponnesian War. Aron concludes, *"The history of events cannot be reduced to that of societies, classes, and economies."* This, Aron insists, is as true today as it was during Thucydides' time (Aron 1978d: 32–3). History is no different today than it was then in the sense of recounting what happened in light of what might have happened but did not. Aron again invokes Weber's spirit by observing that Weber saw that, in the absolute sense, there are no accidents. That is because Weber argued that something may seem to be accidental only in the limited context, but considered in the larger context it makes sense. Aron readily admits that Thucydides does not speculate about necessity and chance in the way that Weber did about probability; none the less, his account of what could have happened is very much like Weber's (Aron 1978d: 35–7). Left unsaid is that Weber's approach to history is tragic, like that of Thucydides. Thucydides experienced tragedy but so do those who in live in the twentieth century. Aron concludes with the observation that as long as there are wars, "politics will rule and individuals [will] act." And historians of today (and tomorrow) will need Thucydides' sense of detachment in order to recount the stories of those heroes in the time of "Lenin, Stalin, Churchill, and Hitler" (Aron 1978d: 40–6).

In the early years of the 1970s, Aron wrote two essays that were more or less concerned with philosophy and history. One essay deals directly with philosophy and history, and that is indicated by its title: "Three Forms of Intelligible History." This article appeared in 1972 and is one of Aron's last writings on the philosophy of history. As in "Dawn of Universal History," Aron chooses not to provide a complete account of "intelligible history" and that is largely because of the problems with each term: "intelligible" and "history" (Aron 1978e: 47). History is difficult to define but he suggests that history is regarded as having four components: first, perceiving one's own past; second, perceiving others' lives; third, perceiving the relations between minds as they occur; and four, perceiving the relations between minds as they are found in institutions. Each of these contributes to the intelligibility of history and they must also be examined together in order to understand history. Aron does not do that in this essay; however, he discusses three types of forms of historical intelligibility.

Similarly, intelligibility is also controversial; this is more than the distinction between explanation and understanding, and revolves around the issue of levels of understanding.[13] By "levels," Aron means, does the historian address the issue of a single soldier, the commander, or the thousands of decisions made by all of the leaders throughout the war? Aron admits that this is a crude example but he insists that it helps to illustrate the problems of understanding historical events. It does so by revealing the varieties in historical intelligibility; none the less, he insists that it reflects the movement from a more or less practical understanding through differing levels until the historian reaches the metaphysical question about the meaning of the whole of history. While men and women can find meaning in history in its lower levels, only God (or those who claim to be like him) knows the ultimate meaning of "the human adventure" (Aron 1978e: 47–8).

Aron suggests that history can be regarded in three ways. The first, and simplest, is as a "train of events" and this is simply the relationship between means and ends. He offers a number of illustrations, one of which is "why did Caesar cross the Rubicon?," but he maintains that the "train of events" approach is too simplistic. What is needed is a conceptual apparatus to accompany these examples and he praises Weber, Shils, and Talcott Parsons for helping to provide basic concepts for historical intelligibility. These also provide the differing approaches, including knowledge, values, symbols, and drives. Aron also stresses that actions can be variously understood based upon the aims of the observer: that is, the observer's own knowledge and values help determine how he or she considers the action. Thus, the action must have meaning for us. But Aron emphasizes that how the observer considers the action rarely fits with how the actor himself had considered the act; therefore, the historian must "emerge" from himself and "recognize" the other. However, Aron immediately notes the dialectic involved by indicating that the historian and the other not only are different, but also have something in common. Without this commonality there can be no understanding and that implies placing the actor and action in the proper context (Aron 1978e: 48–9).

The variations and perspectives eliminate certainty, so history is only probable. Aron does not rule out cause and effect but insists that this is not scientific certainty but "probabilistic determinism." This does not mean that events are arbitrary and mysterious but it does mean that they are understandable – that Napoleon's genius was one crucial factor among others that made him successful on the battlefield (Aron 1978e: 50–1). At the time, certain events seem unlikely to happen but in hindsight they seem almost inevitable – Napoleon determination to march on Russia now seems a certainty but we can envision a situation in which he could have chosen not to do so (Aron 1978e: 52–3). Aron allows that Weber was right and history is the "retrospective reckoning of probabilities." No one can prove that Newton *had* to "formulate" the law of gravity but we can see how probable that was (Aron 1978e: 57).

Aron moves to the question of whether history is like science or like art. He selects Maurice Merleau-Ponty as an example of someone who believes that it is like the former: a Hegelian who thinks that the historian has a "privileged vantage point" in which to survey the unified past and show its inevitability. However, Aron objects to this singularity and counters that history is a plurality. Those like Merleau-Ponty adhere to a philosophy of history that is, in essence, a "camouflaged theology of history." Aron chooses instead the probabilistic approach that lacks the ideal certainty and substitutes the real likelihood that events unfold. It is a provisional discovery that indicates a movement towards a "goal" that is "vaguely outlined by reason" (Aron 1978e: 57–61).

The other essay appeared in 1970 and its title does not indicate the relationship between philosophy and history. Rather, "On the Historical Condition of the Sociologist" investigates the relationship between history and sociology. As Weber's spirit was found in "Thucydides and the Historical Narrative," it is also found here. But Weber's spirit is even more present here: in this essay, Aron refers to Weber more than twenty times. This is largely because Aron contrasts two types of sociological thinking: an idealistic type, as is represented by Durkheim, and a realistic one, as is represented by Weber. Aron confessed to both his allergic reaction to Durkheim's sociology and his elective affinity for that of Weber. While the reasons for both will not be fully revealed until the end of the essay, Aron credits Weber for proving that one may combine "scientific curiosity and political concern" without confusing them. That is, Weber represented the combination of "detached thought and resolute action" (Aron 1978f: 65).

In this essay, Aron is rather personal and he is somewhat apologetic. However, he is convinced that his biographical narrative is crucial for the audience's understanding of his comments on sociology. Beginning in 1930 in Bonn and later in Berlin, Aron sensed the oncoming tragedy – recognizing that, as Toynbee had said, history was moving again. As a result, Aron adopted what he regarded as "active pessimism" (Aron 1978f: 65). It was Weber who provided Aron with an example and a theory of living in such tumultuous times. Aron adopted the life of full lucidity and the theory that helped one to cope with incomplete knowledge and contradictory values. Weber was historically aware, in contrast to his French sociologist mentors (Aron 1978f: 66).

Sociology is the study of modern society, according to Aron, and it is distinguished from the traditional concepts used in politics and economics. Aron notes that socialism is connected to sociology in that it attempts to rectify economic and political inequality by reforming the structure of society (Aron 1978f: 62). Durkheim's socialism was the "state control of economic power." This was a typical "one size fits all" approach: a sociology that stressed the one factor common to all societies. Aron contrasts this with Weber's search for the particular traits in each society. A further difference was that Durkheim studied societies in order to find moral justifications; Weber studied them "to help the individual become conscious of himself and of his environment" (Aron 1978f: 67). As much as they differed, Weber and Durkheim conducted investigations that would be derided as microscopic and empirical:

Durkheim's study of suicide and Weber's study of agriculture in East Prussia (Aron 1978f: 68).

Regarding Weber's Neo-Kantian critique, Aron admits that Weber's language may be outdated but his notions of understanding and the relationships of value are still important, and that is because, no matter what role we have ("father, citizen teacher, journalist, bus rider, tourist"), we conform to certain models of conduct and follow particular customs (Aron 1978f: 69).

Sociology, like every science, "strips nature of its charms." In Weber's words, it is the "disenchantment of the world" ("Entzauberung der Welt") (Aron 1978f: 75). Aron grants that science is incredibly beneficial and credits Weber for indicating how important it is for understanding the world. But he shares Weber's fear that science is turning individuals into "specialists without spirit" ("Fachmenschen ohne Geist"). Like Weber, Aron does not choose between believing in a new Prometheus or awaiting Nietzsche's "last man" – not because of cowardice but because of ignorance (Aron 1978f: 81). This may be the fundamental similarity that led Aron to his "elective affinity" with Weber and prompted his "allergic reaction" to Durkheim – that the latter believed that he knew how the world would progress whereas the former readily admitted that he did not know. History was of little importance for Durkheim but it was crucial for Weber, and Aron was convinced of the need for understanding the historical condition of the sociologist. It was this that prompted Aron to live by de Tocqueville's counsel to "look forward to the future with that healthy fear" (Aron 1978f: 81–2).

## Concluding comments: history and politics

Raymond Aron's "History and Politics" is placed at the end of this chapter for several reasons: first, it is more social–political than it is philosophical; second, his discussion of the tension between science and politics is a precursor to his later writings; and third, it leads to the next chapter, which is on ideology. It is a comparatively short article; none the less, it contains a wealth of insights and indicates how his war-time experiences, as well as his post-war life, helped shape his understanding of the complex relationship between history and politics.

Aron insists that one can be neither indifferent to reality nor a slave to it, and he suggests that the correct approach is to maintain a detached stand to reality. In this, Aron is in agreement with Weber, but when Aron insists that facts influence values and values influence facts, he is disavowing Weber's command to separate facts and values. In

Aron's opinion, politics is "impure" in that it is moralizing while being scientific, and its moralizing is influenced by reality (Aron 1978h: 237). Neither raw observation nor utopian ideas are able to contribute much; rather, it is something closer to the middle that contributes to political philosophy. Political philosophy looks to earlier societies; however, one type does so in order to learn from it while the other type seeks what is new. Aron again promotes a combination of these two tendencies. First, seek to understand the present through learning from the past; and second, apply these lessons to different situations. This is the type of political thinking that Aron endorses but he recognizes that there are three different types: millenarian, conservative, and progressive.

The millenarian believes in a final end to history, regardless of whether this end is Hegelian or Marxist. However, the Hegelian pales in comparison to the Marxist because the latter believes in using any means necessary to bring the "Kingdom of God" to earth (Aron 1978h: 242). The conservative does not believe in any final goal but is convinced of the order and regularity of human life. The millenarian attempts to ignore human nature; in contrast, the conservative recognizes that human nature helps determine society. None the less, conservatives are not necessarily any more tolerant than millenarians (Aron 1978h: 242–3). Progressives reject the idea of an end to history as well as the belief that history is orderly. Rather, the progressive recognizes plurality and change, and embraces the variations and contrasts in history. Aron does not explicitly state his preference for progressivism but it is obvious that he prefers it to either millenarianism or conservatism and that is because of its fundamental political realism (Aron 1978h: 247–8).

Aron insisted that, in "calm and happy eras," all three of these approaches to politics have something of value to contribute. Millenarianism teaches us never to be satisfied with what has been achieved because there is always more to do. Conservatism teaches us that, regardless of the changes in times, there are some needs that are timeless. Progressivism teaches us that the statesman should seek that which is between the "dream of the ideal" and the "understanding of evil": that is, the middle between ideal and real. But Aron also insisted that during less calm and less troubling times, these three approaches no longer seem to be compatible but appear irreconcilable. That is because the tension between ideal and real is heightened and we tend to forget that relativism is part of the human condition. There is no final goal in history, the past cannot guarantee the future, and understanding reality is more important than dreaming of an ideal. Aron's point is that history contributes to our understanding of politics and that its relativism teaches us about ourselves. Aron writes, "Relativism is the authentic experience of political man." The religious believer has two advantages: the lack of real interest in mundane political quarrels and the conviction of having absolute values. In contrast, the atheist lacks these but is content to know that human history is formed through "doubt and error." Thus, political history teaches us about the need to "accept the limits of human existence" (Aron 1978h: 248). Unfortunately, the believers in Marxism and similar ideologies reject this advice because they are optimists who believe that history progresses in a linear fashion. There is, then, no need to try to learn from history because history is on the march. History is not important; what matters is only the end. There are also pessimists who think that history has nothing new to tell us because it has already been known. In contrast to the optimists and the pessimists, Aron believes in a "cyclical conception of history" (Aron 1980b: 6, 16). Accordingly, Aron believes not only that we must value history, but also that we must try to learn from it. That is why Aron continually looked back to Thucydides, Clausewitz, and Weber because they were in positions to teach him about crucially important things. And Aron learned from Clausewitz about what is most likely the most important thing: war. That is because, like Clausewitz, Aron recognized the devastation that war brings, but unlike the famous general, Aron lived during a time in which the devastation caused by nuclear war would be far greater than anything Clausewitz experienced. However, Clausewitz's genius lay in understanding the nature of warfare and Aron recognized that Clausewitz's account was just as applicable in the twentieth century as it had been in the nineteenth century. Before taking up Aron's examination of Clausewitz and the nature of war, it is time to discuss Weber's considerable impact on Aron's conception of responsibility in politics. After all, Aron shared with Weber the insistence that if one is to engage seriously in political activity, then one absolutely needs to have a proper sense of responsibility.

## NOTES

1. This quotation comes at the conclusion of Part One of *The Century of Total War* (Aron 1954: 98).
2. This is apparent with regard to some of the recent work on Aron. Of the fourteen essays in *Political Reason in the Age of Ideology* (Frost and Mahoney 2007) and the nineteen essays in *The Companion to Raymond Aron* (Colen and Dutartre-Michaut 2015), only one is ostensibly devoted to Aron's concept of history: "Raymond Aron and the Notion of History: Taking Part in History" (Simon-Nahum 2015). Writing about Aron, Perrine Simon-Nahum observed that "History was at his life's center"; however, Simon-Nahum does

not examine Aron's conception of history as much as the role that it plays in his political writings. The possible exception in this essay is the page and a half that is devoted to Aron's dissertations (Simon-Nahum 2015: 105–6). At least, Robert Colquhoun devoted considerable space to Aron's early conception of history in the first volume of his biography of Aron. Even here, the emphasis is less on what Aron meant as on the reception of Aron's dissertations (Colquhoun 1986a: 129–39 versus 119–20 and 140–54). None the less, Colquhoun's comments on the dissertations are enlightening and his account of their reception entertaining.

3. The phrase "pure philosophy" is Pierre Manent's (Manent 2007: 17). In his memoirs, Aron explained that, after the war, he regarded his earlier preoccupation with epistemological questions with indifference and that he preferred dealing with reality. He attributed this to having been "infected by the virus of politics." Later in his memoirs, he referred to it as the "drug of politics" ("la drogue politique") (Aron 1990: 139–40; Aron 1983b: 196–8, 335).

4. Aron later regarded the first dissertation as a difficult book and the second dissertation as resistant to summary (see Aron 1978b: xviii–xix; Aron 1990: 78–9; Aron 1983b: 111, 115–16).

5. The second edition from 1950 carries a different title: Raymond Aron (1950a) *La Philosophie critique de l'histoire: Essai sur une théorie allemande de l'histoire.*

6. Colquhoun noted that Aron had originally envisioned the second dissertation to be a continuance of the first and that he was going to focus on Karl Mannheim and Ernst Troeltsch (Colquhoun 1986a: 120). The latter's *Historismus* may not be among the most difficult works in the philosophy of history but it is exceptionally long. Mannheim's article on "*Historismus*" is relatively short but is rather difficult to understand.

7. Aron wrote: "dans la conscience de l'historien, interprète de tous."

8. The account offered here is a very brief overview of some of the aspects of Aron's notion of causality in history. A full account is, unfortunately, not possible here.

9. Aron (1961: 160–1). These notions are fundamental to Weber's sociology but are notoriously difficult. According to Sam Whimster, the "classical explication" of these concepts is found in Turner and Factor (1981). See Weber (2012: xxvi).

10. It is interesting that Aron suggests that the lawyer and judge do not have complete certitude regarding the assumption of responsibility and that only God has total knowledge of responsibility (Aron 1961: 172; Aron 1948: 175).

11. "L'existence humaine est dialectique" (Aron 1961: 337–47; Aron 1948: 335–50).

12. "The philosophy of history is, in France, a literary genre so discredited that no one dare confess interest in it" (Aron 1961: 282; Aron 1948: 285).

13. In his memoirs, Aron clarifies the distinction between understanding and explanation. One can understand why Hitler chose to invade the Soviet Union in 1941 by considering his personality and his ambitions. However, one is seriously misguided if one tries to explain this in a manner similar to that used in order to explain storms or embolisms (Aron 1990: 469; Aron 1983b: 735).

# CHAPTER TWO

# *On Weber*

"the consciousness of our responsibility *before history*"[1]

## INTRODUCTION

Durkheim, Machiavelli, and Marx are among the numerous thinkers who figure prominently in Raymond Aron's political sociology. There is no question regarding Aron's interest in them but there is considerable doubt regarding how much he admired them and their work. There is little such doubt regarding a number of other thinkers and this list would certainly include Thucydides and de Tocqueville. None the less, there is one other thinker who was even more important and more influential for Aron than Thucydides or even de Tocqueville. That thinker was Max Weber.[2] From the time Aron began reading Weber until his death, Aron continually invoked his name and constantly employed his methods. This is not to claim that Aron always shared the same convictions and values as Weber because it is clear that he did not. However, there are a number of factors that help explain these infrequent discrepancies. Even on the rare occasion when Aron fundamentally disagreed with Weber's beliefs, he continued to have a high degree of respect for his thinking, as well as a large measure of enthusiasm for him as a political sociologist. As this chapter will demonstrate, Weber was far more influential in shaping Aron's political philosophy than anyone else, even including de Tocqueville and Clausewitz. There are likely to be a number of factors that contributed to Aron's interest in, and respect for, Weber and his ideas but there is one that stands out. That is Weber's insistence on the need for political responsibility. This notion is found throughout Weber's writings, from some of his earliest ones to his last ones.[3] However, its most fully and clearly articulated version is found in his 1919 lecture, *Politik als Beruf.* Unfortunately,

Aron's relation to, and dependence upon, Weber and his thinking has largely gone unnoticed by most scholars and the few who have recognized this influence have tried to show that it was probably misplaced or that it was plainly wrong.[4] These two approaches affect not only our understanding of Max Weber, but also, much more importantly, our understanding of Raymond Aron. Without a proper understanding of Aron's appreciation for Weber's thinking in general and Weber's emphasis on political responsibility, we cannot have a full appreciation of Aron's own political philosophy.

That Aron closely followed Weber regarding scholarly thinking and political action should not be surprising for several reasons. First, both men were political sociologists of the highest rank; indeed, there are those who regard Aron as the greatest political sociologist since Weber.[5] Second, both shared similar traits in that both were passionate and coldly analytical at the same time. Third, both insisted on seeing things as they really are and personally rejected the temptations of idealism and ideology. Aron himself acknowledged many of these similarities. For example, in "On the Historical Condition of the Sociologist," Aron wrote of "my elective affinity to the thought of Max Weber" and specifically thanked Weber for demonstrating that one could believe in the conjunction of "scientific curiosity and political concern" (Aron 1978b: 65). Indeed, the second chapter in the second volume of *Main Currents in Sociological Thought*, which is devoted to Weber, is entitled "Science and Action" (Aron 1970b: 229). As Aron had written just before, Weber was always preoccupied with the relationship between science and politics. For Weber, this was important philosophically as well as personally. Aron granted that Weber was never a politician but he insisted that Weber "always dreamed of being one." None the less, Weber chose to be a teacher and a scholar, not a politician; however, he always wondered about the intersection of science and values (see Aron 1970b: 222–3). Aron thought that this intersection was also vitally important and he chose to live his scholarly life with many of the same ideas and principles as Weber had lived his. Aron was perhaps even more sensitive to history than Weber was, and he might have appreciated the impact that politics had on his life more than it had on Weber's. Weber lived during the years of German industrialization, the war, and its revolutionary aftermath; Aron lived through the rise of Hitler, the Second World War, and the Cold War with the threat of nuclear annihilation. Weber might have wished at one time to regard war as a gentlemanly quarrel but the First World War put an end to that. The Second World War may not have matched the horrors of Verdun, but it had more than its share of horrors on the battlefield. Furthermore, the anti-Semitism that was prevalent in Weber's day cannot be compared to the Holocaust. Yet it was Weber's unwavering rejection of easy solutions and the acceptance that life was primarily a struggle that helped to fortify Aron in his life of politics, as well as in scholarship. Weber insisted that scholarship and politics involved different spheres: the former rested on facts while the latter involved values. And he insisted that they be kept separate, although that was because he objected to the conflating of the two. It was permissible to discuss politics and scholarship at the same time, as long as it was made clear when one shifted from scholarly analysis to political judgment. For Weber, one of the most important scholarly virtues was intellectual honesty and the most critical virtue in politics was the sense of responsibility. In other words, honesty and responsibility are conjoined. Therefore, it is the purpose of this chapter to explore Weber's influence on Aron regarding politics in terms of both thought and action.

## Scholarship

The best place to find Aron's views on Weber's thinking about scholarship and science is very likely in his early work, *Die Deutsche Soziologie der Gegenwart*.[6] It was first published in the later 1930s and drew some attention. Aron published it again in 1950 and a German translation appeared three years later. It is a remarkable book in part because of its subject but more so because of the author. Aron sought to justify the fact that he was a French thinker writing on German sociology. He wrote that he could justify it on the basis that Karl Mannheim thought highly enough of the book to suggest that it be translated into German.[7] However, Aron did not wish to rest his claim solely on that; instead, he pointed to the fact that he had spent a number of years in Germany studying sociology. Therefore, he regarded himself as an expert on the subject. But he added that being a non-German provided him with a certain amount of distance that allowed him to provide a more objective overview than a German author might have. He also suggested that the book was prompted in large part by a comment that Mannheim made to Aron. Despite Aron's rather critical assessment of Mannheim's philosophy and his treatment of ideology, Mannheim had encouraged Aron to write the book, thus adding to Aron's justifications for going ahead with it.

Aron's book on German sociology has three parts: the first is devoted to Systematic Sociology and in it Aron discusses six sociologists (Georg Simmel, Leopold von Weise, Ferdinand Tönnies, Hermann Schmalenbach, Alfred Vierkandt, and Otto Spann). The second part is focused on Historical Sociology and there Aron examines the thinking of three other sociologists (Franz Oppenheimer, Alfred Weber, and Karl Mannheim). The third part, which is the longest, is devoted exclusively to Max Weber, whom Aron regarded as a kind of synthesis between Systematic Sociology and Historical Sociology.

Aron begins by stating that Max Weber is, without doubt, the greatest German sociologist and he explains that part of his greatness stems from the fact that he was a specialist in many different disciplines: law, economics, history, and philosophy. Another part of Weber's greatness was his special ability to combine scholarship and politics. Finally, a third element of Weber's greatness was his ability to focus on the "concrete" individual. While other sociologists insisted on the importance of constructing great abstract theories, Weber insisted on the importance of focusing on reality (Aron 1953: 92–3).

One should not be very surprised at Aron's extremely competent examination of Weber's philosophical thinking; after all, Aron's dissertation was on German Neo-Kantian philosophy. Like many commentators, Aron regarded Weber as one who followed Heinrich Rickert. Again, this is unsurprising since Rickert, along with his teacher, Wilhelm Windelband, was a leading figure of the Southwest School of Neo-Kantianism. Both Rickert and Windelband had striven to determine the method through which the historical sciences could be placed upon a secure foundation and thereby have the same degree of respectability as the natural sciences. Rickert, in particular, searched for a way to categorize the historical individual and he achieved it by demonstrating that the historian selects from the manifold of historical phenomena. Aron maintained that Weber adopted his focus on the individual from Rickert and much has been written about this. It is true that Weber often relied on his friend and colleague's philosophical writings but recent scholarship has begun to undermine the widespread opinion that Weber was a disciple of Rickert. While Weber did adopt Rickert's conviction that reality was infinite and so the historian needed to select the relevant portions in order to provide a coherent account, Weber chose to employ different instruments in constructing this social reality. Aron spends a fair amount of time on Weber's notion of the ideal type. Aron explains that an ideal type is not a normal concept but is something more like a particular type of class concept. Furthermore, Aron emphasized that the ideal type was not representative of that which is found in reality but was simply a heuristic device that allowed fruitful comparisons. Furthermore, it is developed by increasing the number of instances until one can reach conceptual unity. But Aron cautions against confusing Weber's ideal type with the concept of essence. Thus, when someone speaks of the "essence of Christianity" (as the theologian Adolf Harnack did), there is an implicit value judgment. When Weber employs an ideal type, there is never any implicit value judgment; rather, it is used purely as a scholarly tool (Aron 1953: 99–100). Aron thought highly of this conceptual tool but he suggested that Weber left it "incomplete." By this, Aron meant that Weber never fully developed a theory of the "ideal type" (Aron 1953: 103–4).

Aron spends some time and considerable effort on setting out what Weber meant by "Verstehen" ("understanding") and what his theory of historical causality was. By "understanding," Weber wished to show that the historical world was not a world of things, but was the "becoming [of] *human lives*" ("Werden *menschlichen Lebens*").[8] Here, Aron suggests that Weber had moved away from Rickert's philosophy of knowledge and towards a more psychological approach. Aron attributes this to the influence that Karl Jaspers had on Weber and, from what we now know, Aron was largely correct (Aron 1953: 105–7; Aron 1950b: 110–11; Aron 1967: 505). Jaspers was not very concerned with causality, although Rickert was; however, Weber's notion of causality in history is far more prominent in Weber's writing than it was in that of Rickert. Like Rickert, Weber held that the historical sciences differed from the natural ones in that the former concentrate on the single individual and not on the general, as in the latter (Aron 1953: 109; Aron 1950b: 114). The natural sciences attempt to formulate universal laws, and in contrast, the historical sciences attempt to explain the uniqueness of individual events. In light of this, the notion of causality that is employed in the natural sciences is inappropriate for use in the historical sciences. Aron's description of Weber's notion of causality is noteworthy because it was relatively accurate, and also because he correctly noted that it was bound up with the notion of values.[9]

This leads to the section that Aron devotes to Weber's distinction between scholarship and value judgments: that is, between science and politics. This is the distinction between "being" ("Sein") and "should" ("Sollen"); Aron stresses that science is always dealing with causal connections and that he agrees with Weber in that science can tell us what we want and how to achieve it but that it can never tell us what we should want.[10] Aron contended that one could approach Weber's theory from two different points. One is from the point of view of science and that involves objectivity and the particularity of "cultural science" ("Kulturwissenschaft") (Aron 1953: 114). The other is from the point of view of politics and that involves subjectivity and a multiplicity of values. Aron refers to Weber's radical opposition between science and politics as the separation of "being" ("Sein") and "should" ("Sollen"). Like Weber, Aron believed that every attempt to perform actions that depends upon a "scientific doctrine of morals" ("wissenschaftliche Sittenlehre") is doomed to failure (Aron 1953: 115–16). Aron maintained that Weber's denial of the possibility of having scientific value judgments is dependent on the limits of science itself. Science can help clarify the various moral choices that we may have, but it cannot help us to decide which one to make (Aron 1953: 116–17). Aron moves to tie this to political decisions and their implications and this involves Weber's distinction between the "ethics of responsibility" ("Verantwortungsethik") and the "ethics of conviction" ("Gesinnungsethik"). Because Aron discusses Weber's two types of ethics in several places and places considerable worth on it, it is important to spend some time discussing it here.

Weber outlined the distinction between these two ethics towards the end of his lecture *Politik als Beruf*. This work may be regarded as one of the two "swan songs" that Weber gave to Munich students in 1917 and 1919. *Politik als Beruf* and *Wissenschaft als Beruf* were two of four lectures that were part of the series "Geistige Arbeit als Beruf" and were presented to the Freistudentische Bewegung (Free Student Movement). While most of the listeners responded favorably to *Wissenschaft as Beruf*, many of them were disappointed by *Politik als Beruf*. That is partially a result of Weber's refusal to engage in discussions about the current state of politics in Germany: many of those in the audience wanted Weber's opinions on Germany's recent defeat and the abdication of the Kaiser. And many were disappointed by Weber's harsh words about the revolutions that were occurring in numerous German cities. But many of those in the audience did not respond to Weber's "philosophical" lectures (Weber 1992: 1).

*Politik als Beruf* may be regarded as being composed of three parts. In the first part, Weber discusses the nature of the state and its legitimate use or threat of use of force. Thus, he connects politics with power and the threat of violence. In the second part, Weber sets out the various types of political groups and indicates the differences between politicians and bureaucrats. In the third and final section, Weber addresses the issue of the relationship between politics and ethics. It is here that he initially notes the opposition between the "ethics of responsibility" and the "ethics of conviction." The follower of the former considers the foreseeable consequences of one's actions. Weber grants that a politician can never know exactly what consequences will result from his or her decision but insists that the genuine politician will attempt to foresee the possible consequences of a decision. Weber's point is that one needs to take politics seriously because the consequences are serious. In contrast, the follower of the "ethics of conviction" acts with indifference to the possible consequences. Weber suggests that these are holy individuals who live by the Sermon of the Mount and are therefore not of "this world" (Weber 1992: 234). Weber has considerable respect for these rare saints. However, Weber also suggests that there is another type that claims to follow the "ethic of conviction" and that is the revolutionary. On the one hand, the revolutionary believes in peace but, on the other, insists that it is legitimate to use violence to achieve it. Not only is this logical nonsense; it is ethically wrong. Weber insists that if one is engaging in politics and using force, then one should not be claiming to act according to the "ethics of conviction" (Weber 1992: 235–40, 246–7). For Weber, this is an either/or situation.[11]

Finally, as to the "Realpolitik" of the time, Weber regarded it as a caricature of the "ethics of responsibility" – in contrast to the real one, as exemplified by Machiavelli's willingness to offer his own soul's salvation for the wellness of his city (Aron 1953: 118). This leads to one of Aron's final points about Weber's notion of values: in politics, it is especially important to recognize the multiplicity of values and the competition among them. Finally, Aron suggests that the rejection of scientific value judgments rested with Weber's inner being. He always strived with "scientific asceticism" ("wissenschaftliche Askese") towards purity. There may be purity in science but not in politics (Aron 1953: 118–19). Aron will explain this later in his section on Weber's political thinking.

Aron was rather convincing in setting out the various strands of Weber's thinking, but he was less so in his claim that Weber's work was a unity. Aron maintained that rationalism was the thread that tied Weber's thinking together (Aron 1953: 148). However, Weber's emphasis on the power of rationalism becomes more pronounced in the last decade of his life and it is not reflective of a sense of unity. Furthermore, Weber was also interested in the irrational powers that informed modern life, with the most notable being charisma. Aron was not the only one to try to seek unity in Weber's work but it is surprising that he even tried to do so, given that he had shown a keen sense of appreciation for the many different areas of Weber's interest.

Aron devoted a section to Weber's politics. Aron confessed that it was difficult to grasp Weber's political thinking because it is not a theory that would deal with the traditional political question of what is the best state. However, Aron insisted that Weber's thoughts on politics were never a collection of opinions (Aron 1953: 119). Weber always objected to those who did not take politics seriously, by which Aron meant those who did not think about the responsibility that accompanies power. Weber was always preoccupied with individual facts and with objective reality; accordingly, Aron approved of Weber's approach to idealists. Once again, Aron invokes the question that the French minister had posed to him earlier in his life: "What would you do if you were minister?" and he noted that that question would cause the political novice to fall silent (Aron 1953: 120).

If Weber did not have a political theory, he still had a theoretical conception. This included antinomies – means and ends, morality and politics, and the "ethics of conviction" ("Gesinnungsethik") and the "ethics of responsibility" ("Verantwortungsethik"). For Weber, there was no lack of clarity regarding the definition of the state: it possessed the sole legitimate right to force. It was also clear to Aron that a politician's striving for power was not to obtain it simply for one's self or to enjoy its use; rather, it was always for the state (Aron 1953: 123). Weber also was always clear that private morality differed from public morality and that one who genuinely adhered to the Christian ideal, as set out in the Sermon on the Mount, would necessarily be excluded from participating in politics. For those who tried to mix religion and politics, Weber had contempt; for the true politicians, Weber had respect. In Weber's view, the true leader had the courage to face the truth. This was not to be taken in Nietzsche's sense but in the manner of the Old Testament prophets. The genuine political leader did not live *from* politics but *for* politics (Aron 1953: 126–7). It appeared that Aron was not as sympathetic to the contents of Weber's politics as much as he respected Weber's attitude towards it. Weber's insistence on "absolute clarity" was coupled with the belief that if "politics is the art of the possible," then it is imperative to seek the impossible in order to reach the possible (Aron 1953: 127). Aron may have modified his enthusiasm for Weber's politics, but he never seemed to have reduced his early admiration for Weber's approach to it.

## POLITICS

In *Deutsche Soziologie*, one finds Aron's early interpretation of Weber's politics and much of it is correct. However, it is limited and it is embedded within an approach to Weber's overall thinking, so that it remains both youthful and incomplete. For Aron's later, and more focused, examination of Weber's politics, one needs to turn to Aron's "Max Weber und die Machtpolitik."[12] This was the speech that Aron gave at Heidelberg in 1964. The occasion was the annual conference of the Deutsche Gesellschaft für Soziologie (DGS) and its focus was the centennial of Weber's birth. By 1964, the DGS had long been established and had hundreds of members, but at the inaugural conference in 1910 there were only about thirty people in attendance. Some of these people were unknown and were just beginning their careers, but others were quite well known and rather well established. In this latter group were Ferdinand Tönnies, Georg Simmel, Werner Sombart, Ernst Troeltsch, and Max Weber.[13] Troeltsch had little to do with the DGS after the initial conference and Simmel had nothing to do with it after the second conference. Troeltsch apparently moved on to other projects and Simmel died in 1918. Weber resigned from the DGS in 1912 but left a lasting imprint on it.[14] He not only had an impact on the DGS; he had a massive impact on German sociology too. It is crucial to recognize how great an impact Weber had in developing sociology as a discipline in Germany. In 1910, there were no departments of sociology at any German university and very few thinkers referred to themselves as sociologists. Certainly, Weber had reservations about the title "sociologist" in general and he was uncertain about the future of sociology in Germany. The first chair of sociology was at Bonn in 1920 but this gave little indication of how securely sociology could develop. In "Die Soziologie der Zwischenkriegszeit," M. Rainer Lepsius has suggested that the beginnings of sociology around 1920 were rather precarious. Much of this was because the early leaders in sociological thinking passed away. Simmel died in 1918 and, within a few years, interest in his work faded; Weber died in 1920 and there were not many younger scholars like Karl Jaspers who continued to champion Weber's thinking. Both Weber and Simmel were regarded as worthy of study in the United States, but their reputations did not begin to be fully re-established in Germany until after the Second World War (Lepsius 1981: 10–11).

The second conference of the DGS took place in 1912, and although it was marked with disagreements concerning focus and structure, it seemed that its future was slightly more assured.[15] The war interrupted the plans for the next conference and the third one was postponed a number of times and was not held until 1922. That it was held at all was undoubtedly due to Tönnies's massive efforts, but even then, only two major speeches were given and there were only about ten people in attendance (see *Verhandlungen* 1923). By 1964, the DGS had grown immensely, in size as well as in importance. There were four major speeches and six minor ones. Of the four major ones, Ernst Topitsch spoke on Weber and sociology "today" and Talcott Parsons spoke on value freedom and objectivity. Both lectures generated considerable discussion but nothing like that from the other two major speeches. Herbert Marcuse dealt with the contentious problems generated by industrialization and capitalism, and Aron delivered a paper on power in Weber's politics. Aron's choice of topic would have been controversial by itself but there was another important factor that contributed to the heated debate. Wolfgang Mommsen had recently published his highly contentious book, *Max Weber und die Deutsche Politik: 1890–1920*, in 1959 and it was still generating considerable controversy around Weber's apparently conflicting interests in democracy and power. Furthermore, Mommsen himself was present at the DGS conference and was one of the people in attendance who publicly commented on Aron's lecture.

Aron's "Max Weber und die Machtpolitik" was ignored by many of those who have written on Aron. In the "Personal" section for 1964 in his "Chronological Table" of Aron's life, Colquhoun mentions Aron's October lectures in California but neglects Aron's lecture at Heidelberg (Colquhoun 1986b: 609). Similarly, Scott Nelson and José Colen do not mention "Max Weber und die Machtpolitik" and there is one brief, almost irrelevant, mention of Weber's "Der Nationalstaat und die Volkswirtschaftspolitik", which was Aron's primary focus in his Heidelberg lecture (Nelson and Colen: 2015: 210, note 31). Matthias Oppermann does discuss this work but it is within a section on Weber and the reference is not to Aron's German lecture but to the French version (Oppermann 2008: 333–8, 340). Yet Aron's lecture is instrumental not only for understanding Weber's views on power and politics, but also for understanding Aron's own views on these issues.

Aron began his lecture by referring to a "question of conscience" ("Gewissensfrage") and wondered how he could be justified in giving a lecture on Max Weber. It would be questionable enough if he had been invited to discuss Weber's sociology and philosophy, but it is even more so because was requested to speak on Weber's politics. It is questionable largely because Aron was French and he suggested that, at another time, a Frenchman might have been able to decline such an invitation. However, he felt that he could not do so now and was resolved to give his lecture. Aron fully recognized the high degree of difficulty he had with his topic and that is because of three, interconnected reasons. First, Aron recognized that he would not be able to treat Weber's political theory without making political judgments regarding German nationalism. Second, while Weber died just after the end of the First World War, his theories continued to influence the Weimar government, and according to some critics, led to Hitler and to the Second World War. Third, to a number of people, Max Weber was considered strictly a "Machtpolitiker"; Wolfgang Mommsen certainly believed that Weber was one. Aron noted that Mommsen's *Max*

*Weber und die deutsche Politik* did not just unleash a pure scholarly controversy – implying that it also unleashed a political one as well.[16] Aron's primary focus was Weber's Inaugural Lecture at Freiburg. Entitled "Der Nationalstaat und die Volkswirtschaftspolitik", Weber's "Antrittsrede" was no ordinary academic lecture but was one of his most important political speeches. It was regarded by Mommsen as the most important political statement that Weber gave until the beginning of the First World War. Furthermore, Mommsen agreed with Arnold Bergstraesser's assessment that the "Antrittsrede" serves as the point of departure for Weber's entire social–political thinking.[17] Whether one agrees with Bergstraesser's and Mommsen's assessments is one thing, but it is evident from Aron's lecture that he mostly shared their convictions.

Aron noted that Weber does not belong to the closed-off past; as the furor that was set off by Mommsen's book showed, Weber belongs very much to Germany's present. In light of this, Aron allows that it might be "indiscreet" of him as a Frenchman to involve himself in this discussion about Weber (Aron 1965b: 103). He offers three possible justifications for his intrusion: first, he has not been suspected as being an opponent to Weber, although he allows that he might not write about Weber in such glowing terms as he did in his *Deutschen Soziologie der Gegenwart*. Second, Weber has had a certain political influence on French politics and Aron points specifically to Mommsen's observation regarding the similarity between the constitution of France's Fifth Republic and Weber's ideas about the proposed Weimar constitution. Third, Aron insists that the "deciding reason" ("entscheidender Grund") is that it is the "European community" ("europäische Gemeinschaft") that should prompt each sociologist from every European country to think about nationalism (or "at least today's nationalism") and about "Machtpolitik" (Aron 1965b: 104). He immediately insists that he does not forget for one moment Weber's distinction between science and politics, but he adds that Weber was not always the model to follow.[18] But Aron formulates Weber's distinction well when he adds, "It is good not to mix facts with values, reality with wishes."[19] However, he has Weber in mind when he maintains that while it is good to see the world as it is, and not as one would like it to be, it is just as problematic to see the world as how one could fear it to be. This pessimistic approach is just as dangerous as the idealist's approach (Aron 1965b: 104).

Having finished with his preliminary remarks, Aron turns to more substantial ones, and again he follows Weber by defining "Machtpolitik" or "Powerpolitics" in two ways. The first is a narrow one and defines "Machtpolitik" as the politics that is a type of competition between states and is decided by power. That is because there are "no laws, no courts, or any supra-national authority" with which to decide conflicts. The second definition is a broader one and defines "Machtpolitik" as the type of politics that takes power as the means or even its goal. Aron suggests that every type of politics is partially based upon this second sense. However, regardless of which definition is chosen, Weber is a typical "Machtpolitiker" and is a descendant of Machiavelli and a contemporary of Nietzsche (Aron 1965b: 104). Like these two thinkers, Weber rejected the question concerning which type of ruling was the best, a question that had been of critical importance to the ancients (Aron 1965b: 104–5, see also Aron 1953: 119). For Weber, politics is always a struggle and it is especially so for those states that are destined to play upon the world's stage. Aron had no doubt that Weber believed Germany to have such a destiny and he quoted a lengthy passage from Weber's 1917 "Parlament und Regierung im neugeordneten Deutschland" to show how important this position was. In Weber's view, Germany was much more than a country of "good officials, honest sales people, and dedicated scholars" (Aron 1965b: 105; Weber 1921b: 259). Aron began his quotation with Weber's assertion that "Only 'Herrenvölker' have the calling to grab into the spokes of the development of the world."[20] Aron insisted that he had chosen this passage because it represented Weber's main theme about "Machtpolitik." Furthermore, it showed that Weber did not differentiate between internal and external politics. Like Machiavelli, Weber saw that all of politics involved struggle (Aron 1965b: 105). To deal with "Machtpolitik" in the second and wider sense would require Aron to discuss Weber's entire sociology and politics, an undertaking that he insisted was out of the question there (Aron 1965b: 106). However, Aron insisted that the theme of nationalism ran throughout Weber's works and suggested that, on certain (but unspecified) points, Weber followed the nationalistic impulses of his teacher von Treitschke. In Aron's view, the biggest difference between Weber's views and those of Treitschke was that the former was more pessimistic and even more tragic than the latter (Aron 1965b: 107). Yet Aron believed that Weber shared Treitschke's belief in Germany's "greatness" ("Größe") and that meant the connection between culture ("Kultur") and power ("Macht").[21] What it always meant to Weber was that "The German nation is a culture people" ("Die deutsche Nation ist ein Kulturvolk") (Aron 1965b: 107). That also meant that Germany had the responsibility to participate in the struggle among the great nations. Unlike the Danes, the Swiss, the Dutch, or the Norwegians, Germans had to fight for the future and against the Russians from the East and the

Anglo-Americans from the West. Aron quotes this long passage from Weber's "Zwischen zwei Gesetzen" and he ends it with Weber's words "Rather us. And with right" ("Sondern uns. Und mit Recht") (Aron 1965b: 107; Weber 1921b: 60–1). Aron does not emphasize "Sondern" but Weber did. And Aron did not continue with the quotation: Weber wrote "Because we are a 'Machtstaat'" Germans have the duty to act (Weber 1921b: 61). Aron simply added, "Soweit Max Weber" (Aron 1965b: 107). Aron noted that Weber's nationalism was widely shared but what made his approach to it so original was the admission that power is diabolical. Weber did not attempt to glorify power but assessed it realistically. Furthermore, rather than treat the "little states" ("Kleinstaaten") as something rather comical, as Treitschke had done in his *Politik*, Weber simply regarded them as being destined not to need to engage in the struggles that duty required the larger states to engage in (Aron 1965b: 108). This sense of realism extended to international relations. Weber's siding with Poland during the war was based less on any sympathy for the country than on his recognition of the threat that Russia posed to Poland and especially to Germany (Aron 1965b: 109). This sense of political realism also meant that Weber was not susceptible to ideological considerations. In Aron's opinion, perhaps the only time that Weber was fooled by an illusion was when he seemed to believe that the conditions for peace with Germany would break the tie between France and Great Britain. In Aron's considered view, Weber possessed the ability to see things more clearly than most of his contemporaries (Aron 1965b: 110). This did not mean that Aron was always in agreement with Weber. Aron specifically faulted Weber for being impressed by "the Darwinian social doctrine" ("der darwinistischen Soziallehren") and pointed particularly to a passage from "Zwischen zwei Gesetzen." There, Weber insisted that Germany was engaged in a "merciless economic struggle for existence" ("erbarmungsfremden ökonomischen Kampf ums Dasein") (Aron 1965b: 111; Weber 1921b: 62). Aron admitted that Weber wrote this passage during the war but insisted that it was a reflection of Weber's entire way of thinking. Aron justified his claim by pointing to a passage from the "Antrittsrede" that represented the same view. In the course of one paragraph, Weber mentioned the "economic struggle for existence" twice (Aron 1965b: 111; Weber 1921b: 17–18; Weber 1993a: 558). Aron added two more passages from the "Antrittsrede" where Weber made similar points. Aron took these passages as sufficient indicators that Weber's thinking had not only a Darwinian component (the economic struggle for existence), but also a Nietzschean one (not humanity's happiness but its greatness), an economic one (the scarcity of goods and the permanence of poverty), a Marxist one (class interests), and finally, a nationalistic one (national interests trump all others) (Aron 1965b: 112–13). Aron confessed that when he had first read Weber some thirty years before, he was impressed in particular by the intellectual courage and the knowledge that he saw in Weber's writings. Furthermore, he added that he thought that Weber's work contained teachings that continued to be valid. Now, however, Aron noticed Weber's metaphysical content and his pessimistic world view. Unlike many liberals but like many of his contemporaries, Weber was convinced that the political power of the state was determined by the economic development of its people and regarded the working class as a weapon in this economic struggle. This now appeared to Aron as no longer relevant. Yet Aron appeared to agree with Weber's conviction – he admitted that "A world without conflict is in fact unimaginable." However, Aron immediately added that "A world in which classes and nations are no longer engaged in struggle is not unimaginable."[22] And he insisted that the victor on the battlefield of votes differs in essence and not in degree with the victor on the military battlefield.[23]

Aron shifted to the other philosophical foundation of "Machtpolitik" and suggested that it rested upon the Neo-Kantian distinction between "what is" ("was ist") and "what should be" ("was sein soll"), between "facts" ("Tatsachen") and "values" ("Werten") (Aron 1965b: 114–15). But Aron argued that Weber did not limit the "Seinsollen" to ethics; rather, he made ethics into a type of value along with others. Furthermore, Aron reminded his audience that Weber followed Baudelaire's claim that a thing can be beautiful *despite* its being bad as well as *because* it is bad (Aron 1965b: 115; Weber 1992: 100). This led Aron to make two observations, both of which are related to "Machtpolitik." First, there is no tribunal to which one can appeal to decide the relative values of German versus French culture. Second, it is impossible for one to be both a politician and a Christian – at least in so far as the Christian adheres to the Sermon on the Mount. Both led Aron again to Weber's famous distinction between the "ethics of conviction" ("Gesinnungsethik") and the "ethics of responsibility" ("Verantwortungsethik.").[24] Aron correctly noted that this distinction was controversial when Weber formulated it, and it continued to be so during 1964. It is safe to add that it continues to generate controversy. Instead of immediately dealing with Weber's distinction, Aron noted that it is correct that no one can decide which has the higher value – German culture or French. But Aron asks whether this is a "question of significance" ("Frage von Bedeutung") (Aron 1965b: 116). Aron attempts to answer this but his more pressing concern is Weber's "two forms of ethics." Weber is right that no one forces somebody to go into politics. Weber is also right to complain about the cult of power but Aron concludes that the ethics of responsibility is not designed to extol power. Instead, it is the recognition of reality. Aron claimed that the "two ethics" were really "two antinomies" and that one really has to choose which one to follow: either the "ethics of conviction" or the "ethics of responsibility." Aron believed that Weber fully recognized the importance of responsibility in politics and that he chose the "ethics of responsibility" over the "ethics of conviction." Furthermore, Aron held that Weber's choice was never driven by some personal interest in power but by his belief that it was absolutely necessary for Germany's future. In Aron's view, it was unfortunate that Weber could not become a politician. That was because Weber was unwilling to compromise and he was unable to tolerate intrigue (Aron 1965b: 118).

Aron agreed that Weber was right about no politics without struggle and no struggle without force, but he admitted that two issues troubled him about Weber's theory of politics. First, Aron was worried by the extreme opposition that Weber set up between the two types of ethics and he was concerned that this radical opposition would lead to two equally untenable positions: the "wrong realists" ("falsche Realisten") and the "wrong idealists" ("falsche Idealisten") (Aron 1965b: 119). Second, when Weber takes the interest of power as Germany's final goal, does that not lead him into a type of nihilism? Aron complained specifically that Weber's position leads not to the quality of culture but simply to prestige of power, and he finds it difficult to believe that Weber was willing to sacrifice all values for the sake of power (Aron 1965b: 119). Both objections led Aron to the decisive point that one must reflect upon: Weber never succumbed to the barrage of propaganda from either the German side or the French side and always maintained his "feeling for measure and distance" ("Gefühl für Maß und Abstand") (Aron 1965b: 119). However, he also never questioned the assertion that the nation state was the highest form of a political community. He never differed from his contemporaries regarding the rights and duties of the great power, just as he never differed from them concerning the diplomatic rules of "Machtpolitik" (Aron 1965b: 120). Weber can be genuinely regarded as a sociologist for today, but as a political thinker he was bound by his time. He could not conceptualize either the burden of the Bolshevik revolution or the totalitarian despotism of the single party, and so when he spoke of the charismatic leader he could not foresee its likely results (Aron 1965b: 120).

Aron did not disagree with much of Weber's theory regarding "Machtpolitik" but he certainly expressed his disagreement regarding

Weber's pessimistic world view (Aron 1965b: 104, 106, 113, 120). Yet it seems as if Weber had a realistic sense of what was going to occur in Germany when he was approaching the conclusion to "Politik als Beruf." There he suggested that, when he and his audience would meet in ten years' time, they would not find "summer's blooms" ("Blühen des Sommers") but "icy darkness" ("eisige Finsternis") (Weber 1992: 251). Perhaps Aron recognized this because he added that, since we cannot know the future, Weber's pessimistic vision might be more accurate than Aron's own optimistic one (Aron 1965b: 120). And he also added that we do not know whether humanity will destroy itself or will unify itself. None the less, Aron was convinced of several things: that never again will the interest in power be the final goal of a nation. And, as much as there are those who regard Max Weber as a real "Machtpolitiker", he never believed that power was the highest value. According to Aron, Weber always adhered to two values in his life and his thinking, and they were "truth and the nobility of conviction" ("Wahrheit und Adel der Gesinnung") (Aron 1965b: 120). Aron concluded with the observation that the inheritance that Weber left made it impossible for a future "Machtpolitiker."[25]

In the discussion period, most of the speakers preferred to set out their own views regarding Weber, but some of them responded directly to Aron's speech. Mommsen had high praise for Aron, noting that Aron's "brilliant analysis" had noteworthy clarity and that Aron justifiably chose to focus on the "Antrittsrede" (Stammer 1965: 130–1). Mommsen allowed that he was in "total agreement" with Aron's claim that Weber was foremost a "Machtpolitiker" and that one could certainly describe Weber's sociology as "a sociology of power" ("eine Soziologie der Macht") (Stammer 1965: 134–5). Karl W. Deutsch echoed Mommsen's observation and praised Aron for showing how far removed Weber was from modern internationalism, with its emphasis on responsibility (Stammer 1965: 141). However, Deutsch questioned Aron's assertion that Weber followed Machiavelli and Hobbes. Yet he agreed with Aron that Weber's central thought was "Herrschaft," which is fundamentally another name for "Macht." This is where Deutsch clarifies the difference between Weber and Machiavelli and Hobbes: while power is important to the latter two, it is *legitimate* power that is important to Weber (Stammer 1965: 142–3). Eduard Baumgarten addressed Aron's use of "Soweit Weber," as well as Deutsch's complaint that Aron often used Weber's words for a purpose other than the one Weber had intended (Stammer 1965: 145). However, Baumgarten suggested that Aron had simply shown that Weber's words had different meanings and that they were often confusing. Baumgarten insisted that Weber had little in common with Nietzsche or with Darwin, and that his critics were too quick to label him. Baumgarten reminded the audience that Weber was attacked from the left as well as from the right (Stammer 1965: 147, 149). However, Baumgarten also insisted that Weber's emphasis on the greatness of Germany should not be taken as an indication that, for Weber, power is the highest value (Stammer 1965: 146). Baumgarten concluded his remarks not only by substantiating Aron's claim about the importance of conflicting values for Weber; he even strengthens Aron's assertion. Whether in the "Antrittsrede" from 1895 or in "Wissenschaft als Beruf" from 1917, Weber's main focus was to have major "discussions of value" ("Wertdiskussionen") (Stammer 1965: 150). Adolf Arndt was the final speaker and he praised Aron for his "fascinating lecture" with its "Cartesian clarity" (Stammer 1965: 150). That was the extent of his comment on Aron, and he devoted most of his remaining time to his defense of Weber from the accusation that Carl Schmitt was a student of Max Weber. Weber was far too serious about power; for Schmitt, it was an arbitrary element to play with as he saw fit.[26]

In his "closing words" ("Schlußwort"), Aron admitted that he did not have the time to defend himself against all of the objections to his interpretation. Indeed, he did not have the time to defend himself from his "defender, Dr. Mommsen" (Stammer 1965: 155). Aron granted that it was possible, as Karl Deutsch had insisted, that he had "translated" Weber into French (Stammer 1965: 139, 155) and he suggested that it would be equally possible to translate Weber into "American." Whether one or the other "translation" is better cannot be established without recourse to values (Stammer 1965: 155). Aron also insisted that, with a great thinker such as Weber and with him having "a personality full of contradictions" ("eine widerspruchsvolle Persönlichkeit"), it is naturally possible to find a number of different meanings in his work. That suggests that people's views of Weber can change; in fact, Aron suggested that his own views of Weber might change even in the next year (Stammer 1965: 155). He also maintained that he did not attempt to provide a complete view of Weber's concept of power politics. Instead, Aron insisted that he had tried to discuss only what he thought Weber meant by it and not what he found problematic about it. Accordingly, Aron suggested that his account was not as one-sided as it might have appeared. Furthermore, Aron insisted that he had not tried to assign general blame to Weber's thinking but had tried to understand Weber in his own time. As such, Weber was a nationalist but that was not such a terrible thing at that time. Aron claimed that it is better to honor a great man as he was, rather than to try to evaluate him from a half-century later. In Aron's view, Weber was a philosopher who believed in the "heterogeneity of values" ("Heterogenität der Werte") and in the difference between order and obedience and between money and power. Aron confessed that that might be an attempt to translate Weber into American but that that is not the Weber that he had read. Aron concluded by insisting that he had read Weber many times and upon each reading always "with new admiration" ("mit neuer Bewunderung") (Stammer 1965: 156).

## CONCLUDING COMMENTS

The point of this chapter was two-fold: the primary point was to show how much Raymond Aron learned from Max Weber, both in the area of scholarship and in the arena of politics. Regarding scholarship, Aron learned from Weber the importance of conceptual clarity and the need to avoid generalizations. He learned about the need to focus on the concrete and to avoid oversimplifications. Regarding politics, he learned about the opposition between facts and values and the need to keep them separate. He learned about the complexities of political decisions and the need to be aware of the possible consequences of one's political decisions. Finally, he learned from Weber the centrality of power in politics and its opposition to ethics. While it is clear that Aron's early enthusiasm for Weber's thinking and especially in politics gave way to a more measured response, he never lost his admiration for Weber as a thinker and an actor. One wonders how much he changed his mind or whether he changed what he said according to circumstances. While it is true that Aron came to disapprove of Weber's nationalism, he always thought highly of Weber's insistence on acting responsibly in politics. As indicated in the Introduction, Aron believed that the genuine political actor must ask himself (or herself) "What would you do?" This is the sense of responsibility that Weber insisted upon. Whether Weber was right to frame it in terms of history is almost irrelevant. What is relevant is that the politician makes decisions that impact hundreds of thousands, if not millions, of people's lives. Again, Weber may not have been correct to insist that there are always going to be economic struggles but he was certainly correct to insist that the consequences could be deadly. Weber was interested in economic struggle; Aron was concerned with military battles. While the consequences of economic conflict can be, and are often, dire, wars lead to the deaths not just of the actual combatants, but also large portions of the civilian population. And as much as the casualties in the First World War were staggering, the numbers during the Second World War were even worse. Also, he understood how deadly a nuclear war could be. Thus, Aron took to heart Weber's insistence on acting responsibly in politics.

This leads to the secondary point of this chapter, which was to indicate the enormous impact that Weber had on Aron and how it is manifested throughout Aron's various writings. Max Weber will no longer be so prominently discussed in the following chapters but his presence will continue to be felt throughout this book. Aron spent his entire life studying the thinking of a very large number of people and had considerable respect for some of them.[27] However, no one seems to have held a more prominent place in Aron's own thinking than Max Weber. And, there is no one who seemed to have figured in Aron's political thinking as much as Weber did.

## NOTES

1. The entire quotation is: "Also related to the powerful need of the masses of the nation which burdens the sharpened social conscience of the new generation, we must also . . . confess that what burdens us even more today is the consciousness of our responsibility *before history*." "Auch Angeschichts der gewaltigen Not der Massen der Nation, welche das geschärfte soziale Gewissen der neuen Generation belastet, müssen wir aufrichtig bekennen: schwerer noch lastest auf uns heute das Bewußtstein unserer Verantwortlichkeit *vor der Geschichte*." The quotation is found in Weber (1993b: 571).

2. Numerous Aron scholars acknowledge Weber's importance for Aron's early thinking but maintain that he grew somewhat disillusioned with Weber. They regard this as a healthy progression towards Aron's independence. Most Weberian experts ignore Aron and the only one who does not, agrees with the Aron scholars that Aron changed his thinking about Weber. However, he contends that this was a defect (see Breiner 2011). To state my view at the outset, I do not think that Aron ever changed his mind regarding Weber's influence, even if he did modify his own views on politics.

3. It is clearly found in his 1895 Freiburg Inaugural Lecture, "Der Nationalstaat und die Volkswirtschaftspolitik" and it is more than hinted at in his 1920 Munich course on "Staatsoziologie." See Weber (1993a: especially 565, 573) and Weber (2009).

4. Joachim Stark was an exception but even he did not seem to be too concerned with Aron's conception of Weber as a "Machtpolitiker" and apparently overlooked Aron's 1964 lecture, "Max Weber und die Machtpolitik" (Stark 1986: esp. 98–102).

5. Colquhoun (1986a: 1). Colquhoun quotes Ralf Dahrendorf's observations from 1979: "Raymond Aron is the only social scientist of recent decades who in view of his wide sphere of interest, his combination of analysis and action, commitment and power of understanding, his blend of critical revolt and critical reserve, may be compared in terms of significance with Max Weber."

6. Aron's views on Weber's significance and his work did not seem to change very much between this work, which was first published in 1934, and his later published lectures, which appeared in 1967 with the title *Les Étapes de la pensée sociologique* (Aron 1967).

7. Aron (1953: VII). It is curious that Colquhoun does not mention Aron's acknowledgment of Mannheim's role in prompting him to write this book. Colquhoun suggested that the idea for writing the book came from Célestin Bouglé (Colquhoun 1986a: 99). It is also strange that the chapter entitled "Max Weber and German Sociology" is devoted not to Weber but to the entire book and its reception. Of the eighteen pages in that chapter, only four were actually devoted to setting out Aron's early interpretation of Weber.

8. Aron (1953: 105); Aron (1950: 110). It is worth quoting the original in full because of the emphasis that the translator added: "En autres termes, pour faire saisir l'opposition avec la philosophie de Durkheim, disons que, grâce à la compréhension, le monde de l'histoire n'est plus un ensemble de choses, mais le devenir de vies humaines."

9. Suffice it to say that Weber's notion of causality is rather complex and cannot be treated here. One could write an entire article on Aron's understanding of the Weberian conception of causality in history, not to mention that Weber's conception of causality is notoriously resistant to comprehension.

10. "Die Wissenschaft zeigt uns, was wir wollen und was wir können, niemals aber was wir sollen" (Aron 1953: 117).

11. Weber later modifies this by insisting that these two ethics complement each other and explains by maintaining that politics is done with both the head and the heart – that while the need to keep a critical distance and act with sober calculation is vital, passion is also required. Finally, even the follower of the "ethics of conviction" needs to have a final standard and Weber invokes Martin Luther's "ich kann nicht anders, hier stehe ich" ("Here I stand, I can do no other") (Weber 1992: 249–50).

12. A French version of this lecture, "Max Weber et la politique de puissance," is found in Aron (1967: 642–56).

13. For an account of the first conference of the DGS see Adair-Toteff (2005: 1–41).

14. In his account of the early years of the DGS, Dirk Käsler regarded Weber as one of the five members of its "core" ("Kern") along with Tönnies, Sombart, Leopold von Weise, and Franz Oppenheimer. He also indicated that out of a total of 883 names that were mentioned during the first seven conferences of the DGS (that is, between 1910 and 1930), Max Weber's name was mentioned much more frequently than any other (Weber 116, Marx 81, Tönnies 60, Hegel 48) (Käsler 1984: 37, 608–10).

15. In his opening address to the 1964 DGS conference, Otto Stammer recounted Weber's importance for the founding of the discipline and especially for the DGS. And, despite Weber's differences about value judgments with some of its members, he strongly believed in its future (Stammer 1965: 7–8).

16. Aron (1965b: 103). Mommsen undoubtedly knew that his book would be controversial because the motto that he chose was a quotation from a letter that Weber wrote to Friedrich von Gottl-Ottlilienfeld from 1906: "Bitte

polemisieren *so scharf wie möglich* gegen meine Ansichten in den Punkten, wo wir differien" ("Please polemicize *as sharply as possible* against my views on those points where we differ") (Mommsen 1959: V). In the second edition, Mommsen insisted that his interpretation of Weber still stood, despite massive criticisms, and added an afterword of more than thirty pages in which he addressed some of those (Mommsen 1974: 442–77).

17. Mommsen (1959: 38); Bergstraesser (1957: 209). Bergstraesser's paper is still worth reading to gain a very insightful and a carefully objective view of Weber's "Antrittsrede." Not only was Bergstraesser an important political sociologist in his own right but he had been a student of Max and Alfred Weber. Unfortunately, Bergstraesser died just before the 1964 conference and it would have been rather interesting to hear his comments on Aron's paper. In fact, he had been the person scheduled to lead the discussion, but after his death, Carl J. Friedrich was chosen to lead it (Stammer 1965: 2, 121).

18. "Ich vergesse nicht für einen Augenblick die Unterscheidung, die Weber zwischen Wissenschaft und Politik macht. Die Art, jedoch, wie Weber selber diese Unterscheidung gehandhabt hat, ist nicht immer vorbildlich" (Aron 1965b: 104).

19. "Es ist gut, Tatsachen nicht mit Werten, Wirklichkeit nicht mit Wünschen zu verwechseln" (Aron 1965b: 104).

20. Weber emphasized his point: "Nur Herrenvölker haben den Beruf, in die Speichen der Weltentwicklung einzugreifen." Aron did not appear to emphasize it.

21. Aron quotes a note to the incomplete manuscript "Machtprestige und Nationalgefühl": "Culture prestige and power prestige are closely connected" ("Kultur-Prestige und Macht-Prestige sind eng verbündet") (Weber 2001: 247; Aron 1965b: 108).

22. "Eine Welt ohne Konflikte ist tatsächlich unvorstellbar." "Eine Welt, in der die Klassen und Nationen nicht mehr im Kampf ums Dasein verstrickt sind, ist dagegen nicht unvorstellbar" (Aron 1965b: 114).

23. "Der Sieger auf dem Wahlschlachtfeld unterscheidet sich dem Wesen, nicht dem Grade nach, von dem Sieger auf dem militärischen Schlachtfeld" (Aron 1965b: 114).

24. Aron (1965b: 115); Weber (1992: 237–8). Nelson and Colen display a lack of understanding of Weber's two ethics when they maintain that the adherent to the "ethics of responsibility" must have "the fortitude to take responsibility for the consequences, intended and unintended, of political action" (Nelson and Colen 2015: 206). They make it seem as if Weber believed that the "ethics of responsibility" was just as absolute as the "ethics of conviction." However, one of Weber's major objections to the latter was that it was absolute; hence could not be expected to be followed by many people but only those few special supra-human beings like Jesus. In contrast, Weber stressed the humanness of the "ethics of responsibility" and this is shown by Weber's insistence that the person must be responsible for "the (foreseeable) *consequences* of his actions" ("die [voraussehbaren] *Folgen* seines Handelns") (Weber 1992: 237). This contrasts with the adherent to the "ethics of conviction," who is absolutely indifferent to any consequences ("ohne Rücksicht auf die Folgen") (Weber 1992: 236).

They also overlook the need to combine hot "passion" ("Leidenschaft") and cool "sense of measure" ("Augenmaß") because the first is necessary in order to do anything well (in scholarship and in politics), while the second is necessary in order not to be caught up in "sterile excitement" in politics. It is needed in large measure to reduce the likelihood of suffering from the "deadly sin" ("Todefeindin") of "vanity" ("Eitelkeit") in politics (Weber 1992: 81, 227–8). "Augenmaß" is difficult to translate; Nelson and Colen's "sense of proportion" is not far off but "sense of measure" is somewhat closer. "Augenmaß" is literally "eye measure" but Weber is clear that "Leidenschaft" brings one very close, if not too close, to the matter at hand, whereas "Augenmaß" pushes one to a safer and more objective distance.

25. "Als Mensch und Philosoph hat Max Weber uns ein Erbe hinterlassen, das keine möglichen Irrtümer des Theoretikers der Machtpolitik beeinträchtigen können" (Aron 1965b: 120).

26. Stammer (1965: 152). The issue of whether Schmitt was or was not a legitimate follower of Weber is still a rather contentious issue. Aron did not voice an opinion on this matter.

27. This list would have to include Thucydides and Clausewitz but for different reasons: the former because of his role as the first historian and the latter because of his role as the formulator of concepts regarding war. These are reasons why both Thucydides and Clausewitz will figure so prominently in this book.

# CHAPTER THREE

# On Clausewitz

"In war everything is simple, but the simple is the most difficult." Clausewitz[1]

Raymond Aron discovered the writings of Max Weber rather early in life but over the years it may have seemed that he had lost some of his enthusiasm for Weber's ideas in general and for his political ideas in particular. In contrast, Aron did not begin to read Carl von Clausewitz's writings until he was considerably older but it seems that his appreciation for Clausewitz's ideas only continued to increase over time. Clausewitz was a soldier and Weber was a professor but they shared the same conviction regarding the importance of thoughtful responsibility. They also believed in the need for intellectual honesty and for political realism. Thus, Weber and Clausewitz shared many of the same convictions about scholarship and politics, and as a result, both exerted considerable influence on Aron's thinking. The previous chapter was devoted to Weber's impact; this chapter focuses on Clausewitz's influence on Aron. In order to do this, the focus will be on Aron's book on Clausewitz's *Vom Kriege*.[2]

## ARON DISCOVERS CLAUSEWITZ

In the Preface to the first volume of *Penser la guerre, Clausewitz*, Aron recalled the three different times in which he had encountered Clausewitz's ideas. The first time was in 1932, when Aron was in Berlin. He had become friends with Herbert Rosinski, who was devoted to understanding Clausewitz's thinking: especially his thinking between the years 1827 and 1830. Aron and Rosinski had discussed Carl Schmitt's highly controversial "Der Begriff des Politischen" but Aron did not offer his opinion about Schmitt. Aron would do that later in his book on Clausewitz. We can gather that Rosinski was more interested in his favorite author, Clausewitz. In fact, Rosinski had intended to write a book on the development of Clausewitz's later thinking; unfortunately, he never did so. Aron attributed part of Rosinski's failure to write the book of his dreams to Rosinski's exhausting life as an emigrant and part of it to his "inner difficulties" (Aron 1976a: 9; Aron 1980a: 17). Rosinski did manage to publish an article on Clausewitz, "Die Entwicklung von Clausewitz' Werk *Vom Kriege*, im Lichte seiner 'Vorreden' und 'Nachrichten,'" in *Historische Zeitschrift* in 1935. Aron confessed that he did not seem to remember sharing Rosinski's enthusiasm for Clausewitz; however, Rosinski's article must have made a fairly substantial impression on him. Aron recalled coming across his copy of that article in the early 1950s and was rather surprised and quite pleased that it had survived during all of the changes and the moves in Aron's life.

The second encounter was in London during the war, when Aron became acquainted with a Polish emigrant by the name of Stanilas Syzmonzyk. Syzmonzyk wrote articles on military science for *La France libre*; he composed them in German and Aron translated them into French. Aron recounted how Syzmonzyk was a passionate follower of Clausewitz and was as dedicated to understanding him as Rosinski had been. However, Aron suggested that Clausewitz had not yet made a significant impact on him and he admitted he had still not bothered to read *Vom Kriege* (Aron 1976a: 10–11; Aron 1980a: 18).

The third encounter with Clausewitz was in 1955 and this was prompted by the publication of *Vom Kriege* in a French translation. It was not so much that Aron was impressed by Clausewitz's theories than that he found *Vom Kriege* to be useful for his own writings. Besides, like many others, Aron found the work to be a "treasure chest" of citations (Aron 1976a: 11; Aron 1980a: 18). However, from 1955 on, Aron began to read *Vom Kriege* seriously, and in doing so, he found a number of things to be surprising. First, he found the work to have multiple meanings and, as a result, it was really difficult to uncover its secret. Second, Aron likened it to a crime novel but it lacked the final clue at the end of the book that revealed everything. That was because Aron believed that Clausewitz had never provided such a clue in his book.[3] And third, Aron found it remarkable that he was often in agreement with Clausewitz. This was surprising because Aron was French and he noted that Clausewitz hated the French. Aron also observed that Clausewitz hated the French people in general but that he really detested Napoleon in particular. However, Aron suggested that, in this manner, Clausewitz was merely expressing the sense of the time. Furthermore, Aron suggested that any Frenchman who condemns Clausewitz for having such sentiments against the French during the period 1806 to 1815 should keep in mind what the French experienced under Hitler between 1940 and 1945 (Aron 1976a: 12–13; Aron 1980a: 20–1). Just as Weber did not wish to conflate facts with values, Clausewitz did not wish to judge but to understand. Aron wanted to do the same. That is why he ended his Preface with the observation that one does not need to be a "German, a Prussian, or an officer" in order to understand Clausewitz.[4]

## Aron on Clausewitz's *Vom Kriege*

In the Introduction, Aron wished to offer more than a general preamble; he intended to provide the theoretical framework for his understanding of Clausewitz's work. Aron noted that Clausewitz was rightly regarded as a writer but he emphasized several critical points. First, Clausewitz published only three pieces during his lifetime and all three appeared anonymously. Second, Clausewitz was more than a thinker; he was a doer. Aron pointed out that while Clausewitz was clearly a "great thinker," he was also someone who knew how to use a saber. Third, Clausewitz was a product of his time but he did not write for his contemporaries. Aron insisted that Clausewitz wrote for himself or – what amounts to the same thing – he wrote for posterity. Fourth, Aron noted that *Vom Kriege* was not just an unfinished work, but also one that Clausewitz labored over for decades. Clausewitz began to work on it seriously in 1816, so Aron believed it important to note the steps of the development in Clausewitz's thinking. These four points reveal that Aron was uninterested in providing an ideal, theoretical account of Clausewitz's work; rather, he wanted to provide an account that was real, if not "positivistic." Clausewitz himself frequently noted the crucial differences between the ideal and the real interpretation of war, and he always chose the latter. Aron intended to do something similarly "real" in his interpretation of *Vom Kriege* and that is why he chose the subtitle, "The Historical Interpretation."[5] However, Aron did not intend his work to be an empirical conception; rather, it was conceived as an analysis and a commentary as well (Aron 1976a: 30; Aron 1980a: 34).

The first part of Aron's book is devoted to Clausewitz the man and his work. The first two chapters of this part are devoted to a discussion of Clausewitz's life, and while they are quite informative and very interesting, they do not have all that much to do with Aron's analysis of *Vom Kriege*. There are, of course, exceptions and these include

Aron's comments regarding Clausewitz's need for "spirit and deed" ("Geist und Tat") but he objected to those biographers who try to separate Clausewitz's life into two separate periods.[6] Another exception is Aron's comments about Clausewitz and his reportedly pessimistic type of philosophy. Aron suggested that Clausewitz's pessimism was over-emphasized and his realism was underemphasized – Clausewitz was free from illusion but not from passion (Aron 1976a: 33; Aron 1980a: 36). Another exception is Aron's observation that, as a philosopher, he never doubted the existence of war, just as a theologian never doubts the existence of God (Aron 1976a: 37; Aron 1980a: 40). And a final exception is Aron's comment about the nobility and their responsibility for many, if not most, of Europe's problems. Aron was inclined to assign blame when and where he saw it. For him, it was bad enough that the German nobility did not allow modernization. Aron held that Germany would not have been a rather poor country if the country had modernized in the East as well as the West. Aron recognized that the industrialization in the Western part of the country brought its own problems but that they were not severe. And he recognized that the continual emphasis on agriculture and the refusal to adopt more mechanical means of farming meant that the Eastern part of Germany was ripe for major unrest. However, Aron was convinced that the problems in Europe were made even worse because of the French nobility. Clausewitz contended that the revolution in France occurred because of their actions. These actions, as well as the nobles' refusal to act on other matters, had finally provoked the peasants into rebellion (Aron 1976a: 63–4; Aron 1980a: 64–5). Both the Germans and the French had acted without thinking through the consequences of their positions. Aron wished to show that Clausewitz's hatred of the French was partially justified, even if he did not completely agree with it. Aron recognized that it would be difficult for his French audience to have an objective view regarding this Prussian general, but he did attempt to demonstrate why Clausewitz is important and worth studying. Aron spent a fair amount of effort in recounting Clausewitz's life and he did so, not just to retell it, but also to prompt some sympathy for Clausewitz (Aron 1976a: 76; Aron 1980a: 75).

Aron often repeated his claim that Clausewitz was a "thinker without illusions" and that in politics, and especially in war, one must not attempt to impose one's ideas on the matter but the matter itself must determine the response.[7] Aron noted the similarity between Clausewitz and Max Weber because both insisted on taking a sensible and sober approach to important matters, and in Clausewitz's opinion, war was a very serious matter. If politicians make frivolous decisions, the repercussions are terrible enough, but when generals make faulty decisions, people die. That is why Clausewitz was so critical of D. H. von Bulow's book on the spirit of the modern system of war. According to Aron, Clausewitz found Bulow's book not just wrong, but almost laughingly so. Bulow's book contained dogma and not science; Clausewitz's writings would be anti-dogmatic and strictly scientific (Aron 1976a: 79–83; Aron 1980a: 80–5). Unfortunately, many scholars seemed to have regarded *Vom Kriege* as a theoretical and normative book, and had not recognized that it was an ethical book as well. The fact that so many scholars misread the book troubled Aron greatly. Aron indicates a number of the major misunderstandings of some of Clausewitz's most famous ideas. These included Clausewitz's belief that the purpose of war was the defeat of the enemy and that this meant either a total defeat or a partial one. Aron noted the similarity with boxing: either a knock-out victory or one on points (Aron 1976a: 103; Aron 1980a: 98). Aron did not appear to have anyone specifically in mind here, but he did regarding Clausewitz's claim that "war is nothing but the continuation of politics by other means."[8] The person he had in mind was Walther Malmsten Schering. Aron objected to several things about Schering: his usual tendency towards exaggeration and sloppy scholarship (Aron 1976a: 104, 106; Aron 1980a: 97, 101). These are some of the criticisms that Aron leveled at Schering; he makes many more about him as well as about others later in his book. Accordingly, they will be treated both towards the end of this chapter and in a later one.

Next to Clausewitz's claim that war is the continuation of politics by other means, his dictum that there are two types of war is perhaps the most famous and the least understood of all of his claims. Aron makes a note of this early in his book but postpones his examination of the claim until later (Aron 1976a: 102; Aron 1980a: 97). For now, it is important to list Clausewitz's two types and, following Aron, postpone a discussion of them until later. In his "Nachricht," Clausewitz insisted that there is a "double type of war" ("doppelte Art des Krieges"): in one, the goal is the *destruction* of the enemy, in which the enemy is destroyed politically or at least made defenseless. The ultimate goal is to ensure a lasting peace. In the other, the goal is more limited and is restricted to the *disarmament* of the enemy's forces. The victor then can make use of this disarmament to ensure peace. Clausewitz readily admitted that the boundary between the two types is fluid (Clausewitz 1973: 179). Aron maintained that when one side destroys the other, then the victor can dictate the terms of peace, but when one side disarms the other, then both sides must negotiate the conditions of the peace.[9] The question is whether war serves a political purpose or a military goal

(Aron 1976a: 109; Aron 1980a: 103). Clausewitz does not provide an answer, if one can call it that, until later in his work. For now, Aron restricts himself to providing a brief overview of *Vom Kriege*. Aron notes that Clausewitz begins by offering a series of definitions, and while they seem to be rather straightforward, they have been the subject of considerable controversy. The most important of those definitions are these three: force, goal, and purpose. Aron does not provide a thorough discussion of them here but makes the point that these are tentative definitions. He makes the related point that Clausewitz noted that an absolute war has not occurred in reality and that it exists as a concept in the "world of ideals."[10] Aron spent most of Chapter Three in the first part in discussing the various interpretations of Clausewitz's own ideas. The second and third parts of Aron's book contain his examination of *Vom Kriege* itself.

*Vom Kriege* is a book that is composed of two parts, which contain six actual "books" and the outlines for two others. Clausewitz refers to each of these as a "book" so in the interest of clarity, these will be referred to as "Buch" so as to differentiate them from the book *Vom Kriege*. Aron began by providing a brief "Buch" as a "Buch" overview. "Buch" One contains the definition of war, its nature, and its purpose. "Buch" Two contains a discussion about the "theory of a theory" and one of the major points is that it is about method and is somewhat similar to an epistemology. The chapter also contains a discussion regarding the relationship between knowledge and power. It is complex and is indicative of the interconnections with both. "Buch" Three is an examination of strategy. "Buch" Four is devoted to combat and "Buch" Five is focused on the fighting forces. "Buch" Six is devoted to defense and "Buch" Seven contains an outline for attack. "Buch" Eight is another outline but this time it is about the relation between politics and war, thus referring back to "Buch" One (Aron 1976a: 151–6; Aron 1980a: 139–43). Aron chose not to follow Clausewitz's own divisions but devotes his Part Two to dialectic and his Part Three to the theoretical plan. Like Part One, Parts Two and Three each contain three chapters that are devoted to specific topics. These chapters, like the earlier ones, contain Aron's analyses of Clausewitz's own ideas in combination with discussions about the interpretations of others. This is evident in Chapter Four of Aron's book, which is entitled "Means and Ends." There, he follows Clausewitz's differentiation between tactic and strategy. Aron notes that Clausewitz had done this in one of his earlier, anonymous publications, but he adds that in *Vom Kriege* Clausewitz is focused on what he calls the "small war" ("klein Krieg") (Aron 1976a: 161–2; Aron 1980a: 147–8). By "small war," Clausewitz meant a type of war that involved combat ("Gefecht") with 20, 50, 100, or 3,400 men. Clausewitz was not assigning a better moral value to the "small war"; rather, it was the type of war that was easiest to understand because of the smaller numbers. Thus, it was more of a heuristic device than an account of reality, and the boundary between the "small war" and a "large war" was not firm nor fixed. If this reminds one of Max Weber's thinking about ideal types being heuristic devices and the boundaries between two types not being rigid, it is with reason. These points are not the only ones that are similar to Weber's; Aron points out two others. First is Weber's insistence on a sober understanding, which is similar to Clausewitz's emphasis on the "Gesunder Menschenverstand."[11] This is important because of a general German inclination towards speculative idealism and its "metaphysical fog" ("metaphysische Nebel"). Second is Weber's emphasis on "purposeful rationality" ("Zweckrationalität"), which is similar to Clausewitz's "means and ends" ("Mittel und Zweck") (Aron 1976a: 161; Aron 1980a: 147). Aron maintained that "Mittel–Zweck" was the highest of the oppositions and that "tactic–strategy" and "war–politics" serve to illustrate it.

Strategy and tactic are not really opposites as they are two parts of a reciprocal interchange; that is why Aron refers to this process as "dialectic" or as a chain (Aron 1976a: 167, 169, 172; Aron 1980a: 152, 154, 157). This is important to keep in mind when considering Clausewitz's famous dictum "Der Krieg ist die fortgesetzte Staatspolitik mit anderen Mitteln" (Aron 1976a: 168; Aron 1980a: 154). Aron pointed out that Clausewitz was not so concerned with peace and noted the contrast with Kant's work on perpetual peace. For Clausewitz, war was a normal, if not natural, condition. As Aron reminded us, Clausewitz never wrote a book on politics or morality, but on the factum of war (Aron 1976a: 174; Aron 1980a: 158–9). Aron also reminds us that "victory" is a strict military concept and is connected to tactics and not to strategy; he warns that one should not confuse war with politics but that war is a result of politics (Aron 1976a: 174; Aron 1980a: 159). Aron clarifies the differences between war and politics by insisting that war is struggle and the single means of struggle in war is combat; the highest goal is to make the enemy powerless (Aron 1976a: 178–82; Aron 1980a: 162–5). These are military goals and not political ones; the first supports the second.

Aron clarifies what Clausewitz meant about morality and war in his fifth chapter, entitled "Le moral et le physique." Here, Aron discusses the origins of Clausewitz's relationship between morality and the physical in war. Aron granted that Clausewitz wrote of morality and of virtues, but stressed that this was not about ethics but about efficiency and victory. Aron made this clear by his extensive discussion of "genius", of knowledge, and of natural talents. Aron also made it clear that while Clausewitz despised Napoleon for what had done, he also regarded him as a military genius. Aron noted that as much as Clausewitz recognized Napoleon's strategic genius, he also recognized that he was humanly fallible.

Aron clarifies Clausewitz's notion of morality in war by emphasizing that this is not a matter of ethics: machineguns kill soldiers regardless of their ethical beliefs (Aron 1976a: 195; Aron 1980a: 177). Rather, Clausewitz's notion of morality in warfare is based upon his understanding of the human will. He recognizes that success in war is often dependent upon the physical characteristics of the soldiers as well as the physical layout of the battlefield, but he placed more emphasis on the soldier's sense of determination and intelligence. Aron spells this out by insisting that Clausewitz maintained that war is a relationship between wills and that physical force serves to determine whether the wills of one side will dominate the other (Aron 1976a: 198; Aron 1980a: 178). Clausewitz often likened war to a card game and he was massively criticized for that. What his critics failed to understand was that Clausewitz was not making this comparison in order to minimize the sense of destruction; rather, it served to explain many of his points about the nature of war. Aron attempted to drive this point home by showing how Clausewitz was correct in using a card game as a means to explain war. Rather than regarding war as some uncontrollable fight, Clausewitz believed that each side tried to calculate whether his side was likely to win. However, as Aron stressed, rational calculation will extend only so far because there are many other factors that contribute to victory or defeat and many of these factors cannot be determined ahead of time. Thus, in war as in a game of cards, luck is important. Moreover, in war as in cards, courage and other "mental" characteristics play critical roles (Aron 1976a: 198; Aron 1980a: 179; Clausewitz 1973: 207–8). As much as one can approach war (and cards) with a rational expectation of winning, each war (and every card game) is different. That is why Clausewitz insisted that war is a chameleon not just because its nature changes in every case but because war has three components: first, hatred of the enemy; second, the play of probability; and third, the role of understanding. The first of these can mostly be found in the general population of a country, whereas the other two are found specifically in the nation's military leaders (Clausewitz 1973: 212–13).

The military leader should possess two elements: understanding ("Verstand") and "feeling" ("Gemüt"). Aron refers to this as a "duality" yet, later, he adds a third element: courage ("Mut"). Thus, there are the three elements of "feeling, understanding, courage" ("affection, entendement, courage"; "Gefühl, Verstand, Mut") (Aron 1976a: 201; Aron 1980a: 180–3). This is another illustration of Clausewitz's employment of dialectic: thesis, antithesis, and synthesis. That is, the "opposition" between "understanding" and "feeling" needs to be developed into a third element – "courage." However, Clausewitz's notion of "courage" is a particularly military virtue. Aron noted that Clausewitz stressed that the three virtues were distinctly military characteristics, and that while these were necessary for ensuring victory, they were not sufficient. That is why Clausewitz added an "antithesis" to this, and that is the combination of other factors that help determine the outcome of the battle and the war (Aron 1976a: 208; Aron 1980a: 188). These factors include the number of troops, the use of artifice, and the element of surprise. Certainly, the number of troops can influence the outcome of a battle but Clausewitz was convinced that artifice and surprise could compensate for a smaller number of soldiers (Aron 1976a: 217; Aron 1980a: 196). Perhaps the biggest and most determining factor in Clausewitz's concept of war is his notion of "genius." However, before Aron discusses that, he wants to clarify Clausewitz's choice of words. Aron focuses on understanding and feeling, and maintains that the question is: how can these two be unified in the military leader (Aron 1976a: 220; Aron 1980a: 198)? Understanding (or intelligence) is necessary in war because of its complexities and its variations. Clausewitz captures each of these in two remarks. The first one is justly famous, the second one less so. Clausewitz wrote: "Everything in war is really simple, but the simplest is difficult."[12] Clausewitz also noted that the military leader's need to calculate is similar to that of Newton and Euler, and that is because if the "multitude of variables" (Aron 1976a: 221; Aron 1980a: 200). Intelligence needs to triumph over the danger, the physical demands, the uncertainty, and the accidental ("Zufall") (Aron 1976a: 222; Aron 1980a: 201). Clausewitz insists that rationality is important but he maintains that there are so many variables that it is difficult to plan and impossible to predict. That is why he stresses how often uncertainties and accidents influence one's battle plans. Thus, possessing the ability to calculate is crucial but possessing just that ability is often insufficient. Besides intelligence, the military leader needs emotion, and by that Clausewitz meant courage. Courage takes two forms: the courage to risk one's life and the courage to take responsibility for what happens. Because of the uncertainties in battle, the military leader must have courage and this courage is in a dialectical process with understanding. It is the understanding that gives the power to stand fast and to remain true to one's self (Aron 1976a: 223–4; Aron 1980a: 201–3). The leader who has the highest level of intelligence and is the most courageous (both in Clausewitz's sense) has the "warrior genius" ("kriegerischer Genius"). In Clausewitz's mind, there were two such leaders who possessed this "warrior genius" as well as political wisdom in recent times: Napoleon and Friedrich II. However, Aron noted that Napoleon's career ended in catastrophe whereas Friedrich II was successful both off and on the battlefield. Aron points to the fact that not only was Friedrich a military genius, but also had the steadfast devotion of his troops and his citizens. And Aron was too polite to mention Clausewitz's personal animosity towards the French leader (Aron 1976a: 229–39; Aron 1980a: 207–8).

Aron appears to have mixed feelings about the chapter on the notions of defense and attack. On one hand, he suggests that it is so complex that only military specialists would be able to understand or evaluate it, and on the other hand, he believes that it is incredibly important for two reasons. First, Clausewitz argues that, in battle, defense is more important than offense. That is why his title is "Verteidigung und Angriff" ("Defence and Attack") and not the reverse. While Clausewitz believed in the dialectic between the two, he placed more emphasis on defense. Aron reminds us that Clausewitz used the terms "Verteidigung" ("defense") and "Widerstand" ("resistance") interchangeably (Aron 1976a: 237–40; Aron 1980a: 213–16) and notes that Clausewitz believes that defense/resistance has three components: "*abwehren, abwarten*, und *erhalten.*" These three may be rendered as turning away, deflecting, or repulsing; waiting, biding one's time, or being patient; and maintaining, preserving, or conserving (Aron 1976a: 240; Aron 1980a: 216). It should be apparent from the last two that Clausewitz believed that patience and resolve are extremely important in battle. He believed that too many battles were lost because the generals made too many hasty decisions or were too indecisive and changed their opinions too frequently. Accordingly, Clausewitz placed more emphasis on defense than he did on attack. Aron suggests that Clausewitz has two justifications for believing that defense is more important than attack: first, on the battlefield as well as in court, defense is more important than attack or prosecution, and second, history suggests that defense is more important than attack (Aron 1976a: 245; Aron 1980a: 220–1). The defending force has many natural things at its disposal: mountains, rivers, and valleys (Aron 1976a: 248–9; Aron 1980a: 223–4). Finally, there is a second reason why Aron thinks so highly of this chapter and that is because it shows the best side of Clausewitz's thinking and the text has lasting value. These pages show his anti-dogmatism, his sense of history, and the constant renewal of his method (Aron 1976a: 247; Aron 1980a: 223).

The first chapter of the third part is on theory and law, and as expected, is devoted to the most theoretical parts of *Vom Kriege*. Aron suggests that they not only are epistemological or methodological, but are fundamentally "theory of theory". He also suggests that they were written late in Clausewitz's life – that is, sometime after 1827 – and that they not only are incomplete but also contain contradictory and confusing passages and references. Aron makes a considerable effort to explain Clausewitz's conception of theory and notes that it differs from the military theories of Clausewitz's contemporaries. Aron begins by setting out the four basic errors that theorists make. First, they focus on only one variable: that is, they do not consider other crucial factors. Second, they focus only on major factors: that is, similar to the first point, here they erroneously believe that only major factors are worth considering. Third, they have the illusion of knowledge through the measurement of major numbers: that is, they do not recognize that what may seem minor, and even trivial, factors often determine the course of the war. And fourth, they ignore the process of reciprocity: that is, they believe that one overarching explanation is sufficient when, as Clausewitz contends, war is a continuous back-and-forth process (Aron 1976a: 288; Aron 1980a: 257). In other words, in their zeal for general abstractness, these theoreticians ignore the complexities and details that make up reality. This complaint is underscored by Clausewitz's demand that theory must respect the complexities of the object of the study as well as his insistence that two situations can never be the same. The human dimension is therefore critical, first, because of human powers and their effects; second, because of people's reaction; and third, because of the uncertainties of numerous factors. Each of these factors plays critical roles in determining the outcome of a battle (Aron 1976a: 288–9; Aron 1980a: 257). Clausewitz admits that theory is critical but he also insists that it cannot be ideal, and this same principle applies equally well to laws.

In the introduction to the section on Clausewitz's conception of laws, Aron reminds us that Clausewitz frequently made use of antitheses throughout *Vom Kriege* and that it should come as no surprise that he has an antithesis regarding laws. This is the antithesis between "necessary laws" ("Notwendige Gesetze") and "probable laws" ("Wahrscheinlichkeitsgesetze").[13] On the face of this, it should be rather easy to distinguish between these two types of laws. However, there are three things that indicate that this is not easy to do. First is Aron's repeated use of question marks in his attempt to decide what the "highest law" is. Second is his admission that he was not readily convinced by Schering's claim that the "highest law" was a "law of occurrence." Third is Aron's suggestion that we look at other passages in which Clausewitz wrote about laws. In light of this, Clausewitz's claim that the choice of weapons is the deciding factor in every type of operation in war should not so much be regarded as the "highest law" as it should be compared to his observation that money is the basis for the exchange of goods. Aron deemed two things important: one, that Clausewitz warned that the concept of war needed to be cut free from the notion of inner necessity and should be considered in terms of probability; and two, necessary laws are not found in reality. Aron concludes from all of this that "necessary laws" do not belong in the real world but in the ideal one, and that the antithesis between "necessary laws" and "probable laws" is indicative of the distance between concepts and reality (Aron 1976a: 295–7; Aron 1980a: 262–5).

Aron notes that Clausewitz has three additional types of laws: "original law" ("Urgesetz"), "universal law" ("allgemeines Gesetz"), and "dynamic law" ("dynamisches Gesetz") (Aron 1976a: 304; Aron 1980a: 271). That Aron is uncertain that these are explicitly found in *Vom Kriege* is indicated by his use of the word "baptized", meaning that he has given them names rather than finding them in Clausewitz's book.[14] The "original law" appears to be the law that the first strike is the most important strike and that successive attacks are generally less meaningful. Aron does not clarify this but it appears that the importance of the initial strike is based upon the first application of force. The "universal law" is even less clear but apparently applies to the double nature of attack: first, to secure the possible retreat and, second, to threaten the enemy. The order of the two might seem odd but it fits with Clausewitz's belief in the need for safety for one's troops. The "dynamic law" appears to cover the movement between the application of force and then the time of rest. It also appears to be the most historically determined of these three laws. Aron suggests that Clausewitz derived the "dynamic law" from the French Revolution and from Napoleon (Aron 1976a: 304–9; Aron 1980a: 271–6).

Aron offers a few comments in the conclusion to this chapter. He notes that Clausewitz emphasized the dual nature of battle – one side is not totally free to inflict harm on the other side; rather, the other side almost always has the capacity to fight back. A similar duality is found in the "dynamic laws," in that there is a flow in war between the tension in fighting and the rest period when the fighting dies down. Both of these observations serve to underscore Aron's observation that the laws that Clausewitz discussed are not part of any theoretical revolution but are part of the reality of historical wars (Aron 1976a: 310–11; Aron 1980a: 276–7).

Chapter Eight continues the previous chapter's concern with laws, but here the emphasis is on their relation to theory and history. At the outset of this chapter, Aron wondered which was more important: historical theory or theory that is always valid. This shows up in the contrast that Clausewitz makes between ancient and modern warfare. He suggested that what distinguished the two was that modern countries were more civilized; however, he warned that being more civilized certainly did not result in less destruction. In fact, frequently it is not the case. Furthermore, while it might seem that more intelligence would minimize the passions against the enemy, in reality that does not often happen. In fact, as Aron noted, the fire-bombing of Dresden and Germany's gas chambers, among many more instances, showed that being more civilized did not lessen the inclination towards barbarity (Aron 1976a: 314; Aron 1980a: 280).

If Clausewitz regarded history as so instructive, why did he not look to the Romans and to the Greeks for examples of warfare? Aron rules out the suggestions that he knew little Latin and no Greek, and believes that, with rare exceptions, Clausewitz did not find their military battles to be very enlightening (Aron 1976a: 315; Aron 1980a: 281). While Clausewitz obviously believed that "history is the laboratory of theory" and that "times and circumstances" play crucial roles, he was also of the opinion that not every historical episode was as instructive as any other. As Aron noted later, Clausewitz believed that every epoch had its own limiting conditions and that Friedrich II and Napoleon were the best examples of military prowess (Aron 1976a: 327–9; Aron 1980a: 292–4). However, even military geniuses make fatal mistakes, and that is what Napoleon did with his march on Moscow. As Aron put it, Clausewitz contended that while Napoleon was able to march all across Europe, he lost in Russia because he had erred in his estimation of his enemy (Aron 1976a: 333; Aron 1980a: 297).

Clausewitz believed in the combination of history and theory, so much of this chapter is devoted to theoretical laws. Aron suggests that they fall into four closely related categories: principles, rules, prescriptions, and methods (Aron 1976a: 318; Aron 1980a: 284). Aron notes that they are not totally theoretical and are based partially upon experience. Aron also appears to note that they seem to overlap and that they are not exactly clear; thus, they lead to a number of questions (Aron 1976a: 322–26; Aron 1980a: 288–90). The first question is about the relationship between the conceptual world and history. Can one construct general concepts from particular historical episodes?

Aron suggests that this question leads to the second one: can one learn about the totality of war from individual battles? Aron again suggests that Clausewitz does not seem to provide clear answers to these two questions and Aron wonders whether his contradictions do not lead him to a dead end (Aron 1976a: 327–8; Aron 1980a: 292). None the less, history offers examples of demonstrative value, even if they are not general principles (Aron 1976a: 330; Aron 1980a: 294).

Aron's final chapter in this volume is about the transition from theory to doctrine, yet it is as much about Clausewitz's earlier work on strategy as it is about *Vom Kriege*. Aron points out that Clausewitz put forth an imperative that appears to him to be unconditional: determine one's greatest and most decisive goal that one can reach, choose the shortest way to get there, and then stay steady on that path.[15] This imperative reflects several of Clausewitz's points that Aron considers to be extremely important: decision on goals, calculation of means, and perseverance. Aron adds that Clausewitz contended that, in war, one should utilize all available power and use the maximum of energy to reach one's goal. In addition, one needs to strike in the shortest time possible (Aron 1976a: 351; Aron 1980a: 313). In Aron's opinion, Clausewitz's writings showed the greatest clarity and the greatest logical simplicity compared to any other military text.[16] None the less, the question remains whether Clausewitz deserves his famous reputation. In order to answer that, Aron insists that it is necessary to determine what Clausewitz himself thought was his main decision (Aron 1976a: 352–3; Aron 1980a: 314–15). Aron suggests that the answer to that question rests upon which years of Clausewitz's life are chosen. Aron recognizes that the years between 1812 and 1830 are important but that he considers the years between 1826 and 1830 to be the most critical. That is because Clausewitz was finalizing his thoughts and revising parts of *Vom Kriege*.

Aron concludes the first volume on Clausewitz with a two-part philosophical discussion. The first part takes up the issue of how much Clausewitz owed to Kant and Hegel, while the second part is a discussion of Clausewitz's connection to Montesquieu. Both parts are intriguing but because of space cannot be given an appropriate examination here.[17] Thus, only a few observations can be offered. Aron notes at the outset that he agrees that Clausewitz believes in the importance of dialectics, a belief that Clausewitz shared with both Kant and Hegel. After all, Aron notes that the second part of this first volume has the title "The Dialectic." However, he immediately adds that it depends on which sense "dialectic" is taken in. And, that is a real indication that he thinks that Clausewitz's notion of dialectic differs from that of Kant as well as from that of Hegel (Aron 1976a: 360; Aron 1980a: 321). Part of this is because Aron believes that Clausewitz's use of conceptual pairs differs from these two philosophers, and part is because he contends that the movement from one pair to another is not the same as either Kant's dialectical movement or Hegel's more famous notion. Aron poses the question of whether Clausewitz ever read Kant or Hegel. Aron notes that while Clausewitz was in Berlin, he supposedly heard some lectures on Kantian thinking, but he also notes that they were neither very philosophical nor true to Kant's own philosophy. Regarding Hegel, Aron remarks that nowhere in *Vom Kriege* is Hegel ever mentioned. If there is no real connection to Kant, what about the apparent connection to Hegel? Clausewitz's "Hegelianism" may be based upon two grounds: during the years between 1820 and 1830, when Clausewitz was in Berlin, Hegel was teaching there and at the height of his fame; and Clausewitz and Hegel shared the same conviction regarding the importance of dialectic (Aron 1976a: 361–2; Aron 1980a: 322–3). However, Clausewitz was not interested in Hegel's philosophy in general nor in his dialectic in particular. Aron argued that, in contrast, Clausewitz shared with Kant the idea that war is political. However, that in itself should not be taken to imply that Clausewitz was a Kantian any more than his real appreciation of dialectics makes him a Hegelian (Aron 1976a: 368; Aron 1980a: 328). Furthermore, Aron insisted that Clausewitz's terminology was only superficially similar to Kant's. Aron's conclusion is that whoever believes that Clausewitz wrote in a philosophical style must also admit that Clausewitz knew very little philosophy (Aron 1976a: 170–1; Aron 1980a: 331).

Aron turns to Clausewitz and Montesquieu. Aron believed that the central problem that preoccupied Clausewitz towards the end of his life was the relationship between "absolute war" and "real war," and maintained that this was the relationship between ideas, or concepts, and the concrete, historical reality (Aron 1976a: 371–2; Aron 1980a: 331–2). This is a relationship that clearly concerned Kant and less so Hegel, but did it concern Montesquieu? This seems doubtful, just as much as Aron's suggestion that Clausewitz was a thinker who was reflective of the eighteenth century rather than of the nineteenth. Certainly, there are elements of the Enlightenment in Clausewitz's thinking, but one can find traces of Romanticism as well. Aron admits that he cannot point to any concrete evidence that Montesquieu influenced Clausewitz but he does insist that there are stylistic similarities as well as a shared manner of thought. What does seem certain to Aron is that, early in his life, Clausewitz fastened on to an idea – an idea about war and how it can be won – and never gave up trying to refine it (Aron 1976a: 372–4;

Aron 1980a: 332–4). But it seems that Clausewitz became less certain of his opinions, just as it seems that Aron became less convinced of the certainty of his reading of Clausewitz. This is evident in the decline in intensity of some of his critical comments of some of his predecessors.

## ARON'S CRITICISMS AND HIS CRITICS

This section of this chapter has two parts: the first is devoted to some of Aron's criticisms of previous Clausewitz scholars while the second part is focused on some of the scholars who provided their own critical assessments of Aron and his Clausewitz book.[18]

There are four, if not more, writers on Clausewitz with whom Aron took issue. The first was the German general Erich Ludendorff, the second was the German scholar Walther Malmsten Schering, the third was the British writer Basil Henry Liddell Hart, and the fourth was the German jurist Carl Schmitt.

Erich Ludendorff was regarded by most Germans as one of the greatest military geniuses, despite having been partially responsible for Germany's defeat in the First World War. He is important here for two reasons: first, because of his assessment of Clausewitz, and second, because of his book on total war. The focus here is on the first theme while the second will be addressed in the next chapter. Aron took issue with Ludendorff, not just because of his misunderstanding of Clausewitz, but because of his attitude towards war and politics in general. Aron confesses that much of his disapproval of Ludendorff is a result of two small books by Hans Delbrück. It is important to remember that Aron thought highly of Delbrück and valued his opinions.[19] That pertained to Delbrück's writings on history and politics but much more so to his work on war. But Aron does credit Ludendorff for moving him further away from Liddell Hart and more in the direction of Delbrück (Aron 1976a: 74–80; Aron 1980a: 735). Aron had complained about Liddell Hart's mischaracterization of Clausewitz; here, he suggests that Clausewitz was perhaps good at tactics, but not so much at strategy. But, he suggests that Delbrück was probably not exaggerating when he suggested that Delbrück seemed to prefer Clausewitz's strategy over that of the French general Foch.[20] Aron faults Ludendorff for a number of things: for not having a decent sense of strategy, for not recognizing military realities, and for not taking responsibility for the loss of the war. In all three cases Aron echoes Delbrück. First, Delbrück argued that Ludendorff was not the military genius that many Germans (and others) thought. In his opinion, Ludendorff was no Gneisenau.[21] Second, he insisted that Ludendorff refused to see that Germany was doomed to lose the war (Delbrück 1920: 15–16). Delbrück accused Ludendorff of having squandered the offensive of 1918 because he had no strategy and no sense of the consequences (Delbrück 1922: 35). And third, he accused Ludendorff of blaming everyone and everything else for Germany's loss rather than accepting that Germany's defeat was mostly a result of his lack of honesty and responsibility (Delbrück 1920: 5, 15–16; Delbrück 1922: 11, 14). In fact, Delbrück wondered whether Ludendorff had ever paid close attention to what Clausewitz had written (Delbrück 1922: 12). Aron seems to have wondered the same.

Walther Malmsten Schering was a well-regarded military expert and wrote on a number of different aspects regarding military affairs, but the focus here is on his writings about Clausewitz. Most scholars thought highly of Schering but Aron's opinion of him was somewhat mixed. Although he objected to a number of Schering's interpretations, he regarded Schering's writings as among the most important books on Clausewitz (Aron 1976b: 346; Aron 1980a: 758). Aron allows that he often refers to Schering, but he objected to Schering's novel interpretation of "Mittel–Zweck." Schering insisted that both "Mittel" and "Zweck" had different meanings during the nineteenth century than they did during the twentieth. According to Aron, Schering made this claim in all of his books so it was not an isolated claim. More importantly, Aron objected to this on a number of grounds: that means can apply equally well to things and to people – to cannons as well as to courage. The play of dialectic between means and ends is not, as Schering suggested, contradictory or exclusionary; rather, it is an ongoing process (Aron 1976a: 189–90; Aron 1980a: 173–4). Aron grants that Clausewitz was never completely clear about the relationship between "Mittel" and "Zweck" but suggests that Clausewitz was not responsible for misunderstanding this relationship. Aron insisted this was the fault of those who could not be bothered to read Clausewitz carefully but merely appropriated his sayings (Aron 1976a: 193–4; Aron 1980a: 175–6). One of Aron's most frequent criticisms of others is that they do not bother to take the time and trouble to read the text carefully. He believed that this certainly applies to Clausewitz but he held that it was also true regarding Weber, Thucydides, and others. Another of Aron's most common criticisms is that scholars often approach an author from a particular point of view and often this is to shape their interpretations to make them match their own ideology.

Basil Liddell Hart was a rather well-regarded journalist and an even more respected author on military history. He wrote numerous books on various famous military figures, including the French general

Ferdinand Foch and the German general Erin Rommel. His relevance here is his interpretation of warfare and especially about how he thought Clausewitz was wrong. Aron observed that Liddell Hart was widely recognized as having written histories of the First World War and the Second World War, and apparently agreed with Liddell Hart's campaign during the early 1950s to rearm Germany in order to serve as a defense against the threat from the Soviet Union. However, he thought that Liddell Hart was mostly wrong in his interpretation of Clausewitz.[22] Aron defended Clausewitz from Liddell Hart's accusation that Clausewitz was somehow responsible for the Nazis' attempts to destroy Great Britain totally and he objected to Liddell Hart's claim that Clausewitz's notion of movement led to the introduction of massive tank movements (Aron 1976b: 87–8; Aron 1980a: 410–11). But Aron objected mostly to Liddell Hart's insistence that Clausewitz was somehow responsible for all of Germany's military strategies. Aron pointed out that most of the military men had been disciples of General von Schlieffen and not General von Clausewitz. Aron faulted Liddell Hart for "appearing" to separate the military issues from the political ones – Aron stressed "appearing" because he believed that it was Liddell Hart's philosophy that prompted him to do so, rather than any objective account of history (Aron 1976b: 414–15; Aron 1980a: 414–15). Finally, Aron faulted Liddell Hart for his "Feindschaft" against Clausewitz, but he acknowledged that Liddell Hart's intentional misreading of Clausewitz led him to think a bit better of Ludendorff (Aron 1976b: 326–8; Aron 1980a: 733–5).

Finally, there is the case of Carl Schmitt. Aron did not wonder whether Schmitt had read Clausewitz closely because he knew that he had. What bothered Aron was that Schmitt attempted to utilize Clausewitz for his own ideological purposes. Schmitt published his "Clausewitz als politischer Denker: Bemerkungen und Hinweise" in the last issue of 1967 of the journal *Der Staat*.[23] However, this was not the first time that Schmidt had examined Clausewitz's ideas; he had done so before, and especially in the *Theorie des Partisanen*. It appears that Clausewitz's writings were of considerable interest to Schmitt for a number of years. However, in *Theorie des Partisanen*, Schmitt utilized a version of Clausewitz in order to justify his "Freund–Feind" distinction and to justify irregular types of combat. And "Clausewitz als politischer Denker: Bemerkungen und Hinweise" is not an essay on Clausewitz but a review essay on four books. Aron recognized that Schmitt tried to use Clausewitz's ideas about military engagement for his own political purposes. Aron objected not only to this, but also to Schmitt's attempt to link the partisans to the state when they are fighting the state (Aron

1976b: 210–11; Aron 1980a: 519–20). In addition, Aron questioned Schmitt's interpretation of Lenin and the use of the notion of absolute war. Finally, Aron faulted Schmitt for claiming that Clausewitz devised a concept of "absolute enemy" (Aron 1976a: 363–5; Aron 1980a: 523–5). It was one thing for someone to misunderstand Clausewitz; it was another for someone to misuse him for political purposes. In Aron's opinion, Schmitt did this in two ways: to discredit Lenin's use of Clausewitz and to promote his own view of state partisanship.

## CONCLUDING COMMENTS

Aron devoted a considerable number of years to the careful study of the writings of Clausewitz. While he concentrated primarily on *Vom Kriege*, he believed that it was crucial to consider Clausewitz's other writings. Aron wanted to understand the man and his thinking, and not just his works. One does not get the sense that Aron felt the same way about Max Weber. It is probably safe to say that as much as Aron admired Weber, he respected Clausewitz more. Although Aron seemed to believe that Clausewitz was as much of a patriot as Weber was, he did not seem to believe that that sense had impacted Clausewitz's thinking as much as it had colored Weber's. Clausewitz's personal hatred of Napoleon never diminished his appreciation for his genius in war. Yet Clausewitz and Weber shared a number of similar traits, including their conviction of the importance of theory and experience. Hans Rothfels maintained that the most significant and the most sin gular characteristic of Clausewitz's analysis of war was his belief in the interrelationship between philosophy and experience: that is, between theory and practice (Rothfels 1980: 264). Aron also believed in the general need for the interrelation between theory and practice, or in this case between thought and action.

## NOTES

1. Clausewitz (1973: 261).
2. This chapter is focused on the first book of Aron's work on Clausewitz because it is here that he examined Clausewitz's theories regarding war. The second book will be the focus of a later chapter because it is there that Aron discussed Clausewitz's contemporary relevance.
3. Herberg-Rothe cites Aron's remark that "every reader solves the secret in his own way" ("Jeder Leser löste das Geheimnis auf seine Weise") with approval (Herberg-Rothe 2001: 19; Aron 1980a: 19). Herberg-Rothe's title suggests that Clausewitz's book is not a secret but a riddle. Furthermore, he suggested that Clausewitz's book is like an onion with multiple layers of meanings.

4. "Nul besoin d'être Allemand, Preussien ou officier pour partager l'aventure de cette âme partagée." "Man muß nicht Deutscher, Preuße oder Offizier sein, um das Abenteuer dieser gespaltenen Seele nachvollziehen zu können" (Aron 1976a: 15; Aron 1980a: 22).

5. "De l'interpretation historique" (Aron 1976a: 17–18). The German subtitle omits Aron's emphasis on historical: "Zur Theorie der Interpretation" (Aron 1980a: 23–4).

6. The phrase "Geist und Tat" ("spirit and deed") supposedly reflects the first part of Clausewitz's life, when he was primarily a soldier and doing things ("Tat"), and the second part of his life, when he was primarily a scholar ("Geist"). Aron intentionally chose the phrase "Geist und Tat" and remarked that he had borrowed this phrase from the book of the same name by W. M. Schering (Aron 1976a: 32; Aron 1980a: 36; see Schering 1942).

7. Aron (1976a: 33, 79); Aron (1980a: 36, 78). Aron offers the first version of this dictum in German: "Die Sache muß entscheiden" (Aron 1976a: 81–2; Aron 1980a: 79–80). It is rather doubtful that Aron did not notice how much Weber's insistence on focusing on the matter itself is similar to Clausewitz's dictum.

8. "[D]er Krieg nichts ist, als die fortgesetze Staatspolitik mit anderen Mitteln." Aron noted that this formula is often given without the word "Staat" (Aron 1976a: 104; Aron 1980a: 99). "[D]er Krieg nichts ist, als die fortgesetze Staatspolitik mit anderen Mitteln" (Clausewitz 1973: 179).

9. Andreas Herberg-Rothe characterizes the two types of war as "absolute" ("absolute") and "limited" ("begrenzte") (Herberg-Rothe 2001: 18).

10. Aron (1976a: 109, 121); Aron (1980a: 103, 114). It is again instructive to compare the German version with Aron's original: the German version reads "Welt des Ideals" whereas the French is "le monde du concept, de l'idéal."

11. Aron provides this phrase in German and then offers "bon sens" and "sens commun" as translations.

12. "Es ist im Kriege sehr einfach, aber das Einfachtes ist schwierig" (Clausewitz 1973: 261). "Dans la guerre tout est simple mais le plus simple est difficile" (Aron 1976a: 221). The German translation of Aron's citation is slightly inaccurate: "Es ist alles im Kriege sehr einfach, aber das Einfache ist schwierig" (Aron 1980a: 200).

13. Aron (1980: 262). In the original French edition, Aron refers to these as "lois nécessaires" and "lois de probabilité" (Aron 1976a: 294).

14. "Drei andere Gesetze, das eine *Urgesetz*, das andere *allgemeines*, das dritte *dynamisches Gesetz* getauft, erfordern eine ebensolche Analyse" (Aron 1980a: 271). "Trois autres lois, l'une baptisée *originelle*, l'autre *générale*, la troisième *dynamique*, exigent une analyse de même sorte" (Aron 1976a: 304).

15. Aron quotes Clausewitz: "Mich dünkt, es sei also, daß die Kriegskunst zu uns redet: Gehe dem größten, entscheindendsten Zweck nach, welchen du zu erreichen, wähle den kürzesten Weg dazu, den du zu gehen *dich getraust*" (Aron 1976a: 344; Aron 1980a: 306–7).

16. About a hundred years earlier Karl Schwarz had offered a similar assessment, in which he claimed that Clausewitz possessed logical sharpness, exactness in concepts, and a precision and clarity of expression (Schwartz 1878: II 493).

17. A proper discussion would require not only a fuller treatment of Aron's comments, but a detailed examination of the books by Rothfels and Schering, among others (see Rothfels 1920 and Schering 1935). It would also demand an excursion into the philosophies of Kant and Hegel, not to mention the thinking of Montesquieu. This would no doubt be enlightening as well as rewarding, but would primarily be of historical interest to philosophers and not so much to political philosophers.

18. Aron approved of a number of scholar's interpretations of Clausewitz. He counted Karl Linnenbach as one of the best-informed Clausewitz experts (as well as editor of an edition of *Vom Kriege*) (Aron 1976a: 278–9; Aron 1980a: 402). He also thought highly of Hans Delbrück's various writing on Clausewitz, as well as those of another scholar and editor of *Vom Kriege*: Werner Hahlweg (Aron 1976a: 362; Aron 1980a: 400, 755–6).

19. Aron also utilizes Delbrück's review of a book on Clausewitz by Karl Schwartz. Although Aron's comments on Delbrück's review are rather interesting, they play no real role here. That is because Delbrück used the opportunity to enter into a conflict about strategy and was not solely focused on Clausewitz (Aron 1976b: 412–14; Aron 1980a: 629–31).

20. Aron (1976b: 326–7); Aron (1980a: 735). Aron cites Delbrück's book, *Ludendorffs Selbstporträt*, in which Delbrück indicated that he had read Foch's two-volume work, *Des principes de la guerre* (Delbrück 1922: 41).

21. Delbrück (1920: 7, 9); see also Delbrück (1922: 7). There, Delbrück writes of the greatness of "Scharnhorst, Gneisenau oder Clausewitz."

22. Aron was not the only person to take issue with Liddell Hart's impression of Clausewitz; others did so as well. See in particular Erich Vad's comments in his *Carl von Clausewitz* (1984: 55–8).

23. Schmitt was one of the few scholars who considered Clausewitz a political thinker. In 1922, Hans Rothfels noted that most scholars regarded Clausewitz as a military reformer and hardly anyone thought of him as a political thinker. Rothfels suggested that this prompted him both to write his book *Carl von Clausewitz: Politik und Krieg* and to publish his collection *Carl von Clausewitz: Politische Schriften und Briefe* (Clausewitz 1922: vii).

# CHAPTER FOUR

# On War

"Better to die a thousand times than to relive this again."[1]

This quotation is attributed to August Wilhelm Anton Neidhardt Graf von Gneisenau by Graf Alfred von Schlieffen in his book *Gneisenau*. Gneisenau was reflecting on his experience in fighting the French on German soil in 1806. He and his troops were outnumbered and out-flanked, and could not retreat because the Elbe river was between them and the safety of the other side. Gneisenau, Scharnhorst, Clausewitz, Moltke, Moltke the Younger, and Schlieffen himself were all Prussian generals who knew exactly how terrible war always was and certainly could be. However, they could not possibly foresee how devastating the wars of the twentieth century would be. Gneisenau, Scharnhorst, and Clausewitz died before the end of the 1830s, Moltke and Schlieffen died before 1914, and even Moltke the younger did not live till the end of the First World War. None the less, they were fully aware of the destruction that wars caused. They wrote about war from their personal experience and because they wanted to ensure that others knew that to enter into a war was dangerous and should not be undertaken lightly. In short, they were responsible for the lives of their soldiers. Their lives were military ones but those who ordered them into war were politicians. These are a few ideas to keep in mind when reading Raymond Aron's writings on war.

That Aron wrote so much on war may seem somewhat perplexing, knowing what we do about him. He always wrote in favor of peace and never thought highly of war. He had never served as a regular soldier; nor did he regard himself to be qualified enough to write about military matters.[2] However, the severity of the events of the first half of the twentieth century drove him to investigate the nature and results of war. He maintained that the twentieth century was the "century of war" and suggested that he had lived through the twentieth-century version of the "Thirty Years War" – his reference to "the German war of 1914–1945" (Aron 1978b: 21). In fact, the "War of 1914–1945" would not be the second "Thirty Year War" – because Aron had written that the Peloponnesian War was a "thirty year war" (Aron 1978b: 32). These are not the only striking comments that Aron made in his remarkable essay "Thucydides and the Historical Narrative." He also maintained that there is a type of dialectics between peace and war and insisted that war is, at the same time, the completion *and* the negation of politics (Aron 1978b: 23–4). Thus, while Aron believed war and peace to be interconnected, in the interest of clarity and focus, they will be discussed separately: the primary topic of this chapter is war, and peace will be the main topic of the next chapter. There is no doubt that Aron regarded both war and peace as being among the most important matters in human history: he wrote on peace because he knew that peace was crucial to the ideals of prosperity and freedom, yet he wrote more on war because he recognized that it was a real and lasting part of politics. He was realistic enough to recognize that peace could be fostered through international relations, and that realization prompted him to write his major work on it. However, Aron devoted much more of his life to examining war, both historically and theoretically.

This chapter proceeds historically: that is, by looking chronologically at Aron's historical topics. This means beginning with Aron's writings on Thucydides, moving to his three books on war – *The Century of Total War*, *On War*, and *The Great Debate* – and ending with an examination of the second part of his work on Clausewitz. It is in that section that Aron deals with the relevance of Clausewitz for twentieth-century issues and addresses the notion of "total war." Of course, Clausewitz belonged to the early part of the nineteenth century and Erich Ludendorff belonged to the early part of the twentieth century, but what they wrote continues to have significance for the issue of war in the beginning of the twenty-first century.

## The Peloponnesian War

"Thucydides and the Historical Narrative" is a remarkable essay for a number of reasons: first, it is about Thucydides and his account of the Peloponnesian War; second, it is a general analysis of war; and third, as will be shown, these two accounts are framed by a Weberian point of view. This makes Aron's essay very rich in knowledge, but it also means that it is frequently difficult to comprehend.[3] In what follows, an attempt is made to try to keep these three accounts separate, but there are times in which the discussion must involve two or even three of Aron's lines of thinking.

It is quite obvious that Aron thought highly of Thucydides. Thucydides joins Weber and Clausewitz as being one of the three individuals who made a significant impression on him. This is shown by the comments that Aron makes about Thucydides and his approach to history. Thucydides approached history from a critical standpoint, from a distance. This need for distance pertains not just to the historian but to the politician as well. Aron does not invoke Weber at this point, but Weber makes the point about the need for distance especially well in *Politik als Beruf*. There, Weber lists the three key traits that a genuine politician must have: "Leidenschaft" ("passion"), "Verantwortungsethik" ("ethics of responsibility"), and "Augenmaß." Weber makes it clear that, to him, the term "Augenmaß" implies a certain degree of distance: that is, "the *distance* to things and men" ("die *Distanz* zu den Dingen und Menschen") (Weber 1992: 227). Furthermore, he adds that the lack of distance leads to vanity, which he claims is the "deadly enemy" of a politician. What is needed to combat it is "the distance to one's self" ("der Distanz sich selbst gegenüber") (Weber 1992: 228). This is similar to what Aron means when he calls Thucydides a spectator: one who simply narrates his account and refrains from intruding with his own personal views. Furthermore, Thucydides placed his actors in the proper context, meaning in their own time and place (Aron 1978d: 29). And he recognized the "quality" of his historical object; thus, his account is about men worthy of remembrance (Aron 1978d: 21–2, 32). This sense of being objective, or just, distinguishes Thucydides from modern commentators with their ideologies and their cynicism. In addition, Thucydides employs two types of historical writing: the general type found in the first book and the more specific type found in the other books (Aron 1978d: 21, 31). Aron distinguishes Thucydides' historical focus from the modern one: his narrative is driven by the actions of individual men in contrast to the modern one, which is mainly preoccupied with economic explanations. This is what lies behind Aron's initial claim that the modern historian is preoccupied with economic factors; thus "The history of war has gone out of fashion" (Aron 1978d: 20, 31). What Aron means by this is that modern historians are concerned with explaining historical activity by means of economic factors, whereas previously, historians explained historical activity by looking at the most significant and most deadly occurrences – war. Aron does not dispute the importance of economics in human conduct; what he takes issue with is the complete dominance of the economic factors. Economics should not be regarded as the only means of explanation but it does need to be employed when appropriate. Aron had learned far too much from Max Weber about the importance of economic factors as determining factors in society to ignore them, and like Weber, he strove to apply them when appropriate.

Aron invokes Weber in an even more explicit manner by suggesting that Aron's own analysis of Thucydides' account is sociological. This admission is accurate in two ways: methodological and substantial. It is methodological in the Weberian manner because it aims to make sense of men's actions and it does so by determining the ends men chose and the means that they employed to reach them. Aron notes that Weber calls this "Zweckrational" and maintains that the Weberian definition covers the conduct of four individual types: the engineer, the politician, the military commander, and the speculator. Aron does not wish to discuss the technical action of the engineer or the speculative action of the speculator but chooses to focus on the diplomatic action of the politician and the strategic action of the commander (Aron 1978d: 26). Thucydides' account is substantially sociological in the Weberian sense because his account of the Peloponnesian War is of a stylized or "ideal" war, in Weberian terminology. That war was "unparalleled" in scope and duration; it included so many contradictions and lasted so long. And its concrete and abstract elements were stylized.[4] Aron does not clarify what he means by this, but a possible explanation can be found in Aron's remark that Thucydides does not discuss the participants' weapons (Aron 1978d: 24–5, 32). Instead, Thucydides focuses on the participants in the war. This means individuals such as Nicias and Pericles, and city-states such as Athens and Sparta, because both individuals and political groups of individuals engage in human action, which is the subject of history. For Thucydides, the most important type of human action is war, and that is why Aron insists that "It was the Peloponnesian war that interested him, nothing else." And that is because "human action" is, again invoking Weber, "the struggle of man over man," which is the central interest of Thucydides.[5] It is also why the most violent part of this struggle is war and it is also why Thucydides' account of that war is "*the* masterpiece of ancient historiography" (Aron 1978d: 21, 27).

Aron finds it somewhat puzzling that, in the century of great wars, the study of war has fallen out of fashion. He argues that historians are not generally warmongers but rather scholars who seek to understand war and its ramifications. However, he has explained that historians do not think that the study of war is valuable because they are now convinced that economic factors explain everything (Aron 1978d: 20–1). He objects to this general interpretation because history cannot be reduced to societies, classes, and economies. Furthermore, he maintains that this is as true today as it was during Thucydides' time. He also objects to the attempt to explain war by economic factors; he allows that they do play some role but believes they did not play a part in the Peloponnesian War (Aron 1978d: 32–3). An additional problem arises because of the influence of economics on the modern notion of politics. "Politics" contains two different meanings: *politics* as the plan of action of humans and *policy* as the plan of action of business. The first belongs to states and the second pertains to businesses (Aron 1978d: 22–3). Aron does not doubt the importance of policy but politics is about the "free men" who live together with others.

Aron has already acknowledged that there is always competition and struggle among humans; war is when those struggles become violent. Politics, according to Aron, is a type of dialogue: one that is the dialectic between persuasion and compulsion. There is a continuum in politics, ranging from mundane conflict to bitter strife to war; Aron contends that Thucydides believed that war is the "supreme act of politics." As such, Thucydides could have never subscribed to the belief that war was "a pathetic and ridiculous commotion on the surface of the 'wave of history'" (Aron 1978d: 22). War reveals man as both human and animal, but the human part of the soldier seeks to channel his animal instincts. This is necessary because war is both cooperation and competition – soldiers need to cooperate in order to defeat the enemy. Like Thucydides, Clausewitz, and Weber, Aron believes that war is waged among equals; it requires mutual acknowledgment, if not mutual respect.

The problem that Thucydides recognized was that Athens had the will to dominate and that meant challenging Sparta's supremacy. The further problem that Thucydides noticed was that the Athenians discarded prudence and reasonableness for hubris and irrationality. Despite this irrationality, Aron insists that both sides involved in this war are understandable – thus reflecting Aron's notion of "intelligible history" (Aron 1978d: 27–30). War is contradictory: it is both the completion and negation of politics; it is cooperation and competition; and it is rational and irrational (Aron 1978d: 23). Aron rejects the notion that something was inevitable and endorses the concept of probability. That means the repudiation of the idea of determinism and the embracing of the notion of chance. In introducing the ideas of chance and probability, Aron is again following Weber: he says that Weber was right to insist on a "calculation of probabilities" (Aron 1978d: 36). That means that, in theory, the Peloponnesian War could have been avoided but real individuals ensured that it happened. People did not heed Nicias' warnings, just as they did not follow Weber's warnings about unlimited submarine warfare. And the Russian Revolution would not have happened when and how it did without Lenin. (Aron 1978d: 36, 38). Thus, chance, irrationality, and rationality play their part in history, but even more so in war.

Aron had many reasons to believe that Thucydides' historical account of the tragedy that was the Peloponnesian War was important. He knew full well that the differences in time and circumstances were immense but he also believed that certain aspects of human nature did not change, particularly in the area of politics and warfare (Aron 1959: 2). Like Clausewitz; Aron studied history for examples to use in politics and war, and like Weber, Aron used a similar methodological approach to understand political (and military) conflicts.

## THE CENTURY OF TOTAL WAR

*The Century of Total War* is a misleading title because much of Aron's book is devoted to topics other than war. One such topic is the contrast between socialism and capitalism, and another is the importance of the relationship between liberty and democracy. Both topics will be discussed in the chapter on liberty and in the concluding chapter devoted to Aron's legacy. The concern in this chapter is primarily Aron's remarks in *The Century of Total War* about the history and the effects of warfare and the continuing threat of total war.

Aron argues in the first part of his book that the manner in which governments respond to war has fundamentally changed since the time of Frederick (Friedrich) the Great. As Aron pointed out, he had no need to try to justify his war; public opinion was basically non-existent and his soldiers had no need for any justification for why they were fighting. By the beginning of the First World War, governments found that they needed to justify going to war – both in the realm of public opinion as well as in the ranks of the soldiers. Aron also indicated that this was intended neither to bolster the morale of the soldiers nor to pacify the population; rather, it had the larger purpose of defending the need to go to war in the first place. In Aron's view, the easiest and perhaps the best way to do this was to claim that the nation had no choice and that the war was morally necessary. Thus, governments claim that the enemy has foisted the war on the nation and that its own conscience is clear. Aron asked about the First World War: "Who were the criminals who had plunged Europe into the abyss of violence?" (Aron 1954: 9).

Historians also examine the justification for war but Aron suggests that they ask two related but distinctly different questions about the legitimacy of that war. The first question is: why did the war come about at that particular time? The second one is: what was the situation that led to it? Aron explains that the first question relates to immediate causes while the second one is concerned with remote origins. Both are important but historians of the First World War have unfortunately centered their attention on the first one when they inquire into what was happening in the weeks leading up to the outbreak of war. Aron suggested that, while it seemed that the war was inevitable, it is not so easy to assign blame. There were too many variables and too many actors. And there was too much of a sense that no one would actually go to war. It is this sense of conviction that Aron believed probably led to war (Aron 1954: 11–12). It was the passing of history that evidently prompted all sides to avoid realizing that war was likely. What Aron meant was that people had forgotten that Europe had been plunged into war during the years 1792 to 1815 and believed that, after a century without a major conflict, war was no longer likely. Aron argues two things: first, there was no "mysterious fatality" that caused the war, and second, wars are basically unpredictable. Aron does not address the fact that these two assertions might seem contradictory but he does insist that the First World War was likely caused by what he refers to as a "technical surprise." This surprise is partially because both of the warring sides were convinced that the war would be over within months, if not weeks, and it was partially because of technical improvements in weapons. However much Aron was interested in the historical causes of the First World War, his larger interest was in the reasons why it became a world war and did not remain a rather localized one. Aron employed the term "hyperbolic" to describe a total war. Aron admitted that he did not invent the term but borrowed it from Pareto. None the less, Aron suggested that, once the initial enthusiasm for the war subsided and once it seemed that it was going to be a protracted one, then it became clearer that it was not going to be a limited war; indeed, Aron argued that both sides should have realized that it was always going to be a "hyperbolic" war. The First World War was devastating enough; however, Aron argued that Germany's defeat and the Russian Revolution meant that the war never really ended. In fact, both countries were humiliated sufficiently that, when offered the chance to seek revenge, both sides did just that. Thus, Aron again justifies his claim that the twentieth century was the century of total war (Aron 1954: 25–31).

Aron insisted that the Second World War was similar to the first: it began mostly because of Germany, it also spread throughout much of the world, and it ended much like the First World War (Aron 1954:

32). Yet, Aron points to the major difference in destruction, noting that the airplanes of the First World War were "spectacular" but relatively harmless, whereas the airplanes of the Second World War were commonplace but exceptionally destructive. Here, Aron limits his comments to the number of bombs dropped on Germany. He uses the figures of 30,000 in 1941; 40,000 in 1942; 120,000 in 1943; 600,000 in 1944; and 500,000 during the first five months of 1945. Aron also asks: to what purpose? He suggests that there was and can be no answer (Aron 1954: 40–1) but is able to provide a number of answers to other questions, such as how Hitler was able to survive for so long. Aron noted that Hitler was a master of controlling crowds and understood that modern war required propaganda. But Hitler was blind to his limitations and refused to face reality (Aron 1954: 46, 52). And it was not just the Germans who believed their own propaganda and refused to see things as they actually were.

Aron acknowledges that moralists have always argued that wars are bad, but insists that historians and sociologists attempt to avoid making moral judgments and instead focus on the study of war and its effects. Aron also notes that it is easy to find reasons to argue against a war but he wonders whether anything can be said for it (Aron 1954: 74–5). On one hand, the sheer number of dead and wounded during the wars of the twentieth century exceeded the previous numbers; on the other hand, different countries suffered differently. For example, Britain was bombed but not invaded whereas the Soviet Union was not bombed but was invaded. Accordingly, Russian losses totaled almost 17 million or close to 10 percent of the population. In comparison, Poland lost between 4 and 5 million people but that number represented close to 15 percent of Poland's entire population. Aron added that Poland's losses were especially peculiar because 3 million Jews were exterminated. This was not a direct result of the war but was a result of a policy (Aron 1954: 77). If considered solely in terms of deaths, the Second World War was costly; if one considers other numbers, such as the economy, however, the result is not so starkly negative. Again, Aron points out that not all countries suffered the same in economic terms; for example, the United States' economy was far more productive during the war than many had expected. None the less, Aron considers the effects of the wars not just from these points of view, but from the larger perspective of a historian. That is his justification for contrasting Hans Delbrück's claim, after the end of the First World War, that the Allies could do many things to the defeated Germans but could not kill them. Hitler proved that one could kill innocent civilians on a massive scale, so instead of wars being confined primarily to soldiers on battlefields, modern war entailed civilian deaths in all parts of a country (Aron 1954: 82).

Aron insists that wars reflect the societies of the belligerent nations, so during the nineteenth century the few wars that occurred reflected the heroic values of the states. That changed during the wars of the twentieth century, when heroism was no longer valued. Instead, wars were violent, which apparently reflected the growing violence of the states. But Aron insists that what does not change is the need for organization and rationalization. In Germany, this was accomplished in the military by Erich Ludendorff and in industry by Walther Rathenau (Aron 1954: 87). Furthermore, Aron insists that the means of production does not change, regardless of what is being produced – it does not matter whether what is made is a gun or a brick. Aron noted that some historians see a link between total mobilization and totalitarianism, and that this is based upon the need to make permanent what was temporary. He has in mind Ludendorff's plan, proposed after Germany's defeat in 1919, and noted how much of it was adopted later by Hitler (Aron 1954: 85). None the less, Aron maintains that, despite some similarities, total mobilization and totalitarianism are different. First, he suggests that while the means of production may be similar, the products themselves are not: guns and battleships are needed, not just bricks and steel. Second, living during times of peace differs from living during times of war. Third, the function of the state differs during wartime from that during peacetime (Aron 1954: 90–1).

In the final chapter of Part One, Aron echoes Thucydides and Clausewitz with the assertion that war is never inevitable but almost always is a result of miscalculation and arrogance. If vanity and arrogance were the "causes" of the First World War, the Second came about because of an almost incredible combination of stupidity and bad luck. Thus, Aron emphasizes the importance of accident over that of necessity. And his conclusion to this part is philosophical: immediate actions may often seem capricious and to have devastating consequences, yet there seems to be some degree of rationality in them when viewed historically.

Aron returns to the theme of necessity and contingency in the final chapter of Part Two, entitled "Logic and Chance." Aron notes that the "present world" encompasses three different processes of development: first, planetary unity and bi-polar diplomacy; second, the diffusion of secular religion (ideology); and third, the development of weapons of mass destruction. These processes were neither random nor inevitable but came about by "one part logic and one part chance" (Aron 1954: 159). Aron asks: "If war is horrible and peace impossible, what is the way out?" In certain respects, the Cold War appeared to be the answer to an atomic war and an impossible peace. Yet the Cold War may be a limited war but that is no guarantee that it would remain so (Aron 1954: 171). Part of the problem was that the two sides – the United States and the Soviet Union – dragged many less powerful countries into the conflict, either by making them the battlefields for wars or by forcing them to choose sides (Aron 1954: 176). As Aron will also emphasize in *Peace and War*, nations do not necessarily stay on one side. But here, Aron writes, "The history of Europe is fertile in reversals of alliances" and he points out that, once defeated, both Germany and Japan became allies of the United States. Aron believes that much of the decision regarding allegiances is based upon the calculation concerning who is better suited to protect the nation. Thus, during the 1950s, most of the Western countries believed that the United States was positioned to protect them, while many of the Eastern nations counted on the Soviet Union to safeguard them (Aron 1954: 202–5). However, when Aron wrote *The Century of Total War*, he believed that the West would win in a "total" conflict between the West and the East. This was partially because of wishful thinking but more because he recognized that the West had superior forces. And part of this was based upon his understanding that the West was willing to learn. As an example, Aron offers the fact that the West learned *not* to disband its forces after winning the Second World War (Aron 1954: 207–8). What was not yet clear to Aron was whether the Cold War was a "preparation" or a "substitute" for "total war." It is intriguing that, throughout his book, Aron never explicitly said what a "total war" was and his references to the past were not always the most enlightening. There was discussion as to whether Clausewitz was the originator of the notion of "total war" and there was Ludendorff's book from the 1930s, entitled *Der totaler Krieg*. Yet, in *The Century of Total War*, Aron never mentions Clausewitz and the two references to Ludendorff are neither helpful nor positive. If one turns to Aron's Clausewitz book, one finds that, much like Hans Delbrück, Aron does not think much of Ludendorff. But he remained uncharacteristically silent on Ludendorff's book on "total war." It would seem that Aron did not think much of it and did not bother to discuss it. It is also curious that, despite its importance, Aron never provided a clear definition of "total war." It seems as if Aron figured that everyone knew what was meant by "total war" and that is indicated by the following comment: "In the last century the American Civil War had offered a fairly good preview of what we call total war" (Aron 1954: 19). Yet the closest he came to explaining that was a reference to "the relentless mobilization of national resources and the competition over new inventions." That quotation does not explain why Aron thought the American Civil War was a preview of what "total war" would be like; nor does it clarify what he thought "total war" was. For Aron, it seems that the phrase "total war" means both a "world war" and the "complete domination" of politics by the subject of war. Considered in this light, it is more understandable that Aron believed that the Cold War was not a "substitute" but a "preparation" for total war. This makes even more sense when one considers that Aron's books on war contain significant warnings about the catastrophe that a nuclear war would be.

When Aron wrote *The Century of Total War*, he seemed less concerned that a nuclear war would break out. He noted that the United States had come to recognize the threat that the Soviet Union appeared to present but that its leaders were careful not to rearm as fully as they would have liked. The rulers of the Soviet Union were also somewhat reasonable – they felt it necessary to provoke the West but did not want to enter into a war; thus the provocations were rather limited. Aron therefore believed that war would not come about unless both countries decided that they wanted it or both believed that it was inevitable (Aron 1954: 227–9).

While the focus of the section "Can Europe Unite?" is on that topic, Aron makes some crucially significant points about modern warfare. Most nations cannot afford modern weapons: for example, Aron cites the fact that the entire French military budget would be depleted if it spent the money on 300 American B-36 bombers. A tank would cost 30–50 million francs and a radar set for an airfield would cost 15 million. Aron adds that the increase in the complexity of machines means that the cost of building and maintaining them has also increased. In 1940, a fighter plane required 10,000 hours of work to build but only a decade later that figure had jumped to 50,000. In addition, the cost of fuel has also seen massive increases: a plane's hourly consumption went from 20 to 1,000 liters. Accordingly, poor nations cannot hope to be able to field a competitive war machine, even relatively well-off countries like France (Aron 1954: 302–3). In contrast, people in the Soviet Union were willing to pay the cost for two reasons: they were used to a lower standard of living and were convinced that a strong military was necessary for the survival of the country. People in the United States were also willing to pay the cost of a strong military because of the strength of its economic growth. Aron concludes Part Four with a warning: economists and generals would be well served not to believe just in wealth and in weapons because they are "not enough to decide the fate of nations" (Aron 1954: 325).

Aron's "Conclusion" may appear anti-climactic, yet he makes some critically important comments. Some of them are rather historical, as when he writes about modern technical progress. He notes that, in the West, food production had sufficiently increased so that most people are not starving, but he wonders whether that phenomenon is due to luck and whether it could be repeated in other parts of the world. And some of his comments are more philosophical, such as his comment about faith. In 1914, the French believed in something, meaning France. But in 1954 there no longer seems to be anything to believe in. As Aron wrote, men never go to war for a "standard of living"; instead, they go to war for a "way of living" (Aron 1954: 361). If Europe (and the West) is to survive any confrontation with the East, it is possible only with the faith that the European way of living is worth fighting for. While material sources are critical in a limited war or a total one, faith, courage, and the will to win are even more critical for the outcome (Aron 1954: 367–8). Once again, Aron does not elaborate on his point, but like the earlier comment, this one is also a matter of values.


## On War

*On War* is written in Aron's normal style; it is composed of a preface, a very short introduction, seven main chapters, and a postscript. There are two things about this work that are unusual: first, it lacks a table of contents, and second, it is written as a narrative. While, for the most part, one chapter leads to the next, Aron frequently returns to points that he had made previously.

Aron begins *On War* with some preliminary remarks on political stances: the optimists, the pessimists, and the realists. The optimists believe that, with the advent of atomic warfare, political leaders will finally come to their senses because of the horrendous destruction caused by atomic bombs. The pessimists contend that humans – being what they have been, what they are, and what they will be, and faced with the inevitability of such catastrophic damage, would still not be able to refrain from such warfare. Aron contends that both realists and pessimists are concerned only about the future whereas realists are focused on the present. He counts himself a realist, not because of conviction, but because of temperament (Aron 1959: 2–3, 5–6).

Aron discusses the failure of disarmament in the chapter called "The Failure of Atomic Disarmament." He recalls that, after the First World War, people believed that wars were caused by misunderstandings and that, after the destruction caused by that war, people would avoid misunderstandings; thus, there would no longer be wars. Aron considers that view to be naïve and believes that people have realized that wars are caused by real threats and not by mere misunderstandings (Aron 1959: 8). That is because nations are sovereign and their leaders believe they have the right to self-defense. This is true when two competing countries are roughly equal in strength; it is more true when the two countries are not. The latter was the situation between the United States and the Soviet Union shortly after the end of the Second World War. Aron noted that, while the United States talks a great deal about peace, it rarely lives up to its ideal. The Soviet Union not only was ideologically convinced that the United States wished to destroy it, but it also had credible information that appeared to back that up. Thus, the Soviet Union pursued the elimination of nuclear weapons while simultaneously developing its own. By 1949, the Soviet Union had exploded an atomic bomb and thereby eliminated the monopoly that the United States had on nuclear weapons (Aron 1959: 13–14). By the 1950s, the Soviet Union had reached parity with the United States in terms of nuclear weapons, so that theoretically there could have been a process of mutual disarmament. Aron noted that the Soviet Union was too mistrustful – what process of verification could ensure that the United States did, in fact, destroy all of its atomic bombs? Aron draws a larger point: Athens and Sparta could have been reasonable and agreed to share the empire but chose the exhausting path that led to an "unattainable ideal" (Aron 1959: 20–3). Certainly, progress in all fields, including weaponry, had been made since the Peloponnesian War; what had not changed was human nature. Aron ended that chapter with the observation that "Science helps men to kill one another by means of mass production; it does not teach them wisdom" (Aron 1959: 23).

In the next chapter, "The Failure of Traditional Rearmament," Aron briefly discusses how, in the course of thirty years (1914–45), humanity had progressed from horses to automobiles and from rifles to nuclear bombs (Aron 1959: 27). But Aron also discusses the stages of the Cold War, beginning with Stalin's response to Truman. Aron debunks the claim that Stalin was weak during the Second World War and then became stronger around 1950. Aron suggests that while Stalin was really afraid of Hitler, he had little to fear from Truman. One does not know what Stalin would have done if the United States had broken the Berlin blockade by force or had resorted to the use of atomic weapons (Aron 1959: 25–6). But we do know what happened during what Aron refers to as the "second phase" of the Cold War. He suggested that the Korean War was something between the international "Cold War" and an international "hot war" – it was a "hot local war." This meant that hostilities were to remain local – no one thought about bombing China or Russia. The Korean War was a "limited war" that never ended but ceased. Thus, Aron made a number of observations about it: first, both sides attempted to recruit other countries to their side; second, both sides sought to keep the fight to a relatively small geographical area; and third, both sides had limited war aims. Because of these three limitations, the end result could only be a negotiated peace. Thus, Aron concludes that MacArthur's dictum "There is no substitute for victory" is either a "truism" or a "dangerous error" (Aron 1959: 28–9). In Aron's mind, it was primarily the latter because it misrepresents how war had changed after 1945. Destruction of the enemy means that the victor can dictate the terms of peace, but when that is not possible, then the peace must be negotiated. But then the military no longer has a say in the negotiations; "Politics must decide." This sidelining of the military underscores Aron's comment that Clausewitz's claim "War is the continuation of politics by other means" has "no military significance at all" (Aron 1959: 29–30).

In the third chapter, "Unity and Plurality of the Diplomatic Field," Aron offers four observations: the supremacy of the United States and the Soviet Union, their global military presence, their mutual ideological antagonisms, and their development of weapons of mass destruction (Aron 1959: 39). However, Aron places the opposition between the United States and the Soviet Union in a historical context along with the previous dual oppositions: Athens and Sparta, Carthage and Rome, Caesar and Antony. He notes that none of these oppositions ended well (ultimately, for either side). He further observes that, when there are only two major powers, then there are four forms that can result: first, they can rule together; second, they can divide up the area; third, they can try to annihilate each other; or fourth, they can attempt to co-exist as enemies. However, Aron reduces these forms to two more general ones: total or partial agreement or total or partial war (Aron 1959: 39–40). The problem is not just that the leaders of the two powers are distrustful; the rest of the world is as well. Aron points out that countries not only fear one dominating country; they also fear the two countries in tandem. The problem is compounded by the fact that each major power seeks to convince the smaller and less powerful countries to side with it by making the claim that it is necessary *"because the other great power exists"* (Aron 1959: 42–3, Aron's emphasis). Aron expanded upon this by discussing how Japan was drawn to America's side while Russia cultivated China. Similar situations played out in the Middle East (Aron 1959: 46–55).

In the chapter called "Polymorphous Violence," Aron states that the fear of war does not eliminate violence; often, violence occurs at a level below the state of actual warfare. He is thinking about guerrilla warfare. He observes that the end of the First World War seemed to indicate that wars would increase in size and destruction, and that happened in the Second World War. However, limited local wars have been the predominant types (Aron 1959: 59, 62–7). Aron discusses guerrilla warfare in other places, but here he insists that guerrilla warfare is not chaos – it "is not a return to anarchy" but is a limited and yet organized type of war. Aron concludes this chapter with the observation that the machinegun and the atomic bomb are the extremes of modern warfare, the former being a type of individual murder and the latter a form of mass destruction. However, both types of warfare are particularly brutal, both physically and psychologically (Aron 1959: 69–71).

Aron turns to a discussion of a war between the United States and the Soviet Union, and analyzes the claim that the initial attack would be similar to the Japanese aerial attack on Pearl Harbor. It would have a similar element of surprise but a much more deadly one because atomic bombs would be dropped instead of bombs with TNT. However, Aron argues that, while the attack on Pearl Harbor was a surprise attack, the early attacks during the Second World War were by ground and followed lengthy buildups (Aron 1959: 76). More importantly, Aron addresses the three claims that there could be a limitation of warfare. He debunks the claim that there could be psychological limitations by noting that the losing side in a nuclear war really has little or nothing to lose. He debunks the claim that there are political limitations by noting that, even in a conventional war, smaller countries would find themselves to be battlefields. Finally, he debunks the claim that there would be geographical limitations by noting that, even if bombs were dropped on airfields, the nearby cities would be damaged as well (Aron 1959: 77–9). In other words, there seems to be little to support the claim that the threat of nuclear war increases the probability of limited war. If anything, Aron was convinced that great battles belonged to the past because big armies cost too much and weapons are decreasing in size. Finally, other countries would not be content to allow only two countries to possess nuclear weapons. When Aron wrote *On War*, only two countries were known to have nuclear weapons; now numerous countries possess them and many other nations and different groups are actively seeking them. He concludes by observing that war remained somewhat human despite the technological advances of rifles, cannons, and even warships. Now, technology inspires horror (Aron 1959: 86–7).

In "History Slows Down," Aron seems to contradict the title of this chapter. Advances in aircraft and rocket science mean that no place is safe from attack. Whereas the United States seemed safely away from Europe and Asia, these advances have destroyed that degree of security. Previously, one could order "'Halt, or I'll kill you'"; now it is more along the lines of "'Halt, or I'll choose mutual suicide'" (Aron 1959: 94). This may seem that history is accelerating but Aron regards the threat of mutual destruction to have slowed history down (Aron 1959: 101–3). Aron did not mean that history stopped, however, as the next chapter showed: "History Continues."

Aron discounts the belief that the threat of nuclear war increases the chances of peace – he claims that people tend to ignore what they choose and that they now ignore the development of nuclear warheads. He points to the hundreds of books written over the centuries, some of which praised or condemned war, while others sought its causes or analyzed its characteristics. What makes today's situation worse is that more countries have nuclear weapons, and he insisted that it would make people long for the days of bi-polar nuclear powers (Aron 1959: 109). However, Aron again looked to history to explain current events. The war between Athens and Sparta was not inevitable; if both sides had been less stubborn and more reasonable, the war could have been averted. Similarly, limited and total wars do not have to occur – they do so because neither side wants to be reasonable and is unwilling to back down (Aron 1959: 113). Yet Aron hopes that people will ultimately see sense; that is why he rejects the pessimists who predict doom while refusing to accept the optimists who believe in a rosy future. He claims his intent is not to advise but to understand; however, Aron believed that a number of conclusions can be drawn from his investigations: first, America was not imperialistic but it has been too nationalistic; second, technology is controlled by people; third, it is fatal to believe that peace can be achieved by the increase in nuclear threats; and fourth, it is reasonable to distinguish between types of war because it may lead to a diminishment of violence (Aron 1959: 117). He grants that both pessimists and optimists will object to his realistic account and that both sides will hold to some variation of "war-as-destiny." Aron's conclusion is that moderation is the wisdom that may save us politically and physically (Aron 1959: 120–1).


## THE GREAT DEBATE

Aron's book *The Great Debate* is focused not so much on the topic of war as it is on strategy: hence the subtitle, *Theories of Nuclear Strategy*. However, since nuclear war was certainly the most deadly and the most likely to occur, it stands to reason that the actual topic is nuclear war. In the Preface to the American edition, Aron briefly recounted the history of his book by indicating that it originated as a series of lectures for a course on nuclear armament and international relations. He added that, by the time he had finished the course and was revising his lectures for the English language edition, several notable changes had occurred (Khrushchev was no longer in power and the Chinese had joined the United States and the Soviet Union as a nuclear power), yet he insisted that the problem remained the same (Aron 1965a: v). He admitted that, previously, generals kept military plans secret and diplomats refrained from discussing them, but since the advent of the nuclear age more people believed it necessary to discuss the possible use of what Aron referred to as "monstrous weapons." This phrase underscores the seriousness of war and provides the proper context for what Aron regarded as two incontestable statements: Clemenceau's claim that "War is too serious a matter to be left to the generals" and de Gaulle's reply to Atlee's claim that de Gaulle was a great general but a bad politician, "Politics is too serious a matter to be left to the politicians" (Aron 1965a: vi–vii). Echoing Plato's claim in *The Republic* that philosophy needs to be joined with politics, Aron insisted that military leaders need political training and policy makers need to learn about strategy, if not about war (Aron 1965: viii).

Aron began his account as he typically did, by looking at the recent history of technological innovations. Towards the end of World War Two, the United States dropped atomic bombs on two Japanese cities – one on Hiroshima and one on Nagasaki several days later. Relying on statistics from the Soviet Union, Aron compared the deaths resulting from the two atomic bombs with the deaths from normal bombs: 279 planes dropped enough bombs to have killed over 80,000 people or left them missing but the planes that dropped the two atomic bombs killed between 105,000 and 140,000 people or left them missing. That was destructive enough but the invention of the thermonuclear bomb drastically increased the possible carnage. Aron calculated that the total number of bombs that the Allies dropped on Germany was close to 600,000 tons or the equivalent of three atomic bombs. However, instead of being calculated in thousands of tons, as the atomic bomb was, the thermonuclear bomb is calculated in millions of tons (Aron 1965a: 2–3). Aron delineates three types of effects that nuclear bombs produce: mechanical, which is the actual blast; thermal, which is the fire that expands further than the blast; and radioactive, which goes far beyond the actual blast and the firestorm. The blast will kill people instantly, the firestorm will kill people in a short time period, but the effects of radiation will continue to kill people for decades. The shift from atomic bombs to thermonuclear weapons was a major one, but it was only one of several. Another was the miniaturization of the weapons and another was the improvement in missile delivery. The first revolutionized energy, the second revolutionized size, but the third revolutionized time (Aron 1965a: 7–9), and the amount of time needed to "improve" in all three areas is decreasing. Aron provided this brief account as a reminder of "the inconceivable horror implicit in the notion of total war" and in order to set the stage for the need to discuss strategy (Aron 1965a: 4–7).

Prior to 1949, the United States had little to worry about in terms of any possibility of being attacked with nuclear weapons; by 1960, it was concerned about the probability of being attacked with nuclear weapons by the Soviet Union and possibly by China (Aron 1965a: 30–2). The United States did not need to worry about strategic deterrence because, as the sole nuclear power, it held the monopoly on these types of weapons. Things changed radically when the Soviet Union caught up because then American military planners needed to address the twin issues of strategic deterrence and strategic use: the first is intended to forestall an attack; the second is intended to respond to such an attack (Aron 1965a: 32–3). Much of the following three chapters is devoted to specific doctrines and is now of interest primarily to historians. However, Aron returns to the general topic of strategy in Chapter Six, entitled "Logic and Paradoxes of the Strategic Theory."

Aron moves from his prior discussions of specific circumstances to a "theoretical synthesis" (Aron 1965a: 194). He begins by suggesting that the threat of nuclear war has not rendered the classical idea that sovereign nations are in a state of nature outdated. However, he maintains that nuclear threats introduce three new factors to that state of nature. First, the destructive force of thermonuclear weapons far exceeds the destruction wrought by any conventional weapon. Second, the danger differs from before because of both its sense of permanence and its instantaneousness. Previously, a country that had been attacked could mount a counterattack, but now the attacked country may cease to exist in too short a time to mount a counterattack. Third, the definition of victory has been fundamentally altered. Clausewitz defined absolute victory as disarming the vanquished country, but now one need not disarm a country in order to annihilate it (Aron 1965a: 196–8).

## Concluding comments

Aron held that war is a part of human history and likely a part of human nature. He believed that humans often started wars because of mistakes and misunderstandings, but that did not mean that he considered wars inevitable. If anything, he was convinced that wars could be prevented by following certain policies and adopting certain approaches. Yet he ultimately believed that "wisdom and moderation" were the only real grounds to avoid a nuclear holocaust (Aron 1959: 74).

Aron recognized that all of the historical wars were tragic, but the two world wars were even more so because of the huge number of deaths and the sheer amount of destruction. The dropping of the two atomic bombs on Japan revealed a new dimension of damage, but that would no doubt pale in comparison to that associated with the newly invented hydrogen bomb. Because of the possibility of the annihilation of whole cities, Aron was convinced that war now needed to be avoided, if at all possible. All throughout history, wars have been destructive, but modern warfare has led to even greater destruction and more suffering. Thus, while peace would have been preferable before, it is imperative now. That is why Aron wrote on international relations and designed them to be used as a blueprint for peace. It is entirely possible to consider that he wrote them especially for politicians who take their sense of responsibility seriously and will work hard to avoid war. And it is certainly possible to read these writings on peace and war through Aron's question of "What would you do?"

## NOTES

1. "Tausendmal lieber sterben, als dies wieder erleben" (quoted in von Schlieffen 1933: 21).
2. Aron chose the title *Peace and War* to reflect what he thought took precedence and there is no glorification of battle in his writings on war. According to Robert Colquhoun, Aron saw "little fighting" because he was serving as a meteorologist for the air force (Colquhoun: 1986a: 211). And in the Preface to *On War*, Aron wrote, "In other times, a sociologist without specialist qualifications would have hesitated to deal with the problems of military strategy (Aron 1959: ii).
3. It may be the high degree of difficulty that accounts for the lack of interest in this essay and in Thucydides. The essay is mostly ignored by almost all commentators. Thucydides is barely mentioned in the collection *Political Reason in the Age of Ideology* and is named a dozen times in a few of the essays in *The Companion to Raymond Aron*. Perrine Simon-Nahum actually spends a paragraph on Thucydides but only to discuss his conception of history. It is to Simon-Nahum's credit that she notices the importance of Weber and Thucydides for Aron. She writes: "In Aron's works, there is a dialogue between Thucydides and Max Weber." Unfortunately, she does not build upon this insight (Simon-Nahum 2015: 110). For my own account of Thucydides on Weber, see "Max Weber's Pericles: The Political Demagogue" (Adair-Toteff 2008).

4. Aron also states that a "great war becomes the ideal type of death struggle" (Aron 1978d: 44).
5. The ideas that life is a struggle for existence and a "struggle of man over man" are found throughout Weber's political writings but they are expressed most strongly in Weber's 1895 Inaugural Lecture, "Der Nationalstaat und die Wirtschaftspolitik" (Weber 1993a: 543, 553, 558, 560, 567–72). For a significant discussion of these ideas, see Lassmann (2000).

# CHAPTER FIVE

# *On peace*

"Troubled times encourage meditations."
Raymond Aron[1]

## PEACE AND WAR

As much as Raymond Aron was preoccupied with the notion of war, he was also very concerned about the concept of peace. Aron did not regard war and peace as independent and separate; instead, he maintained they were related to what he referred to as the "dialectic of peace and war." He further believed that they were the two "typical conditions" of international relations and it was certainly expected that Aron would ultimately decide to write on that topic. The discipline of international relations had been around for decades when he finally felt ready to offer a contribution to it. In 1954, he announced that he was beginning work on a book on international relations and he continued to work on it during the remainder of that decade and into the early 1960s. He finally published it in 1961 and an English version appeared in 1965. The book carries the title of *Peace and War*, which is intriguing not only because it is a reversal of one of Tolstoy's most famous novels, but also because it reveals Aron's belief in a real, but tenuous, relationship between peace and war.

As with virtually every influential book, Aron's *Peace and War* has been interpreted and evaluated very differently. Some commentators have declared Aron's book to be a great success while others have considered it to be a major failure. What almost all of Aron's readers have agreed upon is that it is one of the greatest books in the discipline of international relations. The purpose of this chapter is to offer a brief description and an even briefer evaluation of *Peace and War*. It is intended neither to provide a full account of Aron's conception of international relations nor to offer a defense of Aron against his critics. Either of those two tasks would undoubtedly require a separate book. Instead, the focus here is to show how Aron's theory of international relations functions in accordance with his philosophy of political responsibility. This focus helps explain why I have chosen to spend far more time discussing certain sections of the book in contrast to other sections. Accordingly, I spend more time on Part One, which deals with concepts and systems, and Part Four, which is normative, than I do on Part Two, which is sociological, and Part Three, which is historical. This is not to imply that those two parts are not important, only that they are less relevant to the goals here.

## PART ONE

Raymond Aron begins *Peace and War* by talking not about peace but about war, and consequently draws heavily and frequently from Clausewitz. In fact, Aron begins Chapter One with a famous quotation from Clausewitz: "War ... is an act of violence intended to compel our opponent to fulfill our will" (Aron 2009: 21, 71, 90). For Aron, as for Clausewitz, war and policy were related: if one cannot bend the opponent by persuasion, then one must try to do it by force. Again invoking Clausewitz, Aron insists that war is the continuation of policy (or politics) by other means (Aron 2009: 23). One has a choice between the "art of convincing" or the "art of constraining"; the first is done with words and the second is accomplished with weapons (Aron 2009: 23–4). But one needs to have a realistic idea of what it is that one intends to accomplish and this is as true about war as it is about diplomacy (Aron 2009: 39). Unfortunately, many statesmen and many generals either have little idea about their objectives or have unrealistic expectations. As he asks later, what are the *objectives*, what are the probable *results*, what are the *stakes* of the war (Aron 2009: 87)? Aron suggests that Ludendorff and Hindenburg are great representatives of generals of this kind because they had no real goal other than victory. In addition, their belief that they could do anything led them to think not only that there would be no negative repercussions in launching unrestricted submarine warfare, but also that doing so would lead to Germany's victory (Aron 2009: 37). What Ludendorff and Hindenburg did not realize was that allowing German submarines to attack anyone would inevitably prompt America to enter the war. Max Weber and many others cautioned explicitly about this danger but Ludendorff and Hindenburg did not heed any warnings.

Aron returns again to Clausewitz because the great military philosopher knew that rational planning was necessary for war, while also recognizing how large a factor chance is in it as well (Aron 2009: 53). Aron suggests that there are three key areas in which chance plays a role: in space, in available materials, and in the collective capacity for action. The first factor is space, by which Aron means terrain or distance. The Swiss mountains have prevented many armies from invading Switzerland, just as the enormous distances in Russia helped defeat both Napoleon and Hitler. Regarding the second factor, Aron indicates that while overwhelming force may seem to guarantee success, the fact that many guerrilla wars are won by a much smaller force that lacks major weapons shows that this is not always the case. Finally, there is the related factor of the collective will to fight. If a large army is composed of soldiers who are extremely demoralized, then a smaller and a more motivated force is more likely to prevail (Aron 2009: 55–7).

What are the causes of war? Aron offers a number of answers but suggests that the primary one is security. No country can count on help from other countries, regardless of what sort of friendly relationship they may have. The Hobbesian notion of the "state of nature" plays a large part in the idea of "war of all against all." But history also reveals that many friendly nations end up going to war against one another. For example, the Athenians and the Spartans fought against the Persians, but they ultimately fought each other. Aron puts forth three notions that seem to serve as a cause of war: power, glory, and an idea (Aron 2009: 73, 91). He draws on the Scottish philosopher and historian David Hume to help explain two of these notions. Hume believed in the importance of equilibrium between states and pointed to the lack of it between Athens and Sparta as being a major factor in the Peloponnesian War. Thus, it was not just the need for security that caused wars, but also the fact that the lust for glory was simply too intoxicating to deny (Aron 2009: 73–6, 103). The third possible cause for going to war might be the most troubling because it has no real basis in human nature per se; going to war because of an idea is completely different than the need for security or the desire for glory. That is part of the reason that Aron expended so much effort on exploring ideology.

In *Peace and War*, Aron devotes a considerable amount of effort to the Peloponnesian War. While he admits that no two wars are alike, he insists that that particular war shares a number of things with later wars. First, it was a matter of glory, but second, it was also a matter of power, and third, it was a matter of having many different causes. There was a sense of fear as well as a belief that Athens needed to punish defecting allies contributing to the conviction that war was inevitable (Aron 2009: 141–5). But there was also a belief that the equilibrium between Athens and Sparta had been lost. Again, Aron invokes Hume: while Hume is referring to the Peloponnesian War, the idea of equilibrium in international relations is the only "universal and formal rule" (Aron 2009: 146). Since Aron was convinced of this, it is crucial to investigate the concept in more detail.

What Aron calls "equilibrium" is really the concept of the "balance of power." It is the attempt to maintain a balance among nations, but it really involves only a few states. Aron divides states into two categories, with the larger one being made up of smaller states and the smaller category being made up of larger states. He makes it clear that the smallness or largeness is not dependent on size but on the degree of power that each state possesses. Furthermore, he maintains that the less powerful nations have far less responsibility in contrast to the greater degree of responsibility that comes with greater power. In making these assertions, Aron is not suggesting anything new, as Max Weber had made similar points decades earlier. Where Aron departs from Weber is in his division of history into two categories. There are times in which there are multiple states with roughly equal power and there are times in which there are just two states that each have approximately the same degree of power. He refers to the first as "multipolar" and to the second as "bipolar." These are Weberian "ideal types": in the "multipolar" situation, there are a number of states and any state can be either a friend or an enemy. In the "bipolar" situation, there are only two principal actors and they are enemies either "by position or by ideology" (Aron 2009: 138). Aron indicated that, prior to 1910, the world was "multipolar," in that there were a number of powerful countries, and he included France, Germany, Russia, Great Britain, Austria, Hungary, and Italy in this group (Aron 2009: 128). During this time, alliances were temporary and subject to change as states changed their beliefs about who to trust, based upon the degree of force that each country had. Aron indicates that as one state appears to gain more power, the others will feel it necessary to respond by forming new alliances. Thus, generalizations can be made: first, alliances are temporary; second, the state that is increasing its power should attempt to moderate its claims, unless it seeks domination; and third, if it does seek domination, then it must be ready to confront the other states (Aron 2009: 128–9). In a "multipolar" period, states do not tend to regard others as mortal enemies but simply as rivals. In such cases, diplomacy works rather well, especially if it is realistic. By "realistic," Aron means a type of diplomacy that is "moderate and reasonable" (Aron 2009: 132). It also implies that the state does not regard others as either friends or enemies but simply as other states. A state that has a realistic sense of diplomacy will not act with feelings but with ideas. Such a state recognizes that all states act egotistically and that, while wars are to be avoided, they are not necessarily immoral. It is here that Aron explains why he did not include the United States in the group of "multipolar" states. It is because two of the wars that it had fought were not against other nations but against internal groups. The first war was the one against Native American tribes and the second was the Civil War. Aron suggests that when the wars were won, the United States did not stop conceiving of the opposing forces as the enemy but continued to hate them. For the United States, this was a moral stand. Thus, until 1945, the United States was the "antipode of this traditional and prudent immorality." Even towards the end of World War Two, the United States tended to view the enemy in strictly moral terms: it was wicked and guilty, so it deserved to be punished. However, the United States learned that it was mistaken about its enemies and its allies: Russia and China were no longer allies and friends; Germany and Japan were no longer enemies but were becoming friends (Aron 2009: 132–3). Aron does not belabor the point here that morality has no place in international relations. As he puts it at the beginning of Chapter Five, "Foreign policy, in and of itself, is power politics" (Aron 2009: 125). As he noted earlier, diplomacy is a substitute for war (Aron 2009: 69). Since diplomacy seeks equilibrium, states need to be moderate and rational, not morally good. Aron writes: "Hateful or admirable, baneful or precious, the diplomacy of equilibrium does not result from the deliberate choice on the part of the statesmen – it results from circumstances" (Aron 2009: 133). It is little wonder that, just prior to this assertion, Aron invoked the realism of Machiavelli: changes in alliances do occur but they should not occur frequently.

Aron returns to his examination of "multipolar" diplomacy. He notes that "multipolar" diplomacy is situated between the "state of nature" and the "rule of law"; it is neither all against all nor a single monarchy. It is not designed to foster the "common good of the system" but is the "imperative of prudence" (Aron 2009: 134–5). Unfortunately, the "multipolar" era of the "immoral and measured diplomacy of equilibrium" has passed and the world has entered the time of "bipolar" forces (Aron 2009: 136).

In the "multipolar" system, there was a large number of weaker states and a small number of stronger ones. Because of the transitory nature of alliances, the "multipolar" system was delicate, yet, as long as the major countries employed a modest and reasonable diplomacy, the equilibrium was maintained. This did not mean that there were no wars but rather that, until the twentieth century, they tended not to be as devastating (of course, there were exceptions, such as the Thirty Years War). Nor is the modern era of "bipolar" states the only one that has ever existed in history – the Greeks were divided into two camps: the Athenians and the Spartans (Aron 2009: 140–1). Aron follows Thucydides in laying the blame for the Peloponnesian War on Athens for acting ruthlessly and aggressively when it should have been focused on maintaining the peace within the alliance. He also agrees with Thucydides that Athens relished intimidating others and that the other city-states realized that Athens was no longing acting as their protector (Aron 2009: 137). This was Athens's greatest indication of "hubris" and its biggest mistake. The other was Athens's refusal to allow the individual city-states the degree of autonomy that they wanted and that they believed they deserved. The larger problem was also two-fold: all involved believed that war was inevitable and, according to Thucydides, it seemed that way primarily because of Athens's increasing power and the growing threat of domination (Aron 2009: 141–2). However, we know from Thucydides that Athens's "hubris" ultimately resulted in its defeat.

Referring to Clausewitz, Aron asks what role his distinction between "offensive" and "defensive" can play in "diplomatic–strategic conduct"? Aron clarifies his own use by indicating that "offensive power" is when one has the capacity to force one's will on the opponent, whereas "defensive power" is the capacity to resist the other's attempt at domination (Aron 2009: 82–3). Yet Aron does not make use of Clausewitz as much as he does of Max Weber and that is because, like Weber, he regards individuals as being purposeful creatures. Weber famously called the "means–end" relationship "zweckrational". Aron notes that Weber frequently employed "zweckrational" in his discussions about economics, but Aron has suggested that economics differs from strategy. First of all, the economist does not claim to know exactly what an individual desires but can rank the interests on a kind of scale. Second of all, the economist is most comfortable when describing an individual and less so when discussing a group. Yet strategy involves more than one individual. Finally, an economist thinks in terms of a single fundamental concept like utility and someone in international relations will attempt to do something similar by suggesting that there is also some single fundamental concept such as "power." However, as Aron has already demonstrated with his claim in *Peace and War*, states are motivated by the three notions of security, glory, and idea (Aron 2009: 90–1). Since the concept of "power" cannot serve a role in international relations that is similar to the role that "utility" plays in economics, there cannot be a *"general theory of international relations comparable to the general theory of economy."*[2]

As such, one who writes about international relations cannot look to economics as a similar type of science and must use different means to explain how international relations functions. Aron employs a theory of systems in which he makes what he regards as a fundamental distinction between a "homogeneous system" and a "heterogeneous system" (Aron 2009: 99–100). A "homogeneous system" is one in which the states are similar in type and obey the same conception of policies. A "heterogeneous system" is composed of states that differ significantly in type and adhere to different conceptions of policy. The first type of system tends to be stable because it is "foreseeable" and it tends to be more permanent because it frowns upon violence. In contrast, the second type is unstable because of the inherent contradictions in the nature of the states, which lead to conflicts and violence (Aron 2009: 100–2). Aron raises a question about the system leading up to 1914: was it a "homogeneous system" or a "heterogeneous" one? At first glance, it looked as if it was a "homogeneous system" because all of the countries, including Russia, recognized each other's right to exist. They also recognized the right to travel and cross borders, as well as the right for an opposition to exist and even criticize the government. However, this appearance of "homogeneity" masked a number of fault lines, including those regarding legitimacy and equality. In the aristocratic states, like Russia, sovereignty belonged only to the ruling family and its heirs, while in the more democratic states, like France and Great Britain, sovereignty belonged to the people. However, when war broke out, these heterogeneous fissures grew and the schism began to widen even further because of each state's increasing reliance on nationalism (Aron 2009: 101–3).

In addition to the distinction between "homogeneous systems" and "heterogeneous systems," Aron sets out a distinction between "transnational society" and "international systems." A "transnational society" is not so much a system as it is a collection of societies that share many similar values. Aron points again to the ability to cross borders and to the exchange of goods. Even though different countries had different types of churches, they shared fundamental religious values. He again points to Europe at the time before the First World War as a time of "transnational society." Aron indicates that, during the war, the "transnational society" broke up and it has yet to reconstitute itself. Instead, there is now a slight interest in "international systems." What Aron appears to mean is public international law, yet he thinks that as long as the West and the East regard each other as complete ideological and total physical enemies, a functioning type of international law cannot occur (Aron 2009: 106–7). However, he moves to discuss the juridical basis for international law and how that relates both to peace and to war.

Aron focuses on treaties, which he thinks provide the basis for much of international law, but he notes that that is because they are entered into by states. Once again, the notion of "recognition" plays a large part in international law; treaties are "valid" only if each state recognizes the other and the other's right to be a signatory of that treaty (Aron 2009: 108). He used as an example the states of Estonia, Lithuania, and Latvia because, as they were incorporated into the Soviet Union, they ceased to exist and lost their ability to be recognized. Now that the Soviet Union has collapsed, they do exist and countries recognize them as nations of the world. Aron's notion of recognition points to a larger problem in international law: namely, that jurists in different states have differing views regarding the propriety of international law. For example, all of the signatories to the documents that created the International Court of Justice have pledged to abide by its rulings but in practice each nation has decided what it was willing or not willing to submit to. His point is that "juridical norms" need to be examined and interpreted, and different nations do that differently (Aron 2009: 109). Accordingly, different nations have different interpretations of various conflicts, whether the Korean War or the war for independence in Algeria.

Aron then takes up the question about legalizing or outlawing war. Until the First World War, no one expected that this was even a question – that wars happened, regardless of what jurists or philosophers wanted to believe. Instead, the issues were how to declare war, how to conduct it, what weapons were to be used, and how could it be concluded. The question was never whether it should be made illegal. As long as wars were conducted according to these principles, including the right to attack in order to defend one's nation, there was no question of illegality. Aron points to the fact that philosophers as different as Rousseau and Hegel agreed on at least one thing: that is, that wars were between nations and not people (Aron 2009: 112). However, the death and destruction of the First World War prompted philosophers to take up the question of whether war could be outlawed. We know, however, that the League of Nations failed and the United Nations has not been very successful (Aron 2009: 113, 124).

Aron concludes Part One by insisting that the Cold War was the manifestation of two processes. The first is the increase in nuclear weapons' capability for destruction and the second is the increase in the psychological element. What this intersection leaves is what Aron calls "peace through terror." Peace through terror is "a worldwide and monstrous threat" of total annihilation that reduces men to a "collective passivity." They are all collectively targeted because each one is individually (Aron 2009: 173).

## Part two

In the initial pages of Part Two, Aron reflects on the focus of Part One. He intended that part to be theoretical: that is, it involved concepts. He recounts how he had discussed the interrelationship between diplomacy and strategy, the factor of power, and the objectives that statesmen have. He also discussed the differences between "homogeneous systems" and "heterogeneous systems," as well as the differentiation between "bipolar" and "multipolar" conditions. Thus far, Aron has tended to treat the historian and the sociologist as being similar but now he argues that they are fundamentally different. They are different because the historian looks back at history to explain and seek causes for past events, whereas the sociologist seeks general rules that can be used to help predict the future (Aron 2009: 177). In Part Two, Aron examines two sets of ideas: the first set contains physical properties such as space, numbers, and resources. By space, Aron means primarily territory; by numbers, he means mostly population; and by resources, he basically means economics. His discussions are wide-ranging and he takes up many issues, including geography, the size of nations, and the consequences of imperialism. Aron's discussions of these issues are illuminating, as usual, but are not directly germane to my thesis of political responsibility. In contrast, the other set is relevant because here Aron examines the three historical unities that he calls nation, civilization, and humanity (Aron 2009: 179). In contrast to the three physical members of the first group, which are determinants of situations, the three members of this group are factors in how the political actors behave (Aron 2009: 279).

Aron asks whether all nations act in the same way and answers in the negative. Different states are ruled differently so they can and do act differently. On the one hand, Aron suggests that authoritarian regimes can, in theory, be more flexible in foreign affairs because they do not really need to respond to public opinion. On the other hand, the same authoritarian regime is often constrained by its own ideology. These notions lead Aron back to the idea that all nations always act in accordance with their own national interests. Aron counters by expanding upon the point that he had made in Part One about the lack of a concept in international relations that is akin to the concept of utility in economics. He insists that the economist does not tell anyone what to do with goods, whereas the scholar of international relations tries to determine how the statesman should act. As Aron will explain in great detail in Part Four, international relations is both a descriptive and a normative discipline. Another difference that he emphasizes is that the economist deals with an economic collective that differs from a political one (Aron 2009: 285–6). As an example, Aron points out that some politically disadvantaged groups may be prone to revolutionary tendencies yet not every political group is so inclined. Aron's point is that the belief that nations are somehow superior to regimes is a false one and he wonders why historians (Treitschke), commentators (Walter Lippmann), and statesmen (de Gaulle) continue to insist that they are (Aron 2009: 287).

Aron wonders whether there is some single concept that might be applicable to political collectives and examines several possible options. One is the notion of a nation's "character" but he notes three objections to it. First, does it apply to all citizens or only to those in the military? Second, since the "character" of an individual is a combination of natural traits and learned experiences, can the notion be applicable to a nation? Third, if it does apply to the nation, how many of its citizens must share that "character"? Since "character" appears to apply mostly to individuals and seems inappropriate for states, Aron asks whether Montesquieu's "spirit of a nation" is more applicable. While this second option shares some of the same defects as "character" does, Aron maintains that the notion of the "spirit of a nation" is preferable because it emphasizes the cultural and historical heritage of a nation (Aron 2009: 287–9). To help bolster this case, Aron invokes de Tocqueville's account of the French throughout modern history. Aron accepts it because he believes that it reveals the changes in French attitudes over the centuries. This point is critically important to Aron's account of international relations because it underlines his conviction regarding the changes and movements in a nation's approach to other states. One of the major problems with that notion of "character" is its sense of permanence, which the "spirit of a nation" apparently lacks. Aron insists that much of this entire conversation is provisional and does not offer any demonstrable truths. History is replete with nations that were once considered to be terrible but now they are not. For example, Aron reminds us that the French were reviled during the reign of terror just as the Germans were considered evil during the Third Reich. This additional point also emphasizes the fluidity that occurs in relations between countries and underscores the need for states to be flexible. Although Aron does not explicitly make that point here, it was the rigid ideology of the Soviet Union that outweighed the absence of a freely-formed public opinion and that rendered it less flexible than the United States (Aron 2009: 289–92).

After a brief discussion about people believing that nationalism causes wars, Aron turns to the topic of regimes and military organization. He maintains that there are three types of secular power: economic, political, and military. He further maintains that the power that men assert over others is also based upon three things: wealth, legitimate authority, and arms. Aron qualifies this by mentioning that legitimate authority is most often based upon either wealth or arms. Leaving aside the political regime, Aron indicates that both the military regime and the economic regime must solve two problems: for the military regime, the technical issue is the production of weapons and the human one is relationships. These are either at work in the factory or in service in the barracks (Aron 2009: 299). These relationships are also based upon discipline and trust; thus they are social. Furthermore, different armies have different social strata and differ in outlook. Aron points out that, in 1870, the Prussian army was made up of conscripts while the French army was composed of professionals. A further difference was that Prussian soldiers preferred army life to war whereas French soldiers preferred war to the detested army life. Aron's larger point is that the military does not invariably prefer war to peace. His conclusion is that a political regime may be military but that does not imply that it is necessarily always interested in war (Aron 2009: 301–6).

Chapter Eleven is entitled "In Search of a Pattern of Change" and is devoted to emphasizing the prevalence of change in politics, military matters, and international relations. More importantly, it represents Aron's search to uncover any pattern that can be found in these changes. If the previous chapter was mostly negative in demolishing the belief that there are general laws, this chapter is more positive in showing that there are some patterns to be found. Aron believes that there are two phases that can be found throughout history: one is "times of trouble" and the other is "universal empire." He notes that, while these exist, they exist for different lengths of time. He suggests that during times of "universal empire," a few nations will extend their influence and attempt to maintain stability. During "times of trouble," there will be many states that will band together in order to facilitate an equilibrium (Aron 2009: 321–3). His conclusion is that there fails to be any meaningful qualitative pattern of change; he spends some time investigating whether there might be some quantitative pattern but arrives at a similar negative result. Aron's third attempt is to consider humanity as a whole rather than as a collection of political groups. His conclusion in this area is similarly negative – that one cannot state with certainty that humans are naturally bellicose but that one can state that wars resemble the societies that engage in them (Aron 2009: 336).

In Chapter Twelve, Aron examines whether the interest in going to war is based upon biological, psychological, or social causes. He notes that biologists refer to an animal's tendency to fight as a type of aggression and further observes that not all types of animals share the same tendency. There are certain species that appear to refrain from attacking while there are others that are more prone to do so. However, even the most aggressive species seem to recognize limits and are unwilling to kill their own kind. Aron cites the example of two wolves who fight. The one who is defeated bares his throat in surrender and the dominant one will not continue the attack. He offers another example of two hens. On meeting for the first time, they will fight; on the next several meetings, the length of the fights declines until one decides not to fight but simply to flee. This behavior is what Aron refers to as a hierarchy of force and he observes that it is found throughout the animal kingdom (Aron 2009: 340–3, 354, 356, 366). In contrast, humans do kill each other and even in instances where one admits defeat or tries to flee. On the basis of these examples, Aron suggests that there is no biological impetus to human aggression but he points instead to certain psychological factors like pride and envy. However, he also suggests that these may not be completely innate but may have a social component. He adds that socialization does not necessarily reduce aggression; in fact, it often increases it. He explains that this has been so historically but it has increased as modern societies become more competitive. And he points to reports that indicated that early man did not go to war. He confesses that he is not qualified to state how long this "golden age" lasted but is convinced that he is qualified to state that "war is the conflict of one form of organized behavior with another" (Aron 2009: 347, 349–51). Aron concludes Part Two with two critical observations: first, that "The difficulty of peace has more to do with man's humanity than his animality"; and second, that "The hierarchy of master and slave will never be stable." He concludes that the masters of the future will not need slaves and will have the power to exterminate (Aron 2009: 366).

## Part three

Part Three carries the title "History," and unlike Parts One and Two, which were focused on the present, this one looks to the past. However, it is not completely historical in orientation; Aron makes numerous points about the present and hints about the future. The central focus of my remarks will be on those general points and will leave aside comments about Aron's specific historical judgments.

The present age is the age of thermonuclear weapons and that fact has altered military strategy and diplomacy. To explain these changes is one of Aron's objectives; the other is to provide a description of the concepts and determining factors in a concrete case. Aron insists that these two objectives overlap (Aron 2009: 371).

Aron insists that one of the most significant changes that occurred after 1945 was how the world was fundamentally altered in the way that seemingly small events occurring in faraway countries were now capable of influencing other countries. Aron suggests that the "diplomatic universe is like an echo chamber"; although that does not seem like the most appropriate description, what he apparently meant by it was that the world has "shrunk" so much that events that would not have been noticed before have now become influential (Aron 2009: 373). That is what the title of Chapter Thirteen seeks to capture: "Le Monde fini."

The title of Chapter Fourteen is more straightforward – "On the Strategy of Deterrence" – and here Aron makes a number of important points. Deterrence is not a modern phenomenon but has existed as long as there have been two people or two collectives. He offers two examples: the threat of a slap deters a young child from ruining his father's books just as the threat of a ticket deters a driver from speeding (Aron 2009: 404). A second crucial point is that all countries, including neutral ones, strive to deter. Aron offers recent historical examples. In 1938, France tried to deter Hitler from attacking Czechoslovakia, and the following year, Great Britain hoped to deter him from attacking Poland. Unfortunately, neither attempt was successful but Aron's point is to demonstrate that deterrence existed prior to the nuclear age.

Aron defines deterrence as that which occurs when one country decides that inaction is preferable to action, based upon the likely response from the other country. He adds that deterrence is based upon three factors: first, psychological, meaning that the other side believes that an unwanted response would be forthcoming; second, technological, meaning that the result would be what the country feared; and third, political, meaning what the consequences would be in political terms. He suggests that the technological factor involves weapons and the political involves diplomacy as well as weapons. Finally, the psychological factor is based upon technological and political factors. Aron does not explicitly state it but modern deterrence differs from historical deterrence because the costs are much higher. He cites figures from the dropping of the atomic bombs on two Japanese cities. Nagasaki had a population of 195,000, of whom 36,000 were either killed or went missing, with an additional 40,000 people wounded. Roughly 1.8 square miles were destroyed in the attack. In comparison, Hiroshima had a population of 255,000, of whom 70,000 people were killed or went missing, and an additional 70,000 were wounded. The number of square miles destroyed in Hiroshima amounted to 4.7. Aron notes that, as horrifying as these numbers were, even more destructive nuclear weapons have been developed since 1945. Accordingly, the numbers of dead, missing, and injured, as well as the size of the area destroyed, would be increased exponentially (Aron 2009: 414–15). Aron observes that these figures both horrify and encourage – the sheer numbers prompt people to believe that such a war could not happen (Aron 2009: 417, 429). However, he insists that we must determine what the results of such a "monstrous war" would be; he relies on another study that indicates, with 2 million dead, it would take one year for the economy to recover, and it would take close on 100 years if 160 million died in a "thermonuclear apocalypse" (Aron 2009: 417). Aron deduces from this that both the Soviet Union and the United States have decided that, since they cannot protect all of their population, they should concentrate instead on improving the ability to attack. Aron wonders whether the development of nuclear weapons means that Clausewitz's dictum "war is the continuation of policy by other means" is no longer true (Aron 2009: 439). His answer is that, despite the increase in destruction, war is still possible. The question concerns what type of war – conventional or nuclear?

Aron devotes a number of chapters to explaining the events between 1945 and 1960. The historian would likely find his account fascinating but what is important here is the question that he asks toward the end of Part Three: namely, has the international situation become more stable or less so, or has it remained basically the same? His answer is complex and he suggests that this is so because between 1945 and 1960 there have been periods of crisis and periods of stability. He considers everything – from the blockade of Berlin to the Suez Canal conflict, the Hungarian uprising, and the Korean War – to be times of conflict. These periods were then followed by periods of relative calm. However, Aron is concerned about the ideologies of the Soviet Union and Communist China and warns the West that it ought to take the Communist threat seriously (Aron 2009: 561, 572)

## PART FOUR

Parts One, Two, and Three were primarily theoretical, meaning conceptual, sociological, and historical. Part Four is almost strictly normative; instead of discussing what was or what is, Aron discusses what ought to be. At first glance, it might appear that Aron is violating Max Weber's cardinal rule against conflating values and facts when he writes, "Normative implications are inherent in every *theory*" (Aron 2009: 575). Yet Aron is not violating Weber's rule because he is not conflating them, but rather is drawing normative conclusions from the empirical facts. Weber himself often did that, as, for example, in his Inaugural Lecture at Freiburg when he moved from his discussion about the then current situation in Western Prussia to his advocacy of what should be done to correct that situation. Aron is doing much the same thing here: after providing a conceptual and historical account, he then moves to advocating what should be done. He begins by reminding us that Clausewitz had once said that strategy cannot be based upon theory because there are too many problems and too many variables (Aron 2009: 575). Aron offers the example of Napoleon's failure to conquer Moscow and asks whether Napoleon could have succeeded if he had employed a different strategy. Aron's answer is that the question is basically unanswerable because there is no definite way to know all of the different possibilities. Thus, we cannot have a general theory of strategy; the best that we can have is a few principles. However, these are not really principles as they consist mostly of vague formulas. These are "the principle of the concentration of forces," "the principle of objectives," "the principle of persistence," "the principle of offensive," "the principle of security," "the principle of surprise," and "the principle of the economy of forces." He notes that, even if these are somewhat vague, they are still valuable. He lists them: one should concentrate one's forces; one needs to have clear goals; one must persevere; one should mount attacks but also defend; one should try to deceive the enemy; and one needs to use one's forces fully. Aron insists that, while these are good principles, they cannot determine the best strategy and that is mostly because they are occasionally contradictory. Furthermore, a theory of strategy would seem to imply a rigid plan whereas the strategist needs to be flexible and change with the conditions. The "strategic indeterminacy" is caused by two factors: concrete factors influence decisions and the goal is less clearly determined compared to the goal of the tactician (Aron 2009: 576–7). These concrete factors can include the location of a country, its history, the nature of its citizens, and even its climate. And the goal may be winning or succeeding but Aron has questions regarding the conditions, limitations, and parameters. Aron devotes much of Part Four to examining these questions, and he does so by discussing a number of different issues. The first two chapters are very Weberian, the second two slightly Clausewitzian, but the final two are pure Aron.

The first two chapters carry the heading "In Search of a Morality" and the title of the first is "Idealism and Realism" while the second is "Conviction and Responsibility." The reader will recall that Aron defended Weber's political realism; what he appeared to object to was Weber's extreme nationalism. The reader will also remember the contrast that Weber drew between the "ethics of conviction" and the "ethics of responsibility," with the adherent of the former acting only on principles while the one who practices the latter considers consequences. Aron concurs with Weber's assessment that the true Christian repudiates force and accordingly should not participate in politics. Because force is central to politics, only those who agree to its use should participate. However, Aron also concurs with Weber's insistence on the need to use force responsibly: hence Aron's insistence on the importance of the "ethics of responsibility" for the political actor. With these thoughts in mind, I turn to Aron's discussion of realism and idealism.

Aron notes that the preceding account was primarily conceptual and factual, and was mostly devoid of ethics and values. However, Aron then observes that international politics has a dual nature: on the one hand, most politicians acknowledge the others' rights to exist peacefully, but on the other hand, they realize that inevitably there is conflict. The question then becomes: whether they adhere to ethical principles or should act according to the opportunity of force. As Aron writes, "What role do nations and statesmen accord, or should they accord to principles, ideas, morality, necessity?" (Aron 2009: 579). The subtitle hints at Aron's own view – "From Idealist Illusions to Prudence" – and this subsection deals with idealism that comes in two forms. Both of these believe in an abstract ideal and, because of this, both "have little to do with reality." One form is what is referred to as "ideological idealism" and that idealism is guided by a single idea. All political decisions are ultimately based upon that one notion. The other form is what is called "juridical idealism," which insists that the political actor must act according to some "more or less defined rule." Aron offers four examples but the two that are applicable today are the one that rejects a change that is a result of force and the one that insists that war be outlawed. These are abstract and normative propositions and accordingly their proponents ignore facts and reality. Furthermore, those who believe in "idealistic diplomacy" often become fanatics. Whether it is ideological idealism or juridical idealism is immaterial; what they have in common is an idealistic illusion. Aron maintains that the opposite of the idealist is the person who recognizes that each situation is different; accordingly, that person sees that different facts will determine the proper response. This is what Aron refers to as prudence, which is his cardinal guide in international relations. He writes: "prudence is the statesman's supreme virtue" (Aron 2009: 585, 599).

Aron suggests that he has yet to find the answer to the philosophical and moral issues that he has raised, so he asks three questions: first, whether power politics is animalistic or human; second, whether it is good or bad when a state decides to take matters into its own hands; and third, whether perpetual peace is a worthy or unworthy goal. Aron asserts that Treitschke represented one attitude towards power politics and he utilizes Treitschke's famous Berlin lectures, which were published in 1897–8 in two volumes with the title *Politik*. Treitschke maintained that the state was morally good, that states are naturally in conflict, and that war is noble (Aron 2009: 586). Aron invokes Aristotle's insistence that man is a political animal; thus humans naturally wish to construct a state. Accordingly, for Treitschke, the state is the embodiment of human beings. However, like a person, a state is both juridical and moral, and regarding the latter, the state, like a person, has a will. Therefore, just as it is natural that there will be conflicts between individuals, it is also natural that there will be conflicts between states. Treitschke also maintained that states exist and function together, even in conflict. As a consequence, Treitschke insisted that the idea of a "universal empire is odious" and the "ideal of a state of mankind is no ideal at all."[3]

Treitschke also believed that war was not just inevitable but also noble. He insisted that it was in war that a people really become a people.[4] In other words, Treitschke's power politics is also idealistic and moral; it exhibits humanity's richness and reveals the divinity's plan. And the paramount feature of the state is the fact that it is independent and sovereign. The notion of sovereignty was a major focus of Treitschke's *Politik* so Aron devotes considerable attention to it. Sovereignty is the power to decide to go to war and, according to Treitschke, only powerful states can be regarded as being truly sovereign. As much as Treitschke appears to have glorified war, Aron insists that he was no Machiavellian because he also believed in treaties and law. In fact, Aron emphasizes that Treitschke believes in faith, fidelity, and honor, and has a type of prudence that encompasses moderation, limited objectives, and balance (Aron 2009: 589–90).

116

Aron did not want to examine Treitschke's "Machtpolitik" just for its own sake but to contrast it with the power politics of the Americans. He sums up one of the major differences by once again invoking Weber. Towards the end of *The Protestant Ethic and the Spirit of Capitalism*, Weber insists that the Puritans wanted to live in a world in which a calling or vocation was a necessity but that modern people are forced to do so. Aron maintains that Treitschke and the Germans believed in "Machtpolitik" in itself but that the Americans feel the need to acknowledge "power politics" and its laws. Aron considers the theologian Reinhold Niebuhr as a representative of the American school of political realism. Niebuhr, like Treitschke, believed that man was inherently sinful and evil; thus the realist recognizes the selfishness inherent in human nature and the human tendency to want to have and use power (Aron 2009: 594–5). Aron moves to discuss the political realism of Hans Morgenthau and notes that Morgenthau had two fundamental concepts – power and national interest. In Morgenthau's view, international politics is basically the struggle for power. As a result, he contended that all states had the same type of foreign policy. Aron suggests that, if this is true, it does not tell us very much. Aron believes that Morgenthau is prone to making these types of unhelpful declarations because he may be a realist but he is also a "crusader of realism." Despite its realism, it is still a type of idealism. Again, Aron counters this type of idealism with his own insistence on the importance of prudence, balance, and moderation. This is what he calls the "morality of prudence" and he maintains that it is a compromise and not a synthesis between the "morality of struggle" and the "morality of law" (Aron 2009: 599, 611).

In the second section of "In Search of a Morality", Aron asks whether his "morality of prudence" is viable in the age of thermonuclear weapons. The answer, he says, depends upon two things: the type of war and the type of consequences. Aron offers a rather idealized notion of what war had been. He claims that it was a test of wills with the combatants seeking to subjugate each other. While he admits that there were wars in which the combatants were neither honest nor honorable, he insists that, for the most part, the sides regarded each other as equals and were entitled to some respect. The type of nuclear war would be more of an annihilation rather than subjugation; it would be the complete elimination of the other country and not its domination. Some of this is dependent on which type of war occurs and he offers six different types. The first is the "Rotterdam" type, in which a country destroys a city for the other country's real or perceived transgression. The second is the "limited reprisal," in which a country attacks a city but with limited aims. The third is the "traditional war," in which both nuclear powers seek to destroy each other's nuclear forces but mostly leave the citizens alone. The fourth is the threat of "execution," in which a weaker country may threaten a stronger one. The fifth is a "free for all," in which, once hostilities begin, there is no moderation. The sixth is "extermination," in which one side totally destroys the other, even if that side has unconditionally surrendered (Aron 2009: 612–13). Aron notes that some might object that these are distinctions without differences but he responds by arguing that there would be degrees of destruction. He suggests that the "Rotterdam" war would be regarded as moral or immoral, depending upon what circumstances prompted the attack. If it were in response to being attacked, then it would carry more moral weight. He links the second and third types by indicating that he does not believe that the damage incurred in these types of nuclear war would be much greater than if the warring parties used conventional weapons. He also combines the last three types because they would be not only destructive but also "absurd." He bases this on the American notion of "playing chicken" to see which side blinks or swerves (Aron 2009: 614–15).

Aron moves to discuss the consequences of nuclear war. We have a fairly good idea about the possible destruction that a nuclear war could cause. The two historical examples were terrible but did not result in the elimination of the human race. In other words, there are risks and variables that we can only imagine. He wonders what a treaty would be like: would it really minimize the risk? And what if smaller powers gain nuclear capabilities: how would that impact any treaty between the two superpowers? He concludes by observing that, like individuals, states also want life and security but they also want dignity and honor (Aron 2009: 629). But he ends the section by referring to Weber's claim that the pacifist embraces the "ethics of conviction" and that "unilateralists" are today's pacifists. What is needed is not the sense of idealist conviction, but the realistic sense of responsibility. And that means being reasonable in calculating risks and in judging possible consequences (Aron 2009: 629, 634–5).

"To Arm or Disarm" is the subtitle of the first of the two chapters called "In Search of a Strategy." Aron's conclusion from the previous chapter was that the introduction of nuclear weapons does not fundamentally alter the nature of war. In his opinion, what has changed is the attitude towards war, meaning that Treitschke's vision of war as noble is no longer appropriate in the age of Hiroshima and Nagasaki. If unconditional disarmament and eternal peace are both unrealistic, is there some way to achieve some form of peace? Aron's answer is possibly yes: "peace by fear." Aron explains that "peace by fear" has three versions. First, there would be a sufficient amount of fear shared by the entire world that would ensure peace. Second, the two nuclear powers would have a sufficient amount of fear that would ensure that they would probably not employ nuclear weapons. Third, nuclear war is impossible because the fear of destruction is too great. Aron discounts the first one as being too idealistic; he notes that many people find it attractive but that is because they are not being reasonable. The second and third ones may seem reasonable because they assume that countries will fear reprisals. However, Aron insists that both of these versions of "peace by fear" assume too much, meaning that statesmen are reasonable and cautious – which Aron believes to be untrue (Aron 2009: 636–43).

The other possibility of gaining peace is "peace by disarmament." However, the sheer fact that Aron refers to this as an illusion, just like "peace by fear," suggests that he holds no hope of it being viable for two reasons. One is that treaties are often poorly written and encourage cheating. Another is that it is often difficult to verify whether the signatories of the treaties would allow attempts at verification. The assumption that this is also an illusion is strengthened by his assertion that his goal may not be peace, but rather the "diminution" of violence (Aron 2009: 643). However, even this is problematic because it seeks to minimize the frequency of wars as well as to limit the damage. History has shown, though, that reducing the frequency has resulted in even more terrifying wars (Aron 2009: 648).

The second chapter devoted to the "search for a strategy" is entitled "To Survive is to Conquer" and here Aron notes that the goal of the West is not just to avoid a nuclear confrontation but to avoid being defeated, if not actually to defeat the Soviet Union (Aron 2009: 665). Aron allows that the United States may not exist after a nuclear war but he is also adamant that it will not exist if it capitulates (Aron 2009: 666, 673). Furthermore, he is convinced that the Soviet Union does not wish for peace but actively seeks the destruction of all capitalist countries (Aron 2009: 689, 700). The question then becomes: how does a country survive in the nuclear age? Aron gives his answer in the final two chapters of *Peace and War*.

International politics has been regarded as power politics for its entire history. This is Aron's claim, which he modifies by noting that, in recent times, there have been some jurists who erroneously believe in their concepts while others are deluded by their idealism. However, modern times also dictate that the world must move beyond power politics. As Aron writes, "History must no longer be a succession of bloody conflicts if it is to pursue its adventure" (Aron 2009: 703). If power politics is no longer viable, then the question becomes: what can and should take its place? He offers a summary of Max Scheler's eight types of pacifism and notes that there are many who share Scheler's hope for peace. However, Aron reminds us that Hobbes is certainly right, to some degree, in observing that conflict is a natural state of human affairs. Furthermore, Hobbes's claim that each state retains the right to arms implies the continuation of war. If peace is to be achieved, can it be determined by the international acceptance of the rule of law? Aron's answer is that history has demonstrated that peace cannot be achieved by international institutions and he points to the past failure of the League of Nations and the present difficulties with the United Nations. He traces the problems to the fact that laws are insufficient to guarantee peace and that international law has failed in theory as well as in reality (Aron 2009: 709, 717, 720). Aron identifies three ways in which international law fails: first, the lawyers have tried to start from a municipal basis; second, they have tended to consider it from a communal point of view; and third, they have believed that any imperfections in it can and will be dealt with later. Aron's response is that they were wrong with regard to the first two points. His reply to the third point was that they did not have any realistic basis for their optimism (Aron 2009: 723–5). In part, it is because pacifists want the world to be as it should be and they refuse to recognize it as it is. This is true regarding independence; they do not want to acknowledge that, in numerous countries, there are people who are fighting to break free. As a French writer who was writing during the early 1960s, Aron was especially concerned about the fights for freedom in Africa so it is not surprising that he focused on Algeria. However, he also looked to Europe and there he identified the earlier uprising in Hungary. He also points to one of the main problems with uprisings: that different countries will take sides. The people demonstrating are patriots and heroes to one country but heretics and traitors to another (Aron 2009: 729–30).

The subject of the final chapter is sovereignty. Before, Aron had used the term but had not "rigorously defined" it. Now, he defines it as a type of authority that is both "legitimate and supreme," and insists that it is not monolithic. He suggests that different groups possess sovereignty and points to the Supreme Court in the United States and to the Cabinet in Great Britain. And different countries have gained or lost sovereignty; he offers Tunisia, Morocco, and Cuba as examples and says that the issue of sovereignty largely depends upon the criterion that one wishes to use (Aron 2009: 738–43). He summarizes the various meanings of sovereignty: besides the legal use of the valid system of norms, there is the justification of a particular idea (the type of government); the justification of a particular tribunal (the kind of court); or the justification of a particular group of individuals (the Assembly). However, in international relations, there is no supreme authority; there is no higher sovereignty because all nations claim sovereignty for themselves.

Aron admits that there seems to be a transnational sovereignty and considers some likely candidates for such an entity. There is the "Common Market" but he argues that this is an economic order and not a political or legal entity. Then there is the United Nations. On the one hand, there is the notion of "sovereign equality," which is invoked to ensure that no country can legally meddle in the affairs of another country. However, Aron argues that, while this notion appears to grant considerable standing to all nations, in reality there is still a hierarchy of stronger states at the top of the power structure and weaker states at the bottom of it (Aron 2009: 743–4). Aron moves to clarify what he thinks sovereignty is. He believes that sovereignty is, first, the supreme authority that legislates; second, the constitutional organ; third, the people who possess this type of authority; and fourth, that which can enforce the laws (Aron 2009: 745–6).

In the "Final Note," Aron offers some final observations. One such observation, which has been present throughout the book, is his claim that coercion is "not illegitimate as such." He bases this claim on historical records: namely, that almost all states were originally founded upon it. In addition, coercion has been practiced throughout history and even by the most ideal of nations. Even the United States had the Civil War. His second observation is that a war today would be far worse than prior wars: not because men are worse than they were before, but because they now know more (Aron 2009: 781, 784). By "knowing more," Aron means knowing how to build deadlier weapons, not having more general knowledge. His third observation is that humanity is actually in its "childhood." His basis for this claim is that one must consider how long *Homo sapiens* has existed and then one should consider the several million years for which the galaxy will likely exist. Given these, we have not been here all that long. However, Aron restricts his case to one million years and on that basis we have lived for about one-tenth of that period: thus his claim that humanity is approximately "ten years old." He explains that humanity was unable to recognize the differences between humans and other animals for the first "six" or "seven years" of its existence. He maintains that we learned to read and write about a "year ago," the Parthenon was built about "three months" ago, and Christ was born about "two months" ago. We discovered experimental science "fifteen days" ago and finally, in just the last "two days," we invented electricity and airplanes. Thus, we should have the proper perspective regarding the likelihood of war and the possibility of a future. Aron admonishes us not to be too despondent about the present situation and instead counsels us to live up to the "obligations ordained" for each of us. He ends with the command "to think and act with the firm intention that the absence of war will be prolonged until the day when peace has become possible – supposing it ever will" (Aron 2009: 786–7). This theory of politics is neither idealistic in the ideologues' way of thinking nor realistic from the American thinkers' point of view. Instead, it is based upon Weber's "ethics of responsibility," which Aron has transformed into his own politics of prudence, moderation, and responsibility.

## PEACE OR WAR?

It appears that, along with Clausewitz, Treitschke, and Max Weber, Aron believed that wars were inevitable and that there was no real possibility for Kant's notion of perpetual peace. The question that remained was "what kind of wars?" Clausewitz knew about war from personal experience, while Treitschke and Weber knew about it second-hand, by virtue of their military training and Germany's history. They differed in how they responded to the notion of war: Treitschke believed that it was a noble struggle that formed the population into one "Volk." Weber was more cautious about war; the First World War began well enough for the Germans but Weber quickly realized that the early victories would not be followed by others. Furthermore, he warned German officials about the great dangers of unleashing unlimited submarine warfare. As a result of defeat and incompetence, Weber was concerned about Germany's future. Clausewitz certainly agreed that war was inevitable but was convinced by Prussia's defeats in 1806 that Prussia needed to have a valid and an applicable theory of war. Taken in this light, Aron's cautious views regarding the possibility of diminishing wars through international relations make sense. What makes even more sense is his description of the person who deals in international politics: he, or she, must be intelligent, thoughtful, and moderate; must have learned from history but recognize that history is limited in the advice that can be gleaned for modern conflicts, and must understand that each concrete situation differs from others, so no one rule is applicable. Finally, the political actor must embrace prudence as the superior virtue and must always act with a sense of responsibility. Pacifism and conviction have their place, and just not in international relations.

Aron's discussion of international relations is still informative. As much as things have changed, his belief in the need for a balance of power is as relevant today as it was when he wrote *Peace and War*, and that is because nations still base their actions on their own convictions as well as their beliefs about other states. And while the "bipolar" world of the United States and the Soviet Union has disappeared, there still appears to be a "bipolar" world of West and East. One of the most important distinctions between the two historical groups was the differing acceptance of the importance of ideology. Aron believed that ideological differences contributed to the "bipolar" antagonisms of the twentieth century, and it seems as if they will continue to play important roles in the twenty-first century as well.

## Notes

1. Aron (2009: 1).
2. Aron (2009: 93, Aron's emphasis). Later, Aron writes: "In the last analysis, nations do not fight each other only to maintain a position of strength." Ideas and emotions also are factors (Aron 2009: 99).
3. Aron (2009: 587). "Daher ist die Idee eines Weltreichs hassenswert; die Ideal eines Menschheitsstaates ist gar kein Ideal" (Treitschke 1899: 29).
4. Aron (2009: 588). "Immer und immer wieder wird sich die Wahrheit bestätigen, daß nur im Kriege ein Volk zum Volke wird" (Treitschke 1899: 60).

# Chapter Six

# On ideology and totalitarianism

"Dead Ideologies and Living Ideas"
Raymond Aron

The twin terms "ideology" and "totalitarianism" were two of the major concerns of Aron's political philosophy. In his thinking, ideology predated totalitarianism; however, he held that the terms were reflective of Germany's National Socialism and the Soviet Union's Communism. Yet they were different: ideology was a type of knowledge whereas totalitarianism was a kind of action. None the less, both were fundamentally threats to liberal democracy and to freedom. By shedding light on both concepts, Aron was convinced he could reveal their actual shortcomings and show how they were so dangerous to Western values of democracy and liberty.

The focus of this chapter is, of course, on the writings of Raymond Aron. However, it is beneficial for the understanding of Aron's conceptions of ideology and totalitarianism to place them in the appropriate context. This context includes two other individuals: Edward Shils and Hannah Arendt. For a fuller understanding of Aron's views, it is helpful to consider Shils's writings on ideology and to consider Arendt's writings on totalitarianism. Regarding ideology, Aron and Shils were almost entirely in agreement; regarding totalitarianism, Aron and Arendt were frequently at odds. Aron and Shils became friends in the 1930s and remained close until Aron's death; Aron and Arendt were never friends and seemed to regard each other with some degree of mistrust. This mistrust was mostly because of their conceptions regarding the origins of totalitarianism, but it was also because they disagreed on a number of social and political issues.

## IDEOLOGY

The term "ideology" is difficult to define – in his Introduction to his collection *The End of Ideology Debate*, Chaim Waxman offers eight different definitions of the term. Some of these were from Karl Mannheim, Talcott Parsons, and Edward Shils, and also from Raymond Aron. Waxman insisted that the "end of ideology" debate was less about the issues than it was about a definition of the term and added that "Almost no two writers maintain the same definition" (Waxman 1968: 3). Without us going much further here, ideology can mean a set of political beliefs or a set of social values (see Waxman 1968: 3–4).

Although the concept of ideology was discussed by scholars before 1930, it was the publication of *Ideologie und Utopie* that brought more interest in the term. Published in 1929, this work by Karl Mannheim did not contain a unified thesis. Rather, the book was composed of two parts: the first on ideology and the second on utopia. It drew immediate attention and Mannheim wished to take advantage of that position. As part of this, Mannheim wanted his book to be translated into English, and Louis Wirth, the American sociologist, indicated that he would see what could be done to facilitate this endeavor. Wirth asked Edward Shils to help translate it and the English version appeared in 1936. Like the German version, it was composed of two parts, but it also included a new introduction by Mannheim. It also featured a translation of his article on "Wissenssoziologie," which had been published in 1931 in Alfred Vierkandt's *Handwörterbuch der Soziologie*. At the time, Shils was very impressed with Mannheim's thinking, although he complained that he was not able to explain Mannheim's main points clearly. Later, Shils wrote that he realized that Mannheim's thinking was rather confused and that it appeared to him that nothing could be salvaged from it – even the ideas on ideology. Shils wondered whether he was too harsh on Mannheim, whom he liked personally. Perhaps the biggest problem was Mannheim's preoccupation with Marxism, which, in Shils's view, accounted for "Mannheim's inability to see the world as it was" (Shils 2006: 33–9).[1] In his *Deutsche Soziologie*, Aron apparently agreed with Shils. While noting the importance of *Ideologie und Utopie*, Aron complained about the prominence of Marxist thinking in Mannheim's book and suggested that Mannheim's insistence on the importance of perspectives meant that he had trouble seeing the world as it is and not as it should be (Aron 1953: 70–2, 75–6). Like Shils, Aron was personally acquainted with Mannheim, having met him while both were in Germany in the early 1930s. Like Shils, Aron was initially impressed by Mannheim's thinking. In a note, Colquhoun quotes from Aron – "For six months or a year I was a Mannheimian" (Colquhoun 1986a: 115) – and in his memoirs, Aron admits to having admired Mannheim. Furthermore, like Shils, Aron grew disenchanted with Mannheim's thinking, and like Shils, could not understand how he could have thought so highly of him (Aron 1990: 43, 77–8; Aron 1983b: 68, 108). Finally, like Shils, Aron may not have learned much about ideology from Mannheim, but they both learned that it was sufficiently important enough to investigate.[2]

## Aron on ideology[3]

In the 1936/7 issue of a journal entitled *Recherches philosophiques*, Aron published what appears to have been his first article on ideology. It is quite likely that Mannheim's *Ideology and Utopia* was one of the factors that prompted Aron to write this piece because, in a footnote, Aron explicitly refers to the section on Mannheim that he wrote for his earlier book on German sociology.[4] Much of this 1936/7 essay dealt with psychology and some of it with Pareto, but Aron did take up the topics of ideology and of Marx. He rejected the idea that ideology could be regarded simply as the idea of one's adversary and questioned whether there could be a science of ideology (Aron 1978i: 35). Regarding the first, Aron addresses the claim that ideology is an idea by indicating that what is in play are values and not facts. Regarding the second, Aron suggests that the Marxian notion of false consciousness indicates that the issue is not about psychology as a science but about interpreting the world according to one's ideology. This is true, regardless of whether it is a proletarian ideology or a bourgeois one (Aron 1978i: 42). Aron notes an even larger problem, which is that Marx adopted Hegel's view of history as absolute. This leads to the conception that the opponent's idea is an ideology, but one's own idea is not. If only opponents have ideologies, then it seems impossible to have a science of ideology. Finally, the only thing that approximates a science of ideology is a type of philosophy of history that looks at the past as a matter of choice and in terms of degrees of probability (Aron 1978i: 49–50).

In 1955, Aron published *The Opium of the Intellectuals*, which, without much question, became his most famous book and, with little doubt, also his most contentious one. Aron's title is a clear reference to Marx's claim that religion is the opiate of the masses, but instead of an unwavering belief in God, the French intellectual is devoted to an ideology. Thus, it is somewhat surprising that Aron does not deal with the concept of ideology until rather late in the book, although he does lay out its foundation earlier. His focus is on one specific ideology and on one particular philosophy of history. This ideology and philosophy of history is Marxism; however, the object of Aron's criticism is not Marx or Marxism, but the leftist French intellectuals. His central objection to them is their adherence to myths and their refusal to see things as they really are.

Aron complains that the French intellectuals hold fast to three myths: the myth of the left, the myth of the revolution, and the myth of the proletariat. Regarding the first myth, Aron explains that the opposition between the left and the right is not so much a political opposition as it is an idealistic one. Those on the right tend to be conservative and to value family, religion, and authority; those on the left tend to be progressive and value equality, reason, and liberty. The right is the party of tradition and privilege; the left is the party of progress and intellect (Aron 2011: 4–5). This "classic formulation" is not false but is only halfway true, and that is because it is an oversimplification.

The left was a reaction to traditional power but as soon as it became the ruling group, the right had no difficulty in demonstrating that it was not liberating everyone as it had promised; rather, it substituted one ruling class for another (Aron 2011: 17–18). Aron argues that this shows that history is dialectic and that the left believes that history is progressive. This is what Aron means by the myth of the left: the illusion of a linear movement of progress (Aron 2011: 21, 31, 35).

The myth of the revolution is that revolutions are sudden and necessary changes. Aron counters that the Industrial Revolution was not sudden and that reforms are often better means to achieve necessary changes (Aron 2011: 36–8). Aron observes that, for the left, in order to be considered as a "revolution," it must take place in accordance with its own ideology and is successful if it upends the existing order. To Aron, these are simply prejudices, and they ignore the fact that revolutions are, by definition, illegal as well as tyrannical. They are illegal because they defy the law and they are tyrannical because they substitute one power for another. Instead of equality for all, some gain but others lose (Aron 2011: 39–40). The problem, as Aron sees it, is that the French find politics boring; whereas reform will predictably change something, the French embrace revolutions because no one can predict what they will ultimately change. Aron objects to the prestige of revolution and calls it a cult. He claims that the terms "revolt" and "nihilism" are in vogue and that today's rebels and nihilists criticize the modern world for its imperfections (Aron 2011: 42–3). Aron concludes that the myth of revolution will continue because of French nostalgia and the belief in the perfectibility of humans. However, Aron notes that revolutionaries are often eager to use violent means in their attempts to achieve perfection (Aron 2011: 64–5).

In the myth of the proletariat, the Marxist believes that it is the proletariat and not God that will collectively save the world. This is part of the reason why Aron refers to Marxism as a "new Faith." The Marxist blames the misery of the proletariat on capitalism, yet capitalism has shown that it can reduce some of the proletariat's misery by reducing hours and increasing pay (Aron 2011: 66, 72–4). Aron calls this "real emancipation" in contrast to the Communist "ideal emancipation." The problem is that the Marxist blames the capitalist boss when the problem is low productivity; production and wages have increased in the West, yet not in the East. But, the Marxist is driven by an ideology and not by reality, and insists that it should not be judged by what is, but on what will be. Aron points out that the East German workers, who know something about real liberty, recognize that the "ideal emancipation" is a hoax. In France, left-wing Catholics and Existentialists are "bewitched" by "ideal emancipation" because it contains the "poetry of the unknown, the future, of the absolute" (Aron 2011: 74, 78, 85). "Ideal emancipation" is a "siren call" to intellectuals whereas "real emancipation" is as boring as an "English Sunday" (Aron 2011: 90).

Aron concludes the first part of *The Opium of the Intellectuals* by noting that "Left, Revolution, Proletariat" have replaced the older myths of "Progress, Reason, the People." However, he clarifies that the left continues to believe in the myth of progress, but unlike the older version, which was fundamentally optimistic, the modern version is pessimistic because it sees the right as continuously blocking its progress. Aron further suggests that the leftist intellectuals combine a pessimistic view of reality with a visionary optimism. (Aron 2011: 94–6).

If there was any doubt whether Aron regarded Marxist ideology as the new religion, that doubt is erased by the title of the chapter beginning the second part. The title of the chapter is "Churchmen and the Faithful" and that of the second part is "The Idolatry of History." While there is no question that Marxism was scientifically outdated, Aron insists that, as an ideology, it is alive and well in France. After suffering through the war, the leftist philosopher seeks salvation, but through the new Church of Marxism. But it is not just the French leftists that Aron is discussing; it is everyone who does not want to accept the world as it is but has faith in the idealist world of the future. Aron's discussion is filled with religious expressions: "salvation," "romantic faith," "sacred history," and "the faithful" (Aron 2011: 105–7, 109, 112–13).

Aron takes particular aim at the notion of heresy by looking at the Moscow trials of 1936–7. Unlike the Inquisitors, the Communist authorities had no concern about people's souls; they only wanted the "criminals" to confess, regardless of whether they had or had not committed any crimes (Aron 2011: 120–1). Since the Marxist Churchmen possessed the universal truth, they were empowered to force people to become part of the Church or face persecution (Aron 2011: 126). This truth was not personal but was a historical doctrine; history is made by "inexorable forces" and not by heroic people. Individuals are unimportant but historical logic is all-important. God is not God, but History is; one is not judged by the Creator but by History's tribunal. The faithful believe that it cannot be wrong but Aron insists that a theory that cannot be refuted has nothing to do with the truth (Aron 2011: 133–4). This emphasis on History leads to Aron's next chapter, entitled "The Meaning of History."

In his idolizing of history, the "socialist crusader" believes two contradictory things. The "socialist crusader" is convinced that history is final and absolute, and he believes in relativism. Because he claims to have the universal truth about history, he believes he is justified in interpreting the past in his own manner (Aron 2011: 135–6). The "socialist crusader" views history as a single whole that has one meaning; the sociologist recognizes that history is made up of individual decisions and actions, and has multiple meanings (Aron 2011: 139–43). The "socialist crusader" believes in the "End of History" and, as such, believes himself justified in employing "revolting means" (Aron 2011: 156). The "socialist crusader" is mistaken in his conviction that history has one meaning; reality shows that it has many. The philosopher looks to the future and "knows what man seeks," but it is the historian who knows what "man has found and what, perhaps, he will find tomorrow" (Aron 2011: 159–60).

In the chapter called "The Illusion of Necessity," Aron builds upon his contrast between the Marxist, who views history as linear and determined, and the sociologist, who looks at history as dialectic and composed of chances (Aron 2011: 161). "Secular theologies" believe in their predictive abilities but Aron counters that this is true only when the predictions are so general as not to be helpful. He takes as an example the claim that there will be wars and acknowledges that this is part of the human condition. Unfortunately, the Marxist then shifts his claim to that which insists that capitalism is responsible for wars, and then concludes that, when capitalism inevitably collapses, there will be no wars (Aron 2011: 168, 177–8).

Instead of regarding history as linear, determined, and predictable,

Aron maintains that it is dialectical, undetermined, and unpredictable. He does, however, qualify the claim of unpredictable by pointing to several issues. First, while a choice is never determined, it is also never totally open: that is, the actor chooses between several alternatives (Aron 2011: 184). Thus, the historian studies the past in order to understand it but the Marxist has no use for history – instead, the Marxist insists on the inevitability of the triumph. In Aron's view, this is the triumph of an ideal over reality. This "idolatry of history" is a "caricature" of what he calls "historical awareness." One who possesses "historical awareness" recognizes the limits of our knowledge and teaches us respect for others. Awareness of the past can provide meaning for specific historical acts but nothing can provide the "ultimate meaning of history" (Aron 2011: 193–4).

Part Three of *The Opium of the Intellectuals* is devoted to those who are regarded as intellectuals: that is, to those who live by thinking of their existence rather than simply living. This implies that the intellectuals are divorced from their communities but Aron suggests that this is only partially accurate. He insists that France is the intellectuals' paradise because they are so revered, and maintains that the United States is the intellectuals' hell because they are so despised there (Aron 2011: 209, 217, 220, 230–3).

The second chapter is devoted to Aron's contrasts among many different nations, in terms of economics and politics. The chapter is interesting but has little to do with ideology so it will not be considered except to mention one point. Towards the conclusion of the previous chapter, Aron had mentioned that the English managed to avoid the anti-intellectualism of the Americans and the "uncritical admiration" of intellectuals by the French. Now, in this chapter, Aron praises British education because it is less optimistic than the American and it is less ideological than the French (Aron 2011: 234–5). The implication is that the British approach is far more realistic than either the overly intellectual one of the French or the more moralizing one of the Americans.

In the final chapter of the third part, Aron returns to his discussion of secular religion and notes the similarities between socialism and religion. Aron lists four ways in which socialist ideology is similar to religion: first, both doctrines explain the universe; second, both have crusader-type mentalities; third, both provide a hierarchy of values; and fourth, both cater to the individual as well as the collective. Regarding the lack of a divine being, Aron suggests that many religious believers lack an understanding of God but none the less practice the faith. For secular believers, the absence of a deity does not diminish their practicing their beliefs (Aron 2011: 265). Aron does allow that Christianity and Communism differ in one important way: the former believes that the destiny of man will be fulfilled in the afterlife whereas the latter is convinced that it will be fulfilled on this earth (Aron 2011: 274).

Intellectuals have exchanged Reason for God and have replaced Christianity with a rationalist religion (Aron 2011: 279, 281) but it was the French Revolutionaries who first sought to replace religion with the cult of reason (Aron 2011: 284). "Marx called religion the opium of the people" but Aron argues that Marxist ideology performs the same function. Both tend to urge people to forget their ills, not to cure them; and both are dismissive of the problems of today because they are obsessed with the ideal future. It did not matter that Christians did terrible things in the name of God, just as it does not matter that there are "millions of corpses" as long as it is in the name of the classless society (Aron 2011: 291–2). Aron ends *The Opium of the Intellectuals* with a conclusion entitled "The End of the Ideological Age?," which will be discussed in the next section.[5]


## "End of ideology?"

The issue of the "end of ideology" was a difficult debate. Not only was there the issue of what an ideology was but also there was the issue about its demise. Many of those who contributed to the debate were fairly insistent that the West's superiority to the Communist bloc was well demonstrated: hence the end of ideology. This sense of a definitive ending is indicated by some of the titles: Daniel Bell's "The End of Ideology" and Chaim I. Waxman's *The End of Ideology Debate*. However, not all of the participants in this debate were convinced: Raymond Aron and Edward Shils both included question marks in "The End of the Ideological Age?" and "The End of Ideology?" In addition, Aron and Shils were convinced that some ideologies were pernicious but they also recognized that some were necessary, if not valuable.

When Aron was writing *The Opium of the Intellectuals*, the United States was preoccupied with Joseph McCarthy's ideological pursuit of Communists. Aron recognized how odd it was to ask about the end of ideology in the midst of such an ideological search (Aron 2011: 305). None the less, he was asking this question because the situation had changed over the decades. In 1954, there were two great powers: the United States on one side and the Soviet Union on the other. The United States held to the ideology of liberalism and the Soviet Union held to socialism (Aron 2011: 309). Liberals believe in the plurality of values and are progressive; socialists believe that they too are progressive but have faith in only one belief – the paradise of socialism. Aron has little concern here with liberalism and focuses almost exclusively on socialism. He maintains that socialist ideology is composed of three elements: a particular view of the future; the belief that this future is linked to a particular class; and collective ownership will lead to this future (Aron 2011: 309). However, Aron points out that the working class did not invent this ideology but the intellectuals did. He also points out that the revolutions of the twentieth century have not been carried out by the workers but by the intellectuals (Aron 2011: 312). The problem is that the intellectuals in the West and especially in France have hungered after a faith and they believe they have found one in the socialist ideology. Like the Christian faith, Marxism provides a sense of purpose within a closed group; it furnishes a doctrine in which everyone has an assigned role, and that each individual, as well as the whole, has meaning. Aron admits that one can admire such fanaticism but insists that it is "not for us." Aron is referring to himself when he writes that one likes human beings and likes living in a community. One respects the truth and refuses "to surrender his soul to an abstract ideal of humanity, a tyrannical party, and an absurd scholasticism." He concludes with the admonishment "if tolerance is born of doubt, let us teach everyone to doubt" (Aron 2011: 323–4).

During September of 1955, there was a conference in Milan on the topic of "The Future of Freedom." Edward Shils provided a summary of it for the November issue of *Encounter* and this account is reprinted in Waxman's *The End of Ideology Debate*. Shils's account carries the title "The End of Ideology?" and the similarity to Aron's chapter is only partially accidental. Aron was one of the organizers of this conference and it was he who apparently steered it in the direction of a discussion about the future of ideologies. Shils insisted that the "proponents of freedom" had been successful in revealing the errors of the ideologies of Communism, Fascism, and National Socialism, but he adds that as intellectuals they have a duty to do more than unmask. Shils argued that they needed to study ideologies to see what could be salvaged and he maintained that ideologies provided a much-needed "grandiose vision." The question was not about the "end of ideology" as much as finding the right point between too little and too much ideology (Shils 1968: 60–1).

Shils later suggested that his account of the Milan conference was characteristically flippant but he was serious in his claim that an ideology cannot dominate a country forever. He admitted that his paper was not very original and that his title and that of Aron were "practically identical." He added that Aron had sent *The Opium of the Intellectuals* to him during the summer but he had not read it until his return to Chicago later in the fall (Shils 2006: 96–7). Shils readily admitted to respecting Aron but noted that their interests did not overlap. Shils pointed out that the one area that did was ideology and he wrote that, regarding ideology, "I agreed with him on nearly everything."[6]

In his encyclopedia entry on "Ideology," Shils showed how his understanding of ideology was similar to Aron's. An ideology is a comprehensive value system that lends meaning to the world; it is an intellectual construction that is divorced from tradition and culture, and looks instead to an ideal future (Shils 1972b: 23–30). In "Ideology and Civility," Shils shared with Aron the belief that ideologies were frequently substitutes for religion and its believers insist that they "alone can provide salvation" (Shils 1972c: 43). He also shared Aron's belief that ideologies were predominantly modern phenomena and that they were devised by intellectuals (Shils 1972c: 48). Furthermore, Shils believed in a liberal and civil society, one in which problems were confronted and solved, in contrast to those who adhere to an ideology that despises this world and promises a better one. The statement "Civil society requires compromise and reasonableness, prudent self-restraint, and responsibility" was written by Shils but could have easily been written by Aron (Shils 1972c: 57).

In 1977, Aron contributed an essay to a volume in honor of Shils, entitled "On the Proper Use of Ideologies." In it, Aron recalled the connection between his "End of the Ideological Age?" and Shils's "End of Ideology?" review of the Milan conference. Aron suggests that his contribution to the Shils volume is meant more as an attempt at self-criticism than as an attempt at self-justification. He recalled that, in Germany in the early 1930s, he witnessed how most people believed in systems and that this is an ideology that promises to bridge the gap between the real and the ideal (Aron 1977: 1–2).

In 1966, Aron published a small volume that, in English, carries the title *The Industrial Society*; as the subtitle (*Three Essays on Ideology and Development*) makes clear, however, it has less to do with industry than it does with ideology. The volume contains three speeches that Aron had given in various locations during the preceding years. The three lectures have the twin themes of industrialization and ideology, and while they were written primarily as comments on particular situations, they contain a number of important reflections on ideology. In "Development Theory and Ideology," Aron asks about the similarities and differences in the two great modern industrial powers – the United States and the Soviet Union. He argues that both share what Weber called a "rational attitude" and both were defined by their organization of labor (Aron 1967: 14–15). Capitalism appeared to have stressed the former while socialism emphasized the latter. Marxists claimed that they were superior because the capitalist workers were oppressed. Aron pointed out that, rather than there being an increase in poverty, Western workers were actually becoming richer; thus historical evidence was refuting the Marxist claim (Aron 1967: 20–1). Given this contradiction, Aron asks why Marxism is still popular. Aron offers three reasons: first, it is an official state philosophy; second, it can be manipulated in order to seem true; and third, by insisting that the increase in riches in developed countries comes at the expense of the underdeveloped ones, hence providing Marxists with a foe to blame for their misfortunes (Aron 1967: 22–3). Aron addresses this with two observations: first, that underdeveloped nations tend to focus on one type of raw material and second, that one would think that, when a country lost its colony, it would become less rich. However, he maintains that the former colonial power lacks the standing to force its former colony to adopt a more realistic approach to its economy. And he points to Holland as an example, which, having lost the income from Indonesia, has still managed to become even richer (Aron 1967: 28). Aron locates the problem in how a country is run and uses Cuba as an example. He maintains that Cuba was generally a prosperous country and in no need of a Communist revolution, yet one occurred there. Aron suggests that it was not because of economics that Cuba ended up with a Soviet-style regime but because of an ideology. He maintains that the megalomania, anti-Americanism, and political "progressiveness" typical of certain Latin intellectuals can be found everywhere and he lists Rio de Janeiro, Havana, and Paris (Aron 1967: 39–40).

Aron concludes with some observations on ideology; he notes that there are radically different views of it, with some insisting that there is a deadly struggle between two competing world views while others believe that the time of ideology is ending. He offers four of his own observations. First, since almost everyone believes in industrialization, the question is no longer about ends but only about means. The contrast is between the West, which is relatively indifferent to religion, and the East, which is actively hostile to it. The Soviet ideology claims to be the sole source of truth - a truth that is not transcendental but earthly. Second, in the West, the ideological quarrels of the previous century are losing their strength. Third, in the industrialized West, ideologies have mostly died away, but in developing countries, there is a belief in ideologies as the "total interpretation of world history." Fourth, there may continue to be rivalries between West and East, but in order to avoid war, both sides must embrace the "principle of mutual tolerance"

(Aron 1967: 48). Unfortunately, Aron has shown that, while the West may be hypocritical on occasion, it mostly adheres to this principle; however, the East seems constitutionally unable even to begin to accept the idea of mutual tolerance.

The "Development Theory and Evolutionism" essay is devoted to development and not to ideology, although Aron discusses the topic of whether Western countries and Eastern ones are becoming more alike. He notes that there is a type of rationality that was employed by the Nazis and is used by the Communists – a type of rationality that is efficient. The Nazis' system of transportation was just as rationally organized as those in Paris and New York; it was just the purpose of that system that was so horrific. Rationality as such cannot be condemned and sciences should be embraced – especially the scientific virtues of "prudence, humility, and deference to fact" (Aron 1967: 63, 77).

The final essay is "The End of Ideology and the Renaissance of Ideas" and in this, the lengthiest of the three, Aron returns to the topic of ideology. However, the first part is devoted to the issue of industrial society and a comparison between the capitalist and socialist versions. It is in the second part, which is entitled "Dead Ideologies and Living Ideas," that he focuses on ideology. Aron notes that, for the past ten years, the question regarding the end of ideology has been a popular one. He reminds us that he has written on this topic but his intention here is not to repeat what he has written but to reassess it. He points to the debates about ideology and insists that there should be clarity about what is meant by that ambiguous word. He defines ideology here as "a pseudo-systematic formulation of a total vision of the historical world" and repeats the claim that he made in *The Opium of the Intellectuals* that an ideology is a secular religion. He addresses some of the criticisms regarding his book and suggests that any "fair-minded reader" would read it as a critique of the leftist intellectuals' infatuation with socialist ideology but that it was also a critique of the liberal's infatuation with the "ideal market." The book was a broadside against all those who believed in "models and utopias" but focused mostly on those on the left who wished to construct an ideal world (Aron 1967: 142–5).

Aron returns to the issue of the decline of ideologies and reminds us that this decline is found only in advanced countries. He asks rhetorically whether we should bemoan this decline and wonders whether the opponents of ideology are spreading skepticism and conservatism. He adds that the opponents of ideology are often regarded as pessimists, and since they do not have an ideology, they tend to weaken the West against its foes. Aron takes up the first issue and confesses that he has no real problem with being considered a pessimist. He is realistic and recognizes that it is not easy to shape "either human nature or human society." The deaths of millions of Jews in the Nazi gas chambers, the forced deportations of the kulaks and the imprisonment of thousands of innocent people had caused Aron to be on guard against those who intend to "reconstruct society." He admits that he does not know what the future will be like but is content in realizing that he does not know (Aron 1967: 158–9). These are the reasons why Aron is anti-ideology.

As Aron has frequently stated, the term "ideology" is ambiguous: he mentions that a French sociologist has identified thirteen different meanings. Aron notes that ideology has two specific uses: a pejorative one and a neutral one. In the first, it is regarded as a "mistaken concept"; in the second, it is a formulation of an attitude towards "social or political reality." He recalled that, ten years before, he had defined ideology as "a total system of interpretation of the historic–political world." As to the charge of passivity, Aron allows that perhaps he does not possess the passion that drives the committed political actor. Aron never claimed to be a political actor; he was a political observer and theorist (Aron 1967: 163–6).

By the time Aron published his final article on ideology, the question regarding the "end of ideology" had largely been answered. Like most others, Aron believed that ideologies were part of modern life. Aron's final article is found in the special issue of *Foreign Affairs* that was specifically devoted to "America and the World 1981." As such, Aron's contribution is focused on the specifics of American foreign policy rather than on a general account of ideology. However, that does not diminish its worth because Aron provides a concrete case in which ideology drives policy. The question was: what was going on in the world and what was America's relationship to it? Aron noted that there were crises throughout the world but the newly elected president, Ronald Reagan, concentrated on America's economic problems and, for the most part, tried to ignore most foreign issues. However, Reagan did continue to use rhetoric from the Cold War; thus Reagan's approach lacked concrete ideas and was more of an ideology in search of a policy (Aron 1982: 503–4). Aron observed that the Reagan administration's "anti-Soviet rhetoric" did nothing to explain America's approach to the Soviet Union; rather, it served to obscure the divisions between American foreign policy experts. Some believed that the Soviet Union had greater military capabilities than the United States while others argued the opposite. While it seemed as if the Soviet military had more missiles than the American forces, Reagan was adamant that the United States would ultimately win the arms race (Aron 1982: 505–7). Yet, as

Aron noted, the West was divided over the increase in missile placements in Western Europe, especially in West Germany. In addition, he indicated that the Soviet Union was forced to deal with continued unrest in Eastern Europe, primarily in Poland (Aron 1982: 511–13). Aron continued with a survey of America's relations with Central and South America as well as Asia, but he refrained from commenting on the United States and Africa. His conclusion was that most of these problems were not solvable by military means alone. In conclusion, Aron insisted that America needed to ask why it is that "a totalitarian government with a deprived population remains the leading military power in the world." Aron's point was that ideology and rhetoric are no substitutes for a realistic foreign policy (Aron 1982: 523–4).

In his *Memoirs*, Aron noted that there was no agreement about the definition of ideology but insisted that his definitions were more precise and more specific than those of many other scholars (Aron 1990: 281; Aron 1983b: 412). That does not mean that his definition and his account were not without flaws. He allowed that his account was sometimes misleading but that often it was simply misunderstood. Aron may have been right about the need to alter his wording about ideology and he was probably right to have insisted on placing a question mark in his "End of Ideology?" essay. He was, however, certainly correct in maintaining that "One ideology displaces another, ideologies do not die."[7]

## Totalitarianism

As with ideology, the term "totalitarianism" has been subject of debate.[8] It has been discussed by numerous scholars but perhaps the most famous was Hannah Arendt. Even during her lifetime, Arendt was regarded as "the keenest student of totalitarianism" and she is still considered one today (Bell 1966: 439; Baehr 2010: 2). She devoted much of her life to an examination of it because she regarded it as the "central event of our world" (Arendt 1994c: 308). One of the few scholars who could be considered a competitor for the title of the "keenest student of totalitarianism" would be Aron; Daniel J. Mahoney insisted that Aron and Arendt were the "two great antitotalitarian political thinkers."[9] Aron and Arendt disagreed on the origins and dangers of totalitarianism; however, they shared a number of important similarities. Both were born in the same decade and both were secular Jews. Both were trained in philosophy and engaged in journalism in addition to their scholarly works. Finally, both were greatly interested in politics and both looked to history to help form their political theories.[10] Yet there are significant differences: Arendt's philosophical background was Heideggerian whereas Aron's was Neo-Kantian, and Arendt particularly despised sociology whereas Aron thought it highly useful. Regardless of these differences, they both agreed that one of sociology's leading lights and its specialist on ideology was wrong. They meant Karl Mannheim and their differences are highlighted in their responses to Mannheim's writings.

In her review of Mannheim's *Ideologie und Utopie*, Arendt defended the existential philosophy that he had learned from her mentors Heidegger and Jaspers. She defended philosophy's belief in the truth and in the importance of reality (Arendt 1982: 515–20). In contrast, she criticized Mannheim's devaluation of value and objected to his replacement of ideas with beliefs (Arendt 1982: 522–4). She complained about his emphasis on destruction and his flight from reality (524–7). Finally, she faulted Mannheim for his mistrust of "Geist" ("spirit") and his rejection of the "Sinnfrage" ("question of meaning") (Arendt 1982: 528–9). In short, Arendt objected to Mannheim's substitution of sociology for philosophy.

In contrast to Arendt, Aron examined Mannheim's "Wissenssoziologie" and not just his *Ideologie und Utopie*. Furthermore, Aron had very little interest in Mannheim's turn away from philosophy and instead concentrated on his Marxism. Aron's larger concern was with Mannheim's sociological claim that social factors determine the structure of our thinking and not just its contents. And Aron seemed not to take issue with Mannheim's contention that we cannot know the truth because we have only perspectives (Aron 1953: 75–6; Aron 1950: 80–1). What Aron does object to is Mannheim's mixture of pragmatism, historicism, and relativism, as well as Mannheim's insistence that there can be no impartial science (Aron 1953: 82–3, 86; Aron 1950: 86, 87, 91). When Aron wrote his early book on German sociology, he was moving away from philosophy. Arendt never lost her interest in philosophy and never gained any respect for sociology. None the less, both Aron and Arendt were becoming increasingly aware of the power of ideology. It would not be until after the war, when the full extent of the impact of ideology could be seen, that Aron and Arendt began their serious investigations into ideology.

This is not the place to examine Arendt's discussions regarding totalitarianism for two reasons: first, they already exist;[11] and second, Aron provided a judicious account of them in his lengthy review article of *The Origins of Totalitarianism*. The major issue here is to what extent Aron agreed with Arendt's assessments and to what extent he disagreed.[12]

In "The Essence of Totalitarianism According to Hannah Arendt," Aron offers considerable praise for Arendt's *The Origins of Totalitarianism*. Aron calls it an "important book" and says that her analysis is subtle but strong. He does, however, find fault with some of her discussions. He objects to her treatment of anti-Semitism in Part One on two levels. On one level, Aron complains that Arendt misconstrues and misinterprets the Dreyfus Affair; on the second level, she misunderstands the history of Jews in nineteenth-century Europe (Aron 1994b: 97–100). Aron ignores Part Two on imperialism and concentrates most of his criticisms on Part Three on totalitarianism. He suggests that, in the first two parts, Arendt wrote like a historian and sociologist, but abandons those approaches in Part Three. He does not explicitly accuse her of being a philosopher but he is critical of her metaphysical quest to find the "essence" of totalitarianism (Aron 1994b: 102, 108, 110). This search for the one defining quality not only blinds her to historical reality but distorts her results. Arendt is unable to recognize that the terrible qualities that Stalin had were found first in Lenin. Arendt is misguided in thinking that the Third Reich became totalitarian only at the final stage of the war (Aron 1994b: 102–5). She did not seem to realize that what allows totalitarianism to flourish is the gap between reality and ideology, which appears because of absolute faith in the latter (Aron 1994b: 106). Aron considers an article that Arendt wrote, entitled "Ideology and Terror: A Novel Form of Government."[13] In that article, Arendt claimed that, while there have been dictators and tyrants throughout history, totalitarianism is a modern and novel form of domination (Arendt 1953: 306). Similarly, terror had often been used in the past but Arendt insists that its use is new because it is now used for the "fabrication of mankind" (Arendt 1953: 311). Ideologies are employed along with terror because ideologies are a combination of strict science and philosophical myth (Arendt 1953: 315). Aron notes that, in her article, Arendt appeals to Montesquieu's idea that every government has a nature and a principle: nature is what it is and principle is what prompts it to act. However, Aron maintains that a totalitarian government lacks a principle and that "a regime without a principle is not a regime" (Aron 1994b: 109). In her zeal to find the essence of the German and Soviet totalitarian governments, Arendt seeks to show that totalitarianism is original and that it breaks with traditional forms of government. Instead, Aron suggests that it is a type of revolutionary movement. Finally, Aron summarizes his criticism of Arendt by insisting that she was wrong to search for the essence of totalitarianism. The belief in the metaphysical essence of totalitarianism prompted her to search for one single cause to explain the phenomenon. In contrast,

Aron maintains that, since totalitarianism has many causes, it needs many political explanations (Aron 1994b: 109–10). Aron frequently accused Arendt of slightly distorting history in order to fit her theory and for oversimplifying in order to prove a point. As much as he agreed with many of her warnings about totalitarianism, he was convinced that a less philosophical and a more sociological account was needed. He never provided a complete account but many of his ideas can be gleaned from a series of lectures that he gave during 1957–8. These lectures were published in France in 1965 and appeared in an English translation in 1969 with the title *Democracy and Totalitarianism*. As Aron admitted in his introduction, these lectures are marked by the spoken word and are limited to discussing then current events. None the less, he thought them worthy and important enough to have them published. Despite his concerns about their general limitations, there are three chapters that help clarify what Aron thought totalitarianism means and what it does.

As an indication of the emphasis that Aron places on ideology over totalitarianism, his Chapter Fourteen has the title "Ideology and Terror." It is unclear whether Aron intentionally chose it, but one of his lectures carries the same title as Arendt's final chapter, "Ideology and Terror." What is clear, however, is that Aron believed terror and ideology are essential elements of the Soviet system under Stalin. In this chapter, he notes that an ideological regime often relies on terror and he delineates three types. The first is legal and codified terror, which is the most formal. As with a normal government, there are laws and rules; unlike with a normal government, the accused may not have actually broken a specific law but has done something similar enough to be charged. The second type is terror by tribunal. Here, normal and semi-normal legal institutions are replaced by a tribunal whose members often work according to their own agendas and ensure that the proceedings take place in a matter of days. The third type is terror by deportation. Aron quotes Khrushchev's comments about Stalin: that he was the one who coined the phrase "enemy of the people" and who applied it to whole populations. Aron further quotes Khrushchev's account of the deportations of entire populations of whole republics. Stalin wished to deport Ukrainians but was prevented from doing so because of the enormity of the challenge – it was impossible to find enough land for 40 million Ukrainians. Khrushchev was convinced that, if there had been enough land, Stalin would have deported all 40 million (Aron 1969: 185–6, 189).

Aron moved from formal classifications to more material ones and suggested that Soviet terror occurred in different forms at different times. The first period occurred during the civil war, thus from 1917 until 1921. This terror eliminated the opposition, and in Aron's opinion, did not differ from any of the previous revolutions. The second period occurred during 1929–30 at the beginning of the collectivization of agriculture. The problem that Stalin faced was dealing with those who were resisting the process of collectivization – the kulaks were regarded as class enemies and had to be dealt with. Aron notes that Khrushchev had insisted that the measures Stalin had used were too drastic. Aron agreed but maintained that that assessment is valid in hindsight and that, like the earlier time of terror, this one was understandable. The third time of terror occurred during the period leading up to and including the show trials: thus from roughly 1934 to 1937. This timeframe underscores "the most abnormal aspect of terror": namely, that from 1917 until 1936, when the Soviet regime was becoming more stable, terror increased rather than decreased (Aron 1969: 187–8). The final period of terror led to two institutions: concentration camps and trials. Aron left aside the former and concentrated on the latter. He did so because the trials represented the "apex of ideological terror" and served as one of the essential elements of the Soviet regime. Aron was interested in the questions that resulted from the defendants confessing to crimes that they did not commit and ones they could not have committed. Aron lists three questions: the first concerns the "logic of the confession," the second concerns the "psychology of the accused," and the third concerns the "function of the trial." Aron insists that the answer to the first is simple: "who is not with me is against me." Since the revolution is the Communist Party and thus is the meaning of history, anyone who does not agree with the party is behaving like a traitor. For Stalin, since there was no distinction between behaving like a traitor and being one, both were subject to prosecution (Aron 1969: 189).

The answer to the second question appears complicated but Aron insists there are only three possible answers. To the idealist, the accused had a guilty conscience and, like the kamikaze, were "supreme servants of their cause." The next answer is less idealistic and holds that there was a "secret pact" between the police and the accused – the police would spare the accused if they confessed. The problem was that everybody knew that the promise was a lie and the accused would be executed. Aron suggests that the accused knew that they would not survive but confessed in the hope that their families would be spared. The third answer is most likely the closest to the truth and that was that the accused were tortured into confessing. Everyone knew that the accusations were false and yet no one was brave enough to stand up to these lies. But Aron admitted that the "psychology of the accused was strange" and bemoaned the fact that no one tried to stop the "world of macabre fiction" (Aron 1969: 190).[14]

As the title of Chapter Fifteen indicates, the topic is totalitarianism; none the less, ideology and terror play prominent roles in the chapter. Aron understood why no one stood up to Stalin and he attributed that to the all-pervasive fear. As he pointed out, even Khrushchev did not know when he was summoned by Stalin whether he would be asked his opinion on some major issue or be sent to the Lubianka prison (Aron 1969: 192). Aron noted that some scholars would consider this a matter of simple terror but he argued that it was based upon an ideology. This is shown in the five points that describe the totalitarian phenomena. First, there is a one-party monopoly on political activity; second, the party is armed with an ideology; third, the ideology is the basis for the party's claim to be the sole determiner of truth; fourth, this ideology determines economic activity; and fifth, this politicization ends in ideological terrorism (Aron 1969: 193–4). Aron admits that there are twentieth-century authoritarian regimes that are not totalitarian and that there are totalitarian regimes that are not monopolized by a single party; thus the first point is mostly true. His concern is with two other related issues: how unique is totalitarianism and is the Soviet system similar to or different than the Nazi system? His answer to the first question is relatively straightforward: while totalitarianism shares some characteristics with previous dictatorships and tyrannies, it is mostly a twentieth-century phenomenon. There have been massacres throughout history but the terrorism of industrial extermination is unprecedented (Aron 1969: 203). His answer to the second question is rather involved. One argument is that the two regimes are similar and Aron notes that Hannah Arendt is a strong proponent of this view in her *Origins of Totalitarianism* (Aron 1969: 197–8). However, Aron rejects the claim of similarity and insists that there is an essential difference: the Nazi system led to the gas chambers and the destruction of a race, while the Soviet system led to the labor camp with the will to create a new regime, if not a new man. Aron concludes that the Soviet system had intended to create an angel but ended up creating a beast; the Nazi system showed that when man attempts to resemble a beast of prey, he is only too successful (Aron 1969: 203–4). Chapter Sixteen is entitled "The Theories of the Soviet System," and while Aron concentrates mainly on historical factors, he does make several crucial points regarding "ideological fanaticism" and Soviet totalitarianism. On the one hand, ideological fanaticism and police terror are revolutionary and not bureaucratic; on the other hand, ideological fanaticism combines the revolutionary will with the absolutism of bureaucracy. He con-

142

cludes by pointing out another factor that makes totalitarianism unique – whereas earlier despotisms were based upon religious faith, the Soviet system is founded on an ideology. Yet, as with the earlier despotisms, the modern one also demands orthodoxy from everyone (Aron 1969: 213, 216). This description of ideology as orthodoxy reflects Aron's conviction that ideology is a secular religion, as he had decided more than a decade earlier in *The Opium of the Intellectuals*. And it marks his belief that there will probably never be an "end of ideology."

## Concluding comments

During the 1950s and 1960s, numerous individuals were writing about ideology and totalitarianism. Some of these writers were more political and wrote about the threats posed by ideological proponents and totalitarian regimes. Others were more scholarly and were concerned with studying what ideologies were and how totalitarian regimes ruled. Raymond Aron, Edward Shils, and Hannah Arendt belonged to this latter group but there were differences among them. Shils seemed less interested in totalitarianism and more in ideology; Arendt seemed less concerned about ideology than she was about totalitarianism. Aron was more inclined to Shils's approach rather than Arendt's – but he believed that ideology and totalitarianism were two of the threats to modern political liberalism. Shils mentioned that he rarely disagreed with Aron; Aron never explicitly said that about his friend but it is relatively clear that Aron tended to agree with Shils. Neither Aron nor Arendt ever clarified their opinions regarding each other but it seems that, despite some superficial similarities, there were fundamental differences. Aron never explicitly claimed that Arendt's biggest flaw was that she remained a philosopher and never made the transition to sociologist. None the less, this is what he seemed to believe because, in his comments about Arendt, Aron hints that if she had made this transition, her political theories would have benefited from the empirical information. He fully recognized and clearly acknowledged that he had benefited greatly in making the shift from metaphysics to political theory.

## Notes

1. For a detailed examination of Shils, Mannheim, and ideology see Adair-Toteff (2019).
2. Aron and Shils remained friends from the 1940s until Aron's death in 1983. Aron referred to Shils as "my friend." For his part, Shils maintained that he almost always agreed with what Aron wrote.

3. Scholars have paid little attention to Aron's conception of ideology, despite the fact that it occupied him for almost five decades and he wrote about it numerous times. "Ideology" is missing from the indices of the books by Mahoney (1992) and Davis (2009). It is also absent from the collections from Frost and Mahoney (2007) and from Colen and Dutartre-Michaut (2015). It is particularly strange that it is missing from Frost and Mahoney's book because the title is *Political Reason in the Age of Ideology*. "Ideology" is listed once as "ideology, Marxist" in Anderson (1997).

4. This article was first published in *Recherches philosophiques* VI, 1936–7, pp. 65–84 and was reprinted in *Revue européenne des sciences sociales* in 1978. References are to the later edition (Aron 1978i: 43, note 3; Aron 1950: 80–8; Aron 1953: 72–80).

5. "The End of the Ideological Age?" is reprinted in Waxman (1968: 27–48).

6. Shils (2006: 153–4). Others also thought that Aron and Shils had similar approaches, both to the function of nature and to the question about its end (see Lipset 1977: 15, 24, 30, 38). Aron's respect for Shils was reciprocated, and Shils regarded Aron as being one of his few close friends. That their political thinking was similar may be traced to Weber's influence on both of them (Shils 1997: 6, 53, 59, 71).

7. "Une idéologie chasse l'autre, les idéologies ne meurent pas" (Aron 1990: 379–84, 281; Aron 1983b: 578–9, 606, 411).

8. Charles Turner recently wrote, "The term 'totalitarianism' is an awkward one." He proceeded to offer three reasons why that is so (Turner 2017: 25).

9. Mahoney claimed that Aron and Arendt were the best guides for a modern investigation into totalitarianism because it still has its adherents, even if it is basically a relic of the past (Aron 1994a: 95).

10. There is little to show that they knew each other well. In her biography of Hannah Arendt, Elisabeth Young-Bruehl notes that, after having fled to France in 1933, Arendt occasionally saw Aron and that he helped arrange for Arendt to attend Alexandre Kojève's lectures on Hegel. Young-Bruehl also indicates that Arendt respected Aron for helping German refugees in the 1930s, and in the 1950s believed that, along with Albert Camus, Aron was the best man in France (Young-Bruehl 1982: 104, 116, 281).

11. Readers are encouraged to consider the relevant writings by Margaret Canovan, Peter Baehr, and Ronald Beiner.

12. Peter Baehr devotes a chapter of his *Hannah Arendt, Totalitarianism, and the Social Sciences* to a discussion of Arendt and Aron on totalitarianism. He concludes that Aron's account of totalitarianism was "subtle, sober, and logical" but that in Aron's efforts to show that it was not a novel form of government he made it seem too normal. In contrast, Baehr appears to applaud Arendt for insisting that it was novel and therefore dangerous. Writing as a scholar, Baehr insists that we need Aron's "sociological acuity" as much as we need Arendt's "demonic poetry" but it seems as if his personal preference is inclined towards Arendt. This is not very surprising, given Baehr is one of the leading experts on Hannah Arendt (see Baehr 2010: 87–8, 90).

13. It was published in the July 1953 issue of *The Review of Politics*. It is uncertain why Aron wrote that it appeared in the Festschrift for Karl Jaspers. First, that

was not published until 1957, and second, Arendt wrote a different paper for the Festschrift (Aron 1994b: 109). Arendt added a slightly revised version of "Ideology and Terror" for the second edition, which was published in 1958.

14. Aron does not provide an answer to the third question about the function of these trials.

# CHAPTER SEVEN

# *On freedom*

"What I tried to illustrate in the second lecture is precisely this
dialectic of power and freedom."
Raymond Aron[1]

The focus of this chapter is not on one person or even on one concept
but on a number of ideas. These include democracy, liberalism, and
especially freedom, and they need to be discussed together because, in
Raymond Aron's thinking, they are all related. But as the quotation
above shows, Aron thought that one could not talk about freedom
without talking about power. Unlike the radicals on the right or the
left, Aron recognized that it was human nature to try to dominate:
hence the dialectic of power and freedom. Nor is the focus of this
chapter on a single work, as in the previous chapter. Rather, it takes
into consideration several works, as in some of the earlier chapters.
Then there are a number of preliminary comments that should be
made. First, Aron does not talk only about the West, but often talks
about the Soviet East. And towards the end of *An Essay on Freedom*,
Aron makes a fundamental point about the differences between the
Westerners and the Marxist–Leninists. The former intend to create a
"certain type of man" and the latter want to create a "new man." The
Westerners are content with revising rather than creating because they
do not believe that human nature can be changed (Aron 1970a: 161).
Second, Aron does not often write about liberalism per se, but a certain
type that was promoted by F. A. Hayek plays an important role in his
thinking and therefore is included here. Third, the choice of the word
"freedom" rather than "liberty" may seem to be somewhat arbitrary
but here I follow the English use of "freedom." Fourth, part of the
choice to use the word "talk" is because both of the works that I use
here were lectures. *Democracy and Totalitarianism* is comprised of one

set of nineteen lectures, which Aron presented at the Sorbonne, and *An Essay on Freedom* is composed of the Jefferson Lectures, which he gave at the University of California. In addition, towards the end of his Sorbonne lectures, Aron spoke about the need for further study of the word "freedom" and it is likely that he used the invitation to give the Jefferson Lectures as an opportunity to do part of that study. Thus, the two books not only share the lecture format but also focus on the concept of freedom. Finally, Aron devoted a large portion of *An Essay on Freedom* to Hayek's thinking and in particular to Hayek's book, *The Constitution of Liberty*. To understand Aron's comments on Hayek's thoughts, it is helpful to consider the 1961 review that Aron wrote on *The Constitution of Liberty*.

The title of this chapter could be "On Liberty" because the word "liberty" is closer to the French term "liberté," and second, Hayek's book uses "liberty" instead of "freedom." However, I prefer "freedom" because that is the term used in the English translation of Aron's lectures. However, in what follows, I will use the terms more or less interchangeably and I justify this by appealing to Aron himself. In "The Liberal Definition of Liberty: Concerning F. A. Hayek's *The Constitution of Liberty*, Aron wrote "liberty (which in English is indifferently freedom and liberty)." While there are three sections, there will be a considerable amount of overlap because democracy, liberalism, and liberty are, in Aron's view, interconnected.

## DE TOCQUEVILLE, MARX, AND FREEDOM

The title *Democracy and Totalitarianism* does not accurately reflect the original title, *Sociologie des sociétés industrielles, esquisse d'une théorie des régimes politiques*, but the book is about politics in modern industrial societies. And even if the term "democracy" is hardly found in this work, its spirit and the notion of politics certainly are present throughout it.

In French, the term "politique" has several meanings. Aron focuses on two: the conception or plan for action, which is best expressed by the English word "policy," and the area in which actors struggle for their own aims and policies: this is the arena of politics. Aron notes that people often regard policy making as something benign whereas politics is regarded as something rather impure. However, he insists not only that policy is subservient to politics but that politics is necessary because of the need for the rule of man over man.[2] Aron makes the further observation that democracy requires its citizens to have a basic awareness of the rules that govern the state. It also requires an admission that the state does not always live up to its ideals. All three of these points make up a type of political realism. This is further amplified by Aron's comment that the Greek sense of politics means how the city is actually run (Aron 1969: 5–6). Accordingly, policy is subservient to politics in that the latter is more extensive; Aron refers to this priority as the "primacy of politics" and suggests that this has two meanings. The first one is human and comes from observing that politics is higher than economics because economics is limited to resources and production but politics is devoted to the question of existence. The second one comes from de Tocqueville, who believed that modern societies are democratic. This is because of the increase in equality among citizens. However, Aron insists that this is not a causal connection and rejects the idea of any type of determinism. He also maintains that his goal in these lectures is rather limited: that is, to study one type of political setting but to refrain from attempting to develop a theory of legitimate authority (Aron 1969: 11–13).

Sociologists, Aron insists, are never strictly scholars; rather, they utilize scholarly facts to bolster a course of action. Thus, sociologists have philosophies; these thinkers are not content just to study but also counsel. Aron insists that this double aspect is not a modern invention, but that Aristotle's *Politics* is a combination of political sociology and political philosophy. Aristotle developed his three types of states – monarchy, aristocracy, and democracy – and he asked which one was the best. Although Aristotle's three categories are no longer employed, political thinkers are still concerned with the question of which form of government is the best (Aron 1969: 15–17). Aron looked not just to Aristotle but also to Montesquieu, who also developed categories for types of government. However, Aron's larger concern is with de Tocqueville and with Marx. While he spends more effort on Marx than de Tocqueville in *Democracy and Totalitarianism*, he is concerned with both of them in *An Essay on Freedom*.

Aron refers to de Tocqueville as "the sociologist of democracy" (Aron 1970a: 15). He begins with the observation that de Tocqueville was never precise and he considers two words to be especially lacking in clarity. The one that interests him initially is the term "democracy." De Tocqueville may not have been rigorous in his definition or consistent in its application, but Aron is certain that his meaning was always clear. He maintains that de Tocqueville considered democracy to be a condition of society rather than a form of government, and he contrasted democracy with aristocracy. The "Old Regime" was an aristocracy of the old nobility and its inherent inequality was based upon the ownership of land. Aron further notes that every genuine aristocracy is territorially based and he justifies this claim by insisting that it is the ownership of the land that guarantees continuity. Aron insists that de Tocqueville considered democracy to be the opposite of aristocracy and that the former superseded the latter with the increase in equality. Aron adds that this use of the term democracy is the one that de Tocqueville used most often but that the French thinker also used it to discuss the three types of government. Traditionally, in a monarchy, sovereignty resided with the single individual; in an aristocracy, sovereignty resided with the few; while in a democracy, sovereignty resides in all (Aron 1970a: 9–11). De Tocqueville knew that the aristocracy was no longer viable and that democracy was going to be the form of government of the future; the issue was what the relationship between democracy and liberalism, equality, and freedom was going to be.

The term "freedom" was the other word that de Tocqueville frequently used but never carefully defined. Aron argued that the "clearest definition" of freedom that de Tocqueville offered was in an essay published in 1836. This definition is both negative and indeterminate: the former because it considers what an individual may choose to do and the latter because it considers the individual in relation to others. Aron notes that "freedom from" often becomes "freedom to" because it is a type of independence but it comes only within the security given by political order. For de Tocqueville, this freedom of independence was the highest type of freedom. Aron suggests that de Tocqueville believed this because of personal inclinations but adds that there is also a sociological basis to his preference. That is because only freedom can substitute for the love of money, the desire for fame, or the worries of everyday life (Aron 1970a: 13–14). Although de Tocqueville wrote of freedom in the singular, he recognized that there were a number of freedoms, including the freedom of expression, the freedom from oppression, and the freedom to participate in governing. He shares de Tocqueville's belief that people have more faith in the legitimacy of laws that they have helped make. And he also shares his contention that Americans are not really virtuous but are more concerned about physical well-being (Aron 1970a: 17–18). Aron emphasizes that de Tocqueville's view of freedom is not the opinion that everyone is free to do what one likes and he compares that to an animal's view of freedom. Instead, his conception of freedom is one that is a civil and moral one. Rather than being radically individualistic, de Tocqueville's concept of freedom is pluralistic. One cannot be truly free as a private individual; freedom is found in the public sphere.

Aron justifies his earlier reference to de Tocqueville as "the sociologist of freedom" on three grounds. First, he defined modern society by its "equality of conditions" instead of by its industry, like Comte, or by capitalism, like Marx. Second, he defines it by its emphasis on probability. While we can find patterns and locate movements, there is nothing fully determined. Third, he insists on the primacy of the political over economics. Unlike with Marxism, with its emphasis on class in modern society, de Tocqueville maintains that the differentiation in classes was a major factor in the "Old Regime" but is not particularly present in democracies (Aron 1970a: 18–20).

The following pages are devoted to contrasting Marx and de Tocqueville. Aron does not doubt that the young Marx was devoted to the ideals of the French Revolution but that he wanted to complete it: "Democracy, liberty, equality: these values are obviously his." What Marx objected to was the exclusive emphasis on politics and he intended to provide an account that emphasized economics. That is also why he described personal and political freedoms as "formal freedoms" in contrast to the real freedom of economic freedom. This economic freedom is realized when the capitalistic class is overthrown and its exploitation is eliminated and replaced by a collectivist one, in which each receives what each needs (Aron 1970a: 26–9).

Aron describes how de Tocqueville and Marx were similar: they both rejected opportunism and both believed in themselves and their ideas. And both believed in freedom. However, they had different notions of freedom: de Tocqueville believed in the freedom that is found in the modern liberal democracy whereas Marx believed that it could be found only in some future utopian state (Aron 1970a: 29–32). And, they differed on the importance of the type of freedom: for de Tocqueville, the freedom that mattered was the "formal" freedom; for Marx, the freedom that mattered was "real" (economic) freedom (Aron 1970a: 38–40).

Aron spends the remaining portion of Chapter One investigating the differences between the Western liberal societies and the Eastern socialist ones. He homes in mostly on the contrast in emphasis on formal freedom in the West and on real freedom in the East, and he employs the Hungarian uprising of 1956 as the focus. As much as the 1956 revolution was similar to the French one in 1848, there is a fundamental difference. In the earlier one, the revolutionaries were fighting against the old traditional order whereas the revolutionaries in the later one were fighting for a new order. However, both the French and the Hungarians were fighting against "an external and all-powerful force" (Aron 1970a: 39). Yet the main impetus for the Hungarian uprising was the refusal of the authorities to allow formal freedom – the right to write, to paint, and to make one's own kind of music. Aron is dismissive of those who claimed that the Marxists wished to extend formal freedom: not so much on their aspirations but on the actual results. He adds that it may seem ironic that, in the countries in which real freedom exists, what is desired is actually formal freedom. Aron comments that there is an element of truth in this "dialectic" but insists that it oversimplifies historical reality. That is because, in the Western states, real freedom exists alongside formal freedom; thus, there, the dialectic cannot be reduced to some ironic reversal. It is in the Communist countries that there is real freedom but not formal freedom. The problem is not with the technical progress that made industrial society possible; it is with those who insist that society can be forcibly changed into some kind of utopia (Aron 1970a: 44–5).

Aron concludes with several observations: first, Western liberal democracies demonstrate that formal freedom and real freedom are not contradictory but can exist within societies; second, the historical dialogue between de Tocqueville's liberal democracy and Marx's socialist utopia continues; and third, that de Tocqueville was "a good prophet." He ends with the observation that modern Western societies have three ideals: bourgeois citizenship, technological efficiency, and the right to choose one's own path to salvation. He counsels us not to sacrifice any of the three and not to be so naïve as to believe that it is easy to achieve them all (Aron 1970a: 45–9).

## FORMAL FREEDOM AND REAL FREEDOM

The center of attention in Chapter Two is the contrast between formal freedom and real freedom, and as another indication of Aron's sympathies, he notes that the sociologists and the ideologists are closer to agreement than at any other time. Recall that he had referred to de Tocqueville as the "sociologist of freedom" and that Marxists believe in the ideology of the future perfect state. To substantiate his claim, he reminds us how liberal democracies were under siege. In contrast, in 1961, it appeared that both the West and the East had had continual improvements in their standards of living and he suggests that the ideas of Marxism, Fascism, and even liberalism had lost some of their allure. He mentions the phrase "end of ideology," but as the previous chapter has shown, he did not believe that it had occurred; nor did he think that it would ever happen (Aron 1970a: 49–51).

Despite the fact that the three ideologies have lost some of their attractiveness, Aron believes that it is important to analyze the differences among the three types and to explain the factors that have been prompting a degree of skepticism towards them. Marxist ideology combined a scientific analysis of capitalism with a vision of the inevitable future. In contrast to the revolutionaries of the left, the revolutionaries of the right were not concerned with uprooting all traditions but wanted to keep some and blend them into a form in which the state and society would be fundamentally the same. Conservatism was not so much an ideology as it was a longing for the past, conjoined with an appreciation of the importance of reason. Finally, there is liberalism that is more an anti-ideology than an ideology. It is liberalism in democracy on which Aron mostly concentrates (Aron 1970a: 50–2).

A liberal democracy seeks to accomplish a number of goals. First, it seeks to ensure the rights of the individual. Second, it fosters the spontaneous actions of its citizens. Third, it recognizes the will of the people. Finally, it attempts to raise the standard of living for the individual, thus contributing to "real freedom" while safeguarding "formal freedom." Aron is convinced that the rising standard of living helped reduce the attractiveness of ideologies and he contrasts the modern approach to a historical one. Aron means that the unconditional revolt is unthinkable today; no one would have the attitude of the silk weavers of "la liberté ou la Mort."

Aron returns to his three ideals, with which he had ended Chapter One – personal destiny, bourgeois citizenship, and technical efficiency – and he wonders whether there is unimpeded progress towards them. He answers in the negative and offers five different types of obstacles. First, new states prefer economic prosperity to personal freedom. Second, Soviet states still remain hostile to formal freedom. Third, Communists hold that formal freedom is incompatible with real freedom and point to poverty in rich countries. Fourth, in contrast, liberals argue that socialism is the "road to serfdom." Fifth, there is a fear that, in the age of mass culture and modern industry, the individual will lose his freedom and simply becomes a "cog in the wheel" (Aron 1970a: 53–5). It is not necessary to discuss Aron's response to some of these points and it is better to focus on a few of them. Aron's response is indirect and he approaches the issues by asking whether the term "freedom" has the same meaning for individuals as it does for states. He asks: "Does national liberation have anything in common with the liberation of the individual?" He answers by way of F. A. Hayek. Aron notes that Hayek is partially justified in limiting the notion of freedom to just the individual.[3] It is the individual who is autonomous and reflective, and can make a personal choice. Since a group is made up of two or more individuals, then it cannot be regarded as having freedom. Aron responds by suggesting that, when a group forms a nation, it generates a kind of unity. This is the type of unity that promotes a type of reflection and decision-making that is similar to that possessed by the individual. In this sense, a nation should also be considered free or not free. This "collective person" meets other "collective persons" in the international arena. In this arena, the highest duty is to maintain the security of the "collective person." Aron returns to the notion of liberation of a people and asks whether the Algerians would consider themselves liberated if they were granted independence as long as they followed French laws. Aron's response is that freedom is just as dependent "on men and on manners" as it is on laws (Aron 1970a: 60). That is true within a country: does everyone enjoy the same degree of freedom or is it restricted to some people? People who are discriminated against because of ethnicity cannot be said to have the same degree of freedom as those who are doing the discriminating. This is true during revolutionary times when cohesiveness is a necessity. Some will argue that this is a necessary but temporary state that will inevitably pass. Aron is unconvinced of this and invokes history in support. In many cases, discrimination continues and he reminds us that it can and does exist, even in pluralistic democracies. Aron returns to the notion of liberal democracy and wants us to remember that its prestige has fallen. Now the emphasis is on governmental efficiency, not on citizens' freedom. He also points out that all countries can be said to be "democratic" in the sense that they lay claim to popular sovereignty. However, they differ according to whether they adhere to the rule of law, meaning they are a "nomocracy," or whether they adhere to the belief in future goals, meaning a "telocracy" (Aron 1970a: 63). The Western countries tend to be "nomocracies" and the Soviet ones tend to be "telocracies." The Communists held an ideology in which the proletariat is the "agent of historical necessity" that will lead to humankind's liberation (Aron 1970a: 64). Aron wonders whether it is the liberal democracies that will bring about freedom for all and not the Communist countries. He acknowledges that an answer to such a question can only be speculative but insists that whether one uses a phrase such as "development of the forces of production" or one such as "economic growth" really does not matter. What does is the difference between the probabilism of de Tocqueville and the determinism of Marx. Does the elevation in standards of living bring about the formal freedoms that are personal and political (Aron 1970a: 65–6)?

These questions lead Aron to an analysis of the revolutions of 1848 and 1956. Granted there were some similarities, which Aron had emphasized in the first chapter, but here he wants to stress how the Polish and Hungarian revolutions of 1956 were different in comparison to the earlier ones. He insists that "The events of 1956 have a demonstrative value that transcends all sociological theories." That is not only because they were extremely important but also because they differed in several ways. First, the revolutions were not prompted by any great dissatisfaction with the standard of living or with the privileges of the few. Rather, they were driven by revulsion against the "organized lie" and the "tyranny of the state." Second, the revolutions differed in that they were national, social, and liberal. The Hungarians and the Poles believed that the regime was not one that they had chosen but was imposed from outside. They had no quarrel with its existence in Russia or in China, but it was not their choice. Third, the revolutions did not occur at the height of oppression but when things seemed to be going well. This leads to Aron's observation regarding the mistake made by many commentators. They believe that the "internal contradictions and the precariousness of the regime" lead necessarily to revolution. Aron thinks that this is wrong because history is not inevitable but probabilistic, and because the seeds of revolution are inherent in the nature of a state. However, if the state enjoys respect, there will be continued stability (Aron 1970a: 65–6). With single-party states, it is similar; however, the problem is with the ideology of the lie. Marxism taught that the revolution against capitalism was necessary and inevitable. It was necessary so that the proletariat could take power and instigate the movement towards liberation. Classes would disappear and a unified society would appear. This process is inevitable but this inevitability would be recognized only at the end, when formal liberalism is restored (Aron 1970a: 68). However, Aron does not see the connection between ideology and formal freedoms, and he takes issue with the state's claim that it has the authority to dictate what can be painted and what can be written. And he points to the inherent contradiction in Communist ideology. How can the authorities emphasize the importance of science while denying the importance of independent art and writing? And how can they provide such massive support for those engaged in scientific activities while giving such limited support to those capable of intellectual achievements? Aron insisted that the Soviets did not have "freedom as security" and he undoubtedly had the Gulag prisons and mass deportations in mind. And the Soviets lack formal freedom, which brings about a tension between the ideology that insists on the monopoly on art and the desires of the intelligentsia for artistic freedom (Aron 1970a: 70). This does not mean that Aron thinks that representative democracies have no faults. In fact, he criticizes their institutions for not being able to express the "universal desire for freedom" (Aron 1970a: 71). Freedom as security and freedom of expression are lacking in the Soviet system; however, the liberal democracies seem unable to provide for the economic well-being of all of their citizens. This inequality is, Aron suggests, the central point of "indictment" and he notes that it is not just certain liberals who are making this charge but that it is shown by "irrefutable statistics." Before turning to these, he questions whether the two types of freedom, formal and real, can ever be synthesized (Aron 1970a: 73). He does not answer this question here but points to the problems that arise with the disparity of wealth in the liberal democracies. First, formal freedom can obscure the fact that many people suffer from the lack of real freedom from want. Second, the continual move towards the concentration of wealth in the hands of the few makes the critical unmasking of democratic fictions far more likely, if not inevitable (Aron 1970a: 73–4). Aron spends a number of pages in laying out the case for the problems of poverty. Even if one allows for the rising standard of living in the United States, Great Britain, and France, there is little doubt that there is a great difference in the distribution of wealth, with the result that poverty is widespread. He refers to Michael Harrington's *The Other America: Poverty in the United States* and notes that poverty is not just a sociological problem but is becoming a political one as well (Aron 1970a: 74–8). He remarks that there are three problems. First, poverty is not just a statistical quantity but is also qualitative; it is both what a family lives on and how the family lives. This suggests that there are degrees of poverty. Second, the impoverished are not a monolithic group but are composed of various people. There are the elderly, the very young, the unemployed, and the immigrants. Some of the people who are impoverished are so because of the environment and some have heredity to thank. Third, the concentration of wealth apparently leads to what C. Wright Mills called the "power elite"; however, as much as economic wealth influences the degree of political power one possesses, Aron does not subscribe to this view. Instead, he believes that this is mostly a sociological version of the Marxist–Leninist theory of monopolies, and that theory was "a curious mixture of undeniable facts and false interpretations" (Aron 1970a: 81). Rather than spelling out his objections to the false interpretations, Aron suggests that, as extensive as the problems are with large corporations, they do not put forth a unified front. But socialism does: thus the economic and political problems not only will not be solved, but are likely to grow larger. Aron does not deny the problems associated with the concentration of wealth and political power, but he insists that socialism is not equipped to deal with them. In his opinion, it is too ideological in the "pejorative sense" and it strikes him as being "somewhat ridiculous." Its adherents have consistently predicted the imminent paralysis of capitalism but that has not occurred. Instead, there has been an increase in economic well-being in the West – not even the "ideologists of Moscow" are convinced by the claim that the capitalist economy will necessarily self-destruct. Instead of trying to argue that the capitalistic system is systematically flawed, the Moscow ideologists have shifted to touting how productivity and material well-being have improved compared to in the West (Aron 1970a: 84).

After having critiqued the Marxist–Leninist view, Aron turns his attention to what he refers to as the "liberal–individualist" or "Whig critique." He has chosen Hayek's book, *The Constitution of Liberty*, as his focus because it is the "most systematic and eloquent expression" of the liberal–individualist conception of liberty. The fact that Aron devotes some twelve pages to it is an indication of the importance that Aron accords to it and a sufficient hint that we should take it very seriously. Unfortunately, Hayek's book has had little success and that is a result of Hayek's reputation, which he acquired from *The Road to Serfdom* as well as the rejection of the non-conformists.[4] Aron allows that many people will find his interest in Hayek's thinking to be rather odd. Either they will dismiss Hayek as being a non-conformist or they do not take the liberal–individualist critique seriously. Aron defends Hayek by praising him both for being the "nonconformist par excellence" and for being willing to be shunned and isolated for his ideas. Finally, he notes that the ideal government in which he believes is subject to criticism from the Marxist left and the Whig right. Aron does not detail his ideal form but lists that it is one that is a liberal democracy with a mixed economy and includes the welfare state. In this, Aron's ideal form falls between the planned economy of the left and the radical individualism of the right. Those of the left insist that mankind must be liberated from want and fear; those of the right want to be liberated from the power of the state and its arbitrary authority. Those of the right believe that human flourishing comes with minimizing the state's influence in order to maximize the individual's initiative. Having spent much of the earlier part of his lectures on the ideas and criticisms of the left, Aron now spends a considerable amount of time examining the ideas of the right. However much he may not agree with liberal–individualists like Hayek, Aron admires them for their rejection of ideology and the acceptance of reason (Aron 1970a: 85).

A typical criticism of *The Road to Serfdom* was that Hayek substituted his own version of historical inevitability for that of the Marxists. Aron discounts this and argues that Hayek's view was not overly simplistic and it was not rigidly deterministic (Aron 1970a: 86). One of the problems with *The Road to Serfdom* was that people did not tend to read it, and when they did, they did not read it very carefully. Accordingly, critics accused Hayek of many things. He was not attacking socialism per se but was attacking the notion of planning. He was convinced that too many people in Great Britain and in the United States believed that planning would solve all economic and political problems. Nor did Hayek think that those countries would necessarily end up with totalitarian governments. What he was concerned about was the lack of critical thinking about the present and the foolishness about the great hopes for the future. Hayek was concerned that people in Great Britain, and less so in the United States, were forgetting about the important ideas of liberalism (Hayek 2007: 22–6, 31). The need for serious reflection and the defense of liberalism were ideas that appealed to Aron. His criticisms are not against these but against Hayek's reluctance to consider a more nuanced view.

Returning to *The Constitution of Liberty*, Aron maintains that to understand Hayek's philosophy it is important to consider his definitions of ideas and his hierarchy of values. Hayek does not define freedom either by considering it as democratic (the sovereignty of the people) or by the "absolutism of the general will" (the will of the majority). Aron suggests that Hayek is like de Tocqueville, in that both of them are democrats because they are liberals rather than being liberals because they are democrats. Thus, the emphasis is on liberalism rather than on democracy. Aron quotes a lengthy passage from *The Constitution of Liberty*, in which Hayek first notes the overlap between liberalism and democracy: that "Equality before the law leads to the demand that all men should have a share in making the law." Hayek then argues that, despite this shared view, traditional liberalism differs from democratic movements. The former insists on limiting all coercive powers of government, regardless of whether it is a democracy or some other form. The "dogmatic democrat" insists on only one limitation and that is a limit to the current opinion of the majority. Hayek suggests that this difference is clarified when he names the governments' opposites: for liberalism it is totalitarianism and for democracy it is authoritarianism. He does not insist that this opposition is complete: a democracy may have totalitarian powers and an authoritarian state may have liberal principles (Aron 1970a: 86–7; Hayek 2011: 166). Aron approves of this distinction, although he notes that it has not been well received by everyone. He adds that he is no "dogmatic democrat" and agrees with Hayek that democracy is not so much an end but a means. It is a means to safeguard freedom and it is the "logical conclusion of the liberal philosophy" (Aron 1970a: 87). He allows that political parties, elections, and assemblies are procedures for electing leaders, but as long as these procedures are respected, they help guarantee the transfer of power. However, there is a fundamental disagreement regarding principles between those who value liberalism over democracy and those who assume that democracy has primacy over liberalism. Aron suggests that, in order to understand the difference, it is critical to have the proper definition of freedom. Hayek does define freedom but it is simply the "absence of coercion." Aron cites a number of passages where Hayek does define freedom as the absence of coercion and notes that Hayek's definition is negative: that is, it is freedom *from*. It is the type of situation where each individual is master of himself. Aron suggests that this is the freedom of the entrepreneur who is free to take the initiative and build a business. It is also the freedom of the consumer who is free to buy what the entrepreneur makes. However, Aron objects that this definition of freedom is restricted to a relatively small group of people: a worker on the production line, an employee in a vast organization, a soldier in an army, or even a Jesuit, cannot be regarded as being free. Aron objects that the nature of industrial society is such that it necessarily reduces the number of free people. Aron notes that Hayek seems aware of such an objection and that he seems intent upon meeting it with the claim that there are differences between particular orders and general ones: thus, a difference between an individual who is commanded and another who is autonomous. But what this comes down to is fundamentally the rule of law (Aron 1970a: 89). Aron does not dispute the importance of the rule of law but insists that it is more of an ideal than it is an accurate reflection of reality. That is because, by definition, governments hold power and because human nature is such that one seeks domination over others. This is Weber's concept of "the rule of man over man"; the rule of law is merely the attempt to substitute law for power. Yet, as Weber had argued, law and power necessarily go together. Putting aside this notion for a minute, Aron returns to Hayek's liberal–individualism and suggests that we are not wrong to ridicule those who believe that only formal freedom matters – especially from those who lack sufficient food and by those who are oppressed by foreign rulers. This is not to say that formal freedom is not necessary, because it is. It is to say that the liberal–individual believes that one aspect of freedom covers all and underestimates "the power of egalitarian demands." The consumer has freedom as well as the entrepreneur; the difference is that we all are, in some way, consumers but very few of us are entrepreneurs. Thus, Hayek's account is mistaken; Aron, however, is convinced not only that it can teach us, but that it is quite fruitful. The major difficulty is that its excessiveness "undermines its own force" (Aron 1970a: 91).

Aron limits himself to discussing a few points that he thinks deserve consideration, if not actual approval. The modern state is increasing in power and scope, and this increase means that it is becoming more bureaucratic and less democratic. Aron points specifically to Hayek's critique of labor unions because that is one of the clearest arguments that the "Whig" individualist has against a collective.[5] Aron makes it clear that he does not subscribe to Hayek's belief that labor unions are monopolies and he believes that unions offer workers a way in which to counterbalance the power that businesses possess. However, he applauds Hayek for his bravery in speaking up, even if it means that Hayek would be called a reactionary. Aron writes: "this simply increases my respect for the liberal who is not afraid of and perhaps secretly desires unpopularity" (Aron 1970a: 92). Whether he was right that Hayek secretly wished to be unpopular is not likely but Aron may have been thinking of himself when he wrote about the need to speak the truth.

Another point of agreement appears to be Aron's and Hayek's opinion on the notion of income tax. Both agree that, while there may be a claim to equality, not everyone is in fact equal. The question is to what degree a redistribution of wealth by means of taxes is warranted. Hayek argued that a progressive tax did not work in Germany in the late nineteenth century and it would not work in the United States in the twentieth. It fails in part because it violates the maxim "equal pay for equal work" (Hayek 2011: 436–44). Aron notes that people are not necessarily against inequality and he points to the high salaries of singers and actors. And he notes that attempts at redistribution often lead to unintended results. However, he does not endorse Hayek's rejection of taxes because he believes that it is a necessary function of the state to guarantee that all of its citizens have "the minimum of resources to have a decent life" and that means that it has the right to tax the wealthy (Aron 1970a: 93–4).

Aron provides a lengthy quotation from *Democracy in America*, in which de Tocqueville describes the near future.[6] Each individual lives an isolated life devoted to seeking "petty and paltry pleasures." Above them is the state, which has absolute authority, similar to a parent but one who seeks to keep the child in "perpetual childhood." Aron indicates that Hayek and the "dogmatic Whigs" frequently cite this passage, but Aron insists that it is a "combination of prophetic insights, excessive fears, and obvious errors" (Aron 1970a: 96–7). This future has not come to pass and Hayek would be forced to acknowledge that, as well as the justification for the need for the state to provide a basic standard of living (Aron 1970a: 98). Aron does not provide any more comments on Hayek's liberal–individualism but moves to Chapter Three. However, Aron wrote a lengthy review of *The Constitution of Liberty*. This review reinforces Aron's ideas in his lectures but also expands upon it, thus providing a fuller account of what he found attractive and what he found wanting in Hayek's liberal–individualism. It is worth exploring Aron's review before moving to Chapter Three.

Aron begins his review of *The Constitution of Liberty* by making points similar to those he makes in *An Essay on Freedom*. That is, Hayek's book is mostly ignored in Europe by those who need to read it most and is neglected in the United States because of the prejudice against *The Road to Serfdom*. However, Aron notes that he subscribes to the judgment of J. W. N. Watkins that "In any circumstances *The Constitution of Liberty* would have been an important book. Given the condition of political philosophy in the English-speaking world today, it is outstandingly important." Aron concurs and praises Hayek for his "vigorous mind" and his attempt to determine what constitutes a "free society, that is, a good society." Aron cautions his reader against taking his criticisms to mean a rejection of Hayek's thesis; instead, he believes that Hayek's book is an incredibly important one (Aron 1994a: 73).

Aron's initial focus is on the title; Hayek employs the term "constitution" in a manner that is larger than its legal meaning. Instead, "constitution" is used to describe a political organization and in particular a liberal one. If it is called liberal, then it is an organization that respects the liberty of individuals (Aron 1994a: 74). Aron further observes that Hayek describes liberty negatively – that is, the freedom from coercion – and he notes that Hayek uses 'liberty' in the singular, unlike those who prefer the term 'liberties'. But Aron focuses mostly on Hayek's negative definition of freedom as the freedom from coercion and suggests that Hayek's definition prompts three questions. First, is it possible to have a type of liberty that is individualistic? Second, is it possible to delineate this individual liberty from the other types of liberty? Third, can a good society be determined solely by the criterion of the lack of constraint?

Aron addresses the first question by noting that people may try to live separate lives but that they live in an organized society. Accordingly, it is impossible to think of an individual as living a radical individualistic life. One cannot conceive of liberty simply as a freedom from coercion. A soldier or a Jesuit is not free because he obeys the will of another; the soldier will be constrained as long as he serves whereas the Jesuit will be constrained by his life-long vows. Furthermore, while Hayek can simply claim that the soldier or the Jesuit voluntarily chose servitude, the same cannot be said of the worker (Aron 1994a: 75–7).

Hayek has to admit that life means constraint – it comes from family, friends, neighbors, and even strangers. It comes from customs, traditions, prejudices, and of course laws. Hayek wants to insist that to obey the law means that one has liberty. However, Aron argues that general law constrains everybody and he notes that Hayek's attempt to evade this difficulty by insisting that it is not discriminatory if it applies to the rulers as much as to the ruled is bound to fail. That is because it is still oppressive (Aron 1994a: 79). Aron has a similar response to Hayek's rejection of progressive taxation; the rich minority may feel constrained by being forced to share some of its wealth but the poor majority is also constrained by not having enough to meet its basic needs. These points lead to Aron's general objection: that Hayek thinks that general laws are like natural laws. Aron insists that they are not and he argues from the following points. First, people agree, for the most part, that laws are made by people: that is, they are products of humans and not of God or nature. Second, laws can be skirted and avoided, unlike natural laws. Physical laws cannot be defied but social laws can. And, third, it is often ridiculous to try to match a social law to a natural law (Aron 1994a: 81). Aron's objection is not so much with Hayek's vision of how the world ought to be as it is with his philosophical argument for it.

Aron admits that he shares Hayek's goal of a state that replaces the rule of man over man by the rule of laws over men and he allows that this is not so much a difference in values as it is a difference in the consideration of facts. One major fact is that there are "human communities" and not one single "human collective." Another major fact is that these different states are at times on friendly terms and at other times on unfriendly terms. This leads to Aron's invocation of Locke's notion that governments have two functions: to maintain internal order as well as to maintain external security. Like many liberals, Hayek has no particular interest in international relations because he is interested in personal constraint. Yet just because someone has no interest in something does not mean that it is unimportant; Aron devoted much of his life to the problems of international relations, by writing on war and on peace. However, Aron is not content with criticizing Hayek's philosophical foundation regarding international relations; he is also critical of Hayek's notion of negative freedom. He points out that, as much as Hayek is dismissive of Hans Kelsen's positivistic theory of law, Hayek himself subscribes to a philosophy that holds that metaphysical questions about liberty are senseless (Aron 1994a: 84–5). These are questions such as at what age is an infant no longer "irresponsible" or what amount of education a people needs to have to be considered responsible. In other words, Hayek thinks only in singulars and negatives: he is concerned solely with the individual and only with the absence of constraint. Aron's point can be illustrated by the fact that humans are not like Robinson Crusoe and live alone, but they must live among others. Furthermore, a society must exist before it can be considered free. The problem is that Hayek's philosophy of liberty is based upon economics. He complains that Hayek believes that "Each individual chooses and remains, in all circumstances, in the hands of his own counsel." Yet Aron reminds us that democracy is a form of government of people, and that it is a social order (Aron 1994a: 87–9). Aron concludes by suggesting that he doubts the virtuosity of economists as much as he doubts the Marxist "cunning of reason" and that he will admire Hayek's argument while reserving his faith. Just as the Marxist is convinced by his idea, the economist is also enamored by his concept (Aron 1994a: 90).

The title of Chapter Three is "Political Freedom and Technology" and Aron begins it by alluding to a problem that he had mentioned in the preceding chapter. This problem is what the function of freedom is in the modern industrial age. He notes that "political freedom" is the freedom to participate in elections, by which one is able to exert some influence over the state. He notes that this freedom still exists in the West but has largely disappeared in the Soviet Union. He does not indicate a definitive reason for this lack but suggests it could be because those in the Soviet Union never had that freedom or that they believe that they have other avenues to influence the collective (Aron 1970a: 101).

Aron reminds us that he follows Hayek in distinguishing between liberalism and democracy; the former strives to limit power whereas the latter is a form of power. Liberalism is a means to an end and that liberalism leads to democracy: a form of government that embraces the "principle of equality before the law." However, Aron insists that if the democracy is real and not an illusion, then there must be freedom for the individual. And this political freedom must include the right to expression, the right to associate, and the right to choose. Aron insists that the single-party election is not an election of choice but an election on acclamation. It is the belief of the party that it knows better than the people (Aron 1970a: 101). But if political freedom still exists in the West, then it is undergoing a crisis in some countries. Aron suggests that there are two bases for determining whether a democracy is stable: is it accepted as legitimate by the population and does it possess "adequate efficiency"? He does not spell out what he means by the first basis because he apparently thought it was self-evident. However, efficiency is that manner of competition that results in a stable majority. On the other hand, a democracy is unstable if the population has lost confidence in the government or if the armed forces no longer obey the civilian powers (Aron 1970a: 102). Aron indicates that many of the Western countries are stable democracies but he focuses in particular on France. He suggests that France was a particular problem because of its natural sense of pessimism and because of the charismatic authority of de Gaulle (Aron 1970a: 103–5). Rather than discussing that, I turn to Aron's distinction between the three types of democracy: the French, the British, and the American. His focus is really on the last two – the parliamentary form in Britain and the presidential form in the United States. He maintains that democratic regimes may differ in form but that they are all "constitutional–pluralistic," by which they embody two things: multiple groups existing under rules and the respect for the rule of law (Aron 1970a: 106). And he points specifically to the two major differences between Great Britain and the United States. One difference is in the degree of discipline that the parties have: they are highly disciplined in Great Britain but virtually undisciplined in the United States. That means that it is more likely that one can predict who will be the leader in Great Britain than in the United States. The second major difference is the contrast in the manner of the exercise of power. In Great Britain, party discipline means a reduction in the discussions about using power whereas in the United States the lack of discipline means more discussions. This is found not just in the political parties but between the executive and congressional branches of government. Aron thinks highly of the American system because he is convinced that the greater amount of discussion offers a higher degree of guarantee of political freedom (Aron 1970a: 106–16). However, he does not minimize the fact that racial inequality occurred (and still occurs) in America and suggests that a change in racial preference may have to be made into law in order to effect that. And he notes that it is frequently the minority that pushes the state closer to the ideal of equality (Aron 1970a: 118).

Aron again emphasizes the importance of pluralism: the belief that many opinions help contribute to the stability and well-being of the state. In this sense, the United States continues to be an ideal worth emulating. The second important factor is the sense of representation. Once again, the plurality of voters contributes to the fact that the representative in the United States appears more likely actually to represent the will of his constituency. The third factor is that, in a modern industrial nation, the individual participates in two groups: one is a lesser political group, such as a labor union or an employer's union, while the second is a major political group, such as a political party (Aron 1970a: 122–3). A political party either utilizes its power or acts as a check or obstacle. For Aron, political parties are necessary because they bring competition; the problem with a country that has a single party is that there is no competition and there is no discussion of ideas. This leads to one of Aron's key convictions: that educated people tend to make thoughtful and responsible decisions. Unfortunately, what is relayed by radio and television is not *education* but *information*, and the latter cannot be substituted for the former. Aron acknowledges that the number of educated people who can thoughtfully discuss political issues has always been rather small; the issue is whether today's small group is less competent than those in the past. In other words, are specialists the only ones who are competent enough to make decisions? Aron answers in the negative and explains that important decisions fall into two categories. One is related to the economic situation and the other is primarily military. One need not be an expert on economic issues or a military specialist to understand how the economy affects one or how a war will destroy one. Granted not everyone can understand these issues but Aron insists that "enlightened amateurs" and "men of culture" can. Aron is not a pessimist but he acknowledges that the number of "men of culture" is dwindling and those who still remain no longer enjoy the respect that the liberal professions used to possess (Aron 1970a: 130–3).

The Conclusion begins with a remark and a list of three possible objections to Aron's account of liberty. He insists that his account was no more than an outline and should not be faulted for not being a complete analysis of freedom. He will also not answer the three objections and will only note them. First, his comparison of de Tocqueville and Marx was wrong, just as his comparison of modern-day political situations lacks a basis. Second, he has not understood the notion of freedom with a capital "F" and has restricted his account to various other freedoms. Third, he has dealt only with a social analysis and has failed to treat the individual (Aron 1970a: 142–2). Instead of responding, Aron insists that freedom in a social sense means the freedom to do something or not to do something, independent of another individual. He suggests that he is free to go to a synagogue or a church, or not to go at all; thus, freedom is both the freedom *to* and the freedom *from*. To paraphrase Aron's quotation from Felix Oppenheim: one is free if one is allowed to do what one wishes and not punished for doing so, and if one is not forced into doing something that one does not wish to do (Aron 1970a: 143–4). Aron believes that this type of definition has several consequences.

First, there is a difference between being free to do something and being able to do it. One may not be able to run a four-minute mile but one is still free to do so. Second, an individual is not free in many respects: in the laws that prohibit him from doing something or the ways in which society functions. Aron insists that this analysis shows that there is not one single freedom but many different ones (Aron 1970a: 142, 145). And everyone believes that freedom is a good thing, even tyrants, if only for themselves or according to their own definitions. That is why there is a difference of opinion between those in the West and those in the Soviet Union (Aron 1970a: 147, 151) But, one freedom that is almost universally accepted is the freedom of security. However, this includes the right to property and the right to associate, both of which are incompatible with the Soviet system. The rebuttal could be that, in the West, the only people who are free are the independents such as farmers, trade people, and entrepreneurs, while everyone else labors for someone. If, as Marx assumed, "work is the domain of necessity," then maybe more people need to be liberated. Yet history has shown that the collective ownership of the means of production does not lead to freedom. For Hayek and other liberals who look to economics, the idea of freedom is one with a capital "F." And that is the entrepreneur who chooses the proper means to the proper end. Unfortunately, liberals who think like that do not recognize the dialectic between power and freedom (Aron 1970a: 155–6). It is his recognition of the dialectic of power and freedom that prompts Aron to reject democratic dogmatism as well as liberal dogmatism. Both dogmatisms' adherence to an idea blinds them to reality. Aron also recognizes that totalitarianism is the greatest danger to freedom because absolute power corrupts absolutely. However, the other danger is the belief that freedom means that the individual "is his own master and answerable only to himself." The focus of the Marxist and the Whig on economics minimizes the importance of politics – the living and working within a society. Aron is convinced that intellectual freedoms are just as important as economic freedoms. Intellectual freedoms are not only safeguards against despotism; they are also the means by which people can be made capable of reason and morality. Like de Tocqueville, Aron despises servility, and the antidote to it is to ensure that each individual be as reasonable as possible. Aron is convinced that political freedom helps make its citizens better: neither a conformist nor a rebel, but one who is "critical and responsible" (Aron 1970a: 157–61).

## CONCLUDING COMMENTS

*An Essay on Freedom* is not an easy work to read; Aron's analysis is often complex and it is frequently dated by his examples. It disappoints in that, despite its intended American audience, Aron does not discuss Jefferson, Madison, or any of the other Founding Fathers. His preoccupation with Marx, and less so with de Tocqueville, seems not as relevant for today's readers whereas it probably was more so in the 1960s. However, Aron's *Essay* is more than an analysis; it is a sense of a certain type of freedom, one that recognizes the dialectic of power and freedom and one that avoids the extreme collectivism of the left and the extreme individualism of the right. Like Jefferson, Aron is a believer in the tenets of the Enlightenment but the history of the twentieth century has taught him to be more realistic and more pessimistic than Jefferson. However, as with de Tocqueville, von Clausewitz, and Max Weber, Raymond Aron's view of freedom is crucially connected to a sense of responsibility to one's fellow citizens, one's fellow soldiers, and also to history.

## NOTES

1. Aron (1970a: 156).
2. This is the same point that was made by Weber and was discussed in Chapter Two. Aron suggested that people often think that policy is "noble" but politics is "base" (Aron 1969: 3–4).
3. Aron (1970a: 59). He references the 1960 edition of Hayek's *The Constitution of Liberty* (Chicago: University of Chicago Press, pp. 14–15). It is worth remarking that Aron met Hayek when Aron joined the Reform Club in London. In Aron's memoirs, he relates that the members met every Thursday evening for dinner. Given that Aron devotes a large part of Chapter Two to Hayek, as well as the lengthy and rather positive review, it is somewhat surprising that Hayek is mentioned only twice and merely in passing (Aron 1990: 116, 133). Even Colquhoun devotes fewer than five pages to Hayek and there are two references to Hayek and von Mise, and one to Hayek and Popper (Colquhoun 1986b: 249–52; 17, 104, 381). The only scholar who seems to have accorded Hayek the respect that Aron had for him was Mahoney (Aron 1994a: 67–71).
4. Although *The Road to Serfdom* sold more copies than *The Constitution of Liberty*, both books ended up selling rather well. Writing in 2007, Bruce Caldwell noted that, since its first appearance in 1944, *The Road to Serfdom* had sold more than 350,000 copies. These were the volumes published by the University of Chicago Press. There were no reliable figures from Routledge but Caldwell assumes that these volumes would number in the thousands (Hayek 2007: 1). *The Constitution of Liberty* did not sell well in its first years, but after Hayek was awarded the Nobel Prize, interest in the book increased its sales and

certainly its popularity. Ronald Hamowy wrote in 2011 that there were 250 books and monographs in twelve different languages on it (Hayek 2011: 22).

5. Aron wrote: "The chapter that F.A. Hayek devotes to labor unions will certainly offend the majority of readers on both sides of the Atlantic" Aron (1970a: 91). The chapter is entitled "Labor Unions and Employment," and in it Hayek complained that, in over a century, labor unions moved from being limited in power, if not considered illegal, to being "uniquely privileged institutions" that are beyond the law. His basic complaint was that, originally, labor unions had been defenders of freedom but now they employ coercion (Hayek 2011: 384–90).

6. The quotation is on pages 96–7 and the reference is in footnote 29: "*Democracy in America*, Part II, Book Four, Chapter 56." It is actually Chapter 6 and the quotation is found in de Tocqueville (2000: 861–2).

# Chapter Eight

# Aron's legacy

When Raymond Aron died suddenly in October of 1983, there was an outpouring of grief and praise. Aron was highly regarded by philosophers, sociologists, political thinkers, and many others in a variety of disciplines. Newspapers and journals were filled with his obituaries and most of the authors lauded Aron for his work. Even allowing for some hyperbole, it was understood that the world had lost a great thinker. Since then, Aron's reputation has suffered to some degree; however, there have been a number of scholars who have written about him and their estimation of Aron is understandably high. Finally, there have been a few additions to the literature on Aron, and those indicate a further resurgence of interest in his thinking. Aron was one of the leading sociologists and political philosophers of the twentieth century; his legacy deserves to live on and his writings deserve to be read.

## Aron's legacy: the past

In 1986, Robert Colquhoun wrote in his two-volume biography of Raymond Aron that Aron "is an incomparable guide to anyone seeking to understand our turbulent century." Colquhoun bases his assessment on three factors: Aron lived through some of the momentous occasions of that century; he knew some of the most famous people; and he had an extraordinarily wide range of interests. Colquhoun was able to interview Aron several times and he reported that Aron was unfailingly polite and ready to answer any of his questions. Furthermore, Aron's "liberalism" allowed Colquhoun to follow his research to whatever ends it led to (Colquhoun 1986a: ix–x). One gets the sense that Colquhoun's biography was a labor of love and that he had enormous respect for Aron.

In 1992, Daniel J. Mahoney published his revised dissertation as *The Liberal Political Science of Raymond Aron*. Mahoney began his

Preface by stating that "Raymond Aron is one of the most important thinkers and participant observers of the chaotic and tumultuous twentieth century." He praised Aron for his learning and understanding, and insisted that Aron kept alive what Thomas Pangle had referred to as "a humanistic and politic liberal rationalism." Aron demonstrated that the assumptions of the left were false and unwarranted, and attacked the unrealistic hopes of the adherents to Communist ideology. Instead, he promoted the rational understanding of history and preached a politics of prudence. Like Colquhoun, Mahoney is very sympathetic to Aron's thinking, and like his predecessor, he is objective in his assessment. That is why the subtitle of his book is *A Critical Introduction*. Like Colquhoun, Mahoney believes that Aron's realistic pessimism is still relevant (Mahoney 1992: ix–x, xiv, 133). Two years after Mahoney's book appeared, he published a collection of Aron's essays. There, Mahoney writes of the renaissance of Aron's thinking in France, and while he refers to him as "the political philosopher of '1989,'" he insisted that Aron remains relevant after the events of that year. As he writes, Aron "is an intellectual antidote to any recurrence of the totalitarian temptation, and he teaches the democracies how they can be worthy of their unexpected and somewhat unearned victory" (Aron 1994a: v, ix). Mahoney wrote that in 1994, five years after the Berlin Wall came down, and it seemed as if democracy was spreading throughout Eastern Europe. The developments in Hungary, Poland, and other Eastern European countries indicate that that assumption was premature. It also indicates that Aron's warnings and his prescriptions for liberty are even more relevant now.

In 1997, Brian C. Anderson published *Raymond Aron: The Recovery of the Political*. Anderson lauded Aron for his incredible learning and praised him for his reflection. He also was amazed by how many disciplines Aron was a master of. Above all, Anderson believed that Aron was a master of the defense of political reason. He believed that Aron was the "preeminent political thinker of the post war years." This was largely due to Aron's "sensitivity to the antinomic structure of the political world" (Anderson 1997: 1–3, 187).

In "Raymond Aron's *Peace and War*, Thirty Years Later," Bryan-Paul Frost suggested that "it is doubtful whether more than a handful of students seriously studies it" and that it is "probably 'more quoted than read' today." He was correct when he made those assertions in 1996 and his statement is still correct today when he writes, "*Peace and War* remains a necessary book for anyone who wants to think seriously about the fundamental questions of international relations" (Frost 1996: 340, 361).

The year 2005 was the centennial of Aron's birth and was filled with conferences dedicated to Aron and his thought. Conferences were held in Budapest, Lisbon, and Rome as well as in Paris. The theme of the Paris conference reflected Aron's continuing relevance, as indicated by the title "Democracy in the Twenty-First Century." The same year also saw the publication of some impressive collections of Aron's writings, including *Penser la liberté, Penser la démocratie* (Frost and Mahoney 2007: 3–4).

In 2007, Frost and Mahoney published a collection of essays called *Political Reason in the Age of Ideology*. Its subtitle, *Essays in Honor of Raymond Aron*, indicates the high regard that the editors and their contributors have for Aron's legacy. Frost and Mahoney point to two outstanding features of Aron's political thinking: the ability to see things from a distance and to show the world as it is, and the capacity to offer advice on how the world should be. Although they do not refer to it, Aron, like Weber, tended to keep the issue of facts separate from the question of values (Frost and Mahoney 2007: 1–6). The editors republished Pierre Manent's 1983 essay, "Raymond Aron – Political Educator," in which he emphasizes how Aron's earlier philosophy studies helped shape his writings on strategy and war (Manent 2007: 21–4). As Aron's student and biographer, Manent may be forgiven for his rather extravagant claim that, "In some way, it is in part thanks to the Aronian renewal – Aron's interpretation of Weber as well as Aron's own personal work – that Weber owes his healthiest posterity in European sociology." As Aron had written in the 1930s, Max Weber was widely known throughout Europe and, one can add, thanks to Frank Knight and Talcott Parsons, in the United States. But Manent does not exaggerate the importance of Aron's legacy in philosophy, politics, and sociology; nor does he overestimate the role that Aron played in education (Manent 2007: 13, 17–21, 28–30).

Two years later, Reed M. Davis declared that Aron was "Recognized on both sides of the Atlantic as one of the leading social theorists produced by France" and that he combined the talents of a scholar with those of a journalist. Davis insisted that Aron was the last in a line of classical French liberalism represented by Montesquieu and de Tocqueville. Unlike most other commentators, Davis was far more critical of Aron and argued that, for all of his attempts to find a middle ground between realism and idealism, Aron was too often too idealistic. Furthermore, Davis insisted that Aron frequently imagined a middle way between the two rather than actually finding one (Davis 2009: 1–3). None the less, Davis admitted that Aron's liberalism was founded upon a respect for the law and he admired him for his self-restraint. And he praised Aron for his ability to combine scholarly analysis with journalistic clarity. Finally, Davis observed the "heroic effort" that Aron exerted in attempting to find a synthesis that would resolve the "contradictions of the human condition" (Davis 2009: 1–3, 7, 9, 25, 179).

Finally, there is the recently published *Companion to Raymond Aron*. The two editors have long been recognized as Aron scholars: Élisabeth Dutartre-Michaut has written a number of articles on him in French and has been an archivist at the Institut Raymond Aron in Paris. José Colen has published several books on Aron's philosophy and politics. In their Introduction, they maintain that Aron was "one of the great political thinkers" and that his work "ranges over the most diverse academic disciplines" (Dutartre-Michaut and Colen 2015: 1). In his Foreword, Pierre Manet repeats his earlier claims regarding Aron's erudition, and in his own chapter, Nicolas Baverez insists that "Raymond Aron is *the* greatest figure in French liberalism of the twentieth century" (Manent 2015: ix; Baverez 2015: 3, 14).

## ARON'S LEGACY: THE PRESENT

While I have some serious differences of opinion with Raymond Aron's overall philosophy, it should also be abundantly clear that I believe he was one of the most important political thinkers of the twentieth century. He may have been too harsh in his judgment regarding the student protests of 1968 and too indulgent in defending Europe; however, he was one of the best minds to investigate historical, political, and sociological issues and problems. Unlike many scholars, he insisted that both theory and action were needed to address problems; unlike some others, he believed that concepts needed to be bolstered with historical examples. Finally, he objected to the conviction that some general theory could explain all social constructions; he insisted that one could develop particular generalizations but that they needed to be revised as events warranted. Yet he also believed that there were certain human traits that could be regarded as universal. They included envy, greed, and the wish to inflict pain, but also toleration, fairness, and charity. He acknowledged that rationality could not account for every human action but also believed that human beings were ultimately rational. That is why he was convinced that if people studied an issue sufficiently, they would be more likely to develop the proper response to it. It is on the basis of these points that I can offer one view of Aron's present legacy.

Raymond Aron's *philosophy* of history may be his least successful work and the one that may appear to have the least impact on Aron's relevance today. That is partially because his writings are too philosophical and partially because they represent some of his earliest thinking. Yet they prompted him to appreciate the importance of *history*. He was one of the few scholars of the twentieth century who looked to history to understand the present while recognizing that history could only offer glimpses of what the future might be. He was eclectic in his choice of historical figures; it did not matter to him whether Thucydides wrote 2,000 years ago, that Clausewitz wrote a century before or that Weber wrote in the previous decades. What mattered to Aron was whether these thinkers (and many others) could offer ways of thinking and methods of analysis that could assist him in understanding the present.

Other scholars may disagree with my assessment of Aron's writings on Max Weber. They, like others, will insist that Aron rejected Weber's "Machtpolitik" as well as his nationalism. However, like Weber, Aron recognized the importance of power in politics, regardless of whether it was domestic or international. And, to a large extent, he understood and shared Weber's love of his country. The difference was that Aron found that he could love countries other than his native France, and somewhat surprisingly, that included Germany. But Aron followed Weber in matters of scholarship as well as in political matters; his understanding of causality in history, his employment of ideal types, and his relentless insistence on honesty are most likely derived from his reading of Weber's work. And while he did not share Weber's insistence on separating facts from values, he recognized the importance of Weber's admonishment to make clear to others, and especially to one's self, when one has moved from the field of facts into the arena of values.

Aron's book about Clausewitz was, and continues to be, one of Aron's masterpieces. Not only did Aron build upon the work of his predecessors but he offered a compelling portrait of Clausewitz as a political theorist as well as a military strategist. Aron also made a convincing case for why we should read Clausewitz and not merely cite him. Aron obviously recognized that the Napoleonic Wars would never be repeated. However, he also recognized that Clausewitz was not offering a historical account but was attempting to write a *theory* of war. I believe that it is safe to say that anyone who wishes to understand Clausewitz needs to read Aron's book. Finally, Aron himself was not providing an account of Clausewitz and his political and military ideas, but was showing how and why Clausewitz's ideas are relevant to modern warfare.

Aron's three books on war may seem to be outdated because the "bipolar" situation that he examined no longer exists. However, his studies are still accurate accounts of the nature of the atomic age and the various threats that thermonuclear weapons pose. He carefully combined historical examples with reasonable theories and prudently utilized statistics to support moral judgments. He was able to approach the monstrous issue of thermonuclear war with a clarity of purpose. He was able to spell out his conclusions with clarity and his warnings were reasonable. Aron's historical account of the changes in the nature of warfare and the development of newer weapons remains solid and informative. His judgments about the present danger and his warnings about the future are neither too pessimistic nor too optimistic, but are reflective of his careful and sober appraisal of the issues of modern warfare.

Aron's *Peace and War* has garnered mixed reactions; some readers have regarded it as a compelling book while others have found it wanting. My opinion is that it may be a mistake to evaluate the book as a whole because the four parts differ in content and tone. There is little doubt that sociologists probably prefer Part Two because it is the sociological part of *Peace and War*. Historians are equally likely to approve of Part Three because it contains the most historical examples in the book. Part One certainly has its attraction for political thinkers because of the combination of theory and examples. However, philosophers are most likely to think the most highly of Part Four because it is in that portion of the book that Aron deftly combines morality with politics. Finally, the work as a whole is rewarding because of Aron's reasonable approach to the issue of power in politics and the need to find a workable theory of international relations. In the final analysis, *Peace and War* may not be Aron's best work but it deserves its rightful place among the most thoughtful and thought-provoking books on the problems of war and peace.

The subject of ideology was a crucial one for Aron and one on which he spent considerable effort. He wrote about it often in short essays and, of course, in his *Opium of the Intellectuals*. He believed that ideology introduced two evils to political thinking. First, it made thinking too easy; adherence to any ideology often meant that the individual did not want, or feel the need, to think. Instead, the belief in the one dominant idea was sufficient. Second, it was too dangerous; adherence to an ideology frequently meant that the individual became a fanatic. No amount of evidence can counter the ideologue's single idea or theory. Accordingly, most Communists believed that it was necessary to destroy capitalist society, even when their own theory insisted that it would collapse on its own. Aron's contributions to the "end of ideology" debate are noteworthy. He was never as assured as others were that the "end of ideology" had been reached; that is why he appended the question mark. Furthermore, he thought that many of those who fought against ideology were almost driven by an "anti-ideology" ideology and that they were blinded to the seductive forces of ideology. It is Aron's careful and thorough examination of ideology that is certainly one of the most important parts of his legacy.

Where Aron's writings on ideology were warnings, his words about freedom were hopeful predictions. He had studied enough history to know what terrible things humans were capable of doing and knew enough about human nature to know why they often chose to follow irrational beliefs. Aron, then, was a pessimist. However, he was also an optimist because he believed in reasonableness and prudence, and because he was convinced that human beings could learn to be good and responsible citizens. Aron's writings on war revealed what could happen if people did not choose wisely, but his writings on liberty indicate what the future might hold if they do make wise choices. For Hayek, liberty was the absence of coercion, but for Aron, it is the freedom to choose. Hayek held an economical view of the individual but Aron had a political view of the citizen. It is Aron's ability to note the dialectics of politics and his appreciation of philosophy and history that continue to make his writings an object of study and continue his legacy into the future.

ARON'S LEGACY: THE FUTURE

It was rather easy to discuss Aron's legacy by looking at some of the writers who have written books and articles on him. Similarly, it was not very difficult to offer my own account of Aron's legacy by indicating the value that he had in each of the areas of this book. It is difficult to predict what Aron's legacy will be but it is easier to suggest what it should be.

It may be that Aron's legacy is already being re-examined. I have already referred to the 2007 Frost and Mahoney collection. In 2013, the *Journal of Classical Sociology* devoted an entire issue to Aron's thinking. The guest editor, Peter Baehr, published the second issue of volume eleven. In 2015, Palgrave published *The Companion to Raymond Aron*, and while I have noted my reservations regarding some of the contributors' interpretations in that book overall, I consider it a worthy contribution to Aron studies. Just in the spring of 2018, Routledge published *Raymond Aron and International Relations* and I expect that it will be a major contribution to one central focus in Aron's political philosophy.[1] Finally, I would hope that my own book may also help further this renaissance of interest in the thinking of Raymond Aron.

174

Raymond Aron may not have been the most highly regarded political philosopher in the world but he was one of the best, in that he was able to combine distinctly different, if not opposing, approaches to political thought. He was able to meld a great respect for history with an equally great respect for the limitations of history in the understanding of modern problems. He was also able to combine a fine appreciation of facts with a similar regard for theory, and to mix an understanding of the need for thinking with an equal realization of the requirement for action. Finally, he was able to combine two approaches to political thinking – that politics is an art as well as a science. It was Aristotle who thought that the best politics was a prudent one; Aron is a worthy successor to the Stagirite because of his belief in the necessity of prudence, moderation, and the need for responsibility in politics. Raymond Aron's philosophy of prudence and his ethics of responsibility can be regarded as his answer to the question "what would you do?" – that is, think carefully and clearly and act prudently and responsibly.

## Notes

1. Unfortunately, it was published too late for me to incorporate it (Schmitt 2018).

# Bibliography


Adair-Toteff, Christopher (2005) *Sociological Beginnings: The First Conference of the German Society for Sociology*. Liverpool: Liverpool University Press.

Adair-Toteff, Christopher (2008) "Max Weber's Pericles: The Political Demagogue." *Max Weber Studies*. Vol. 7, No. 2, pp. 147–62.

Adair-Toteff, Christopher (2019) "Shils, Mannheim, and Ideology." In *The Calling of Social Thought: Rediscovering the Thought of Edward Shils*. Edited by Christopher Adair-Toteff and Stephen Turner. Manchester: Manchester University Press.

Anderson, Brian C. (1997) *Raymond Aron: The Recovery of the Political*. Lanham, MD: Rowman & Littlefield.

Arendt, Hannah (1953) "Ideology and Terror: A Novel Form of Government." *The Review of Politics*. Vol. 15, No. 3, July, pp. 303–27.

Arendt, Hannah (1976) *The Origins of Totalitarianism*. New edition with added prefaces by Hannah Arendt. Orlando: Harvest, Harcourt.

Arendt, Hannah (1982) "Philosophie und Soziologie." In *Der Streit um die Wissenssoziologie*. Edited by Volker Meja and Nico Stehr. Frankfurt am Main: Suhrkamp. Vol. 2: *Rezeption und Kritik der Wissenssoziologie*, pp. 515–31.

Arendt, Hannah (1994a) *Essays in Understanding: 1930–1954. Formation, Exile, and Totalitarianism*. Edited with an Introduction by Jerome Kohn. New York: Schocken.

Arendt, Hannah (1994b) "Understanding and Politics (The Difficulties in Understanding)." In Arendt 1994a, pp. 307–27.

Arendt, Hannah (1994c) "On the Nature of Totalitarianism: An Essay on Understanding." In Arendt 1994a, pp. 328–60.

Aron, Raymond (1948) *Introduction à la philosophie de l'histoire: Essai sur les limites de l'objectivité historique*. Paris: Librairie Gallimard.

Aron, Raymond (1950a) *La Philosophie critique de l'histoire: Essai sur une théorie allemande de l'histoire*. Paris: Librairie Philosophique J. Vrin.

Aron, Raymond (1950b) *La Sociologie allemande contemporaine*. Paris: Presses Universitaires de France. 2nd edition.

Aron, Raymond (1953) *Die Deutsche Soziologie der Gegenwart: Eine Systematische Einführung*. Translated and revised by Iring Fetscher. Stuttgart: Alfred Kröner.

Aron, Raymond (1954) *The Century of Total War*. Boston: Beacon Press.

Aron, Raymond (1955) *L'Opium des intellectuels*. Paris: Calmann-Lévy.

Aron, Raymond (1959) *On War*. Translated by Terence Kilmartin. Garden City, NY: Anchor/Doubleday.

Aron, Raymond (1961) *Introduction to the Philosophy of History: An Essay on the Limits of Historical Objectivity*. Translated by George J. Irwin. Boston: Beacon Press.

Aron, Raymond (1965a) *The Great Debate: Theories of Nuclear Strategy*. Translated by Ernst Pawel. Garden City, NY: Anchor/Doubleday.

Aron, Raymond (1965b) "Max Weber und die Machtpolitik." In *Verhandlungen 1965*, pp. 103–21.

Aron, Raymond (1967) *Les Étapes de la pensée sociologique*. Paris: Gallimard.

Aron, Raymond (1969) *Democracy and Totalitarianism*. Translated by Valence Ionescu. New York: Frederick A. Praeger.

Aron, Raymond (1970a) *An Essay on Freedom*. Translated by Helen Weaver. New York: World Publishing Company.

Aron, Raymond (1970b) *Main Currents in Sociological Thought II: Durkeim-Pareto-Weber*. Translated by Richard Howard and Helen Weaver. New York: Anchor/Doubleday.

Aron, Raymond (1976a) *Penser la guerre, Clausewitz. I. L'Âge européen*. Paris: Gallimard.

Aron, Raymond (1976b) *Penser la guerre, Clausewitz. II. L'Âge planétaire*. Paris: Gallimard.

Aron, Raymond (1977) "On the Proper Use of Ideologies." In Ben-David and Clark 1977, pp. 1–14.

Aron, Raymond (1978a) *Politics and History: Selected Essays by Raymond Aron*. Collected, translated, and edited by Miriam Bernheim Conant. New York: Free Press.

Aron, Raymond (1978b) "Introduction." In Aron 1978a, pp. xvii–xxx.

Aron, Raymond (1978c) "The Philosophy of History." In Aron 1978a, pp. 5–19.

Aron, Raymond (1978d) "Thucydides and the Historical Narrative." In Aron 1978a, pp. 20–46.

Aron, Raymond (1978e) "Three Forms of Intelligible History." In Aron 1978a, pp. 47–61.

Aron, Raymond (1978f) "On the Historical Condition of the Sociologist." In Aron 1978a, pp. 62–82.

Aron, Raymond (1978g) "The Dawn of Universal History." In Aron 1978a, pp. 212–36.

Aron, Raymond (1978h) "History and Politics." In Aron 1978a, pp. 237–48.

Aron, Raymond (1978i) [1926/7] "L'Idéologie." In *Revue européenne des sciences sociales*. Vol. 16, No. 43, pp. 35–50.

Aron, Raymond (1980a) *Clausewitz: Den Krieg denken*. Frankfurt am Main: Propyläcn.

Aron, Raymond (1980b) *War and Industrial Society*. Translated by Mary Bottomore. Westport, CT: Greenwood Press.

Aron, Raymond (1982) "Ideology in Search of a Policy." *Foreign Affairs*. Vol. 60, No. 3, pp. 503–24.

Aron, Raymond (1983a) *Clausewitz: Philosopher of War*. Translated by Christine Booker and Norman Stone. London: Routledge & Kegan Paul.

Aron, Raymond (1983b) *Mémoires: 50 ans de réflexion politique*. Paris: Julliard.

Aron, Raymond (1985) *History, Truth, Liberty: Selected Writings of Raymond Aron*. Edited by Franciszek Draus. With a Memoir by Edward Shils. Chicago and London: University of Chicago Press.

Aron, Raymond (1990) *Memoirs: Fifty Years of Political Reflection*. Translated by George Holoch. New York: Holmes & Meier.

Aron, Raymond (1994a) *In Defense of Political Reason: Essays by Raymond Aron*. Edited by Daniel J. Mahoney. Lanham, MD: Rowman & Littlefield.

Aron, Raymond (1994b) [1954] "The Essence of Totalitarianism According to Hannah Arendt." In Aron 1994a, pp. 97–112.

Aron, Raymond (2003) *The Dawn of Universal History: Selected Essays from a Witness to the Twentieth Century*. Translated by Barbara Bray. Edited by Yair Reiner. With an Introduction by Tony Judt. New York: Basic Books.

Aron, Raymond (2009) *Peace and War: A Theory of International Relations*. With a new Introduction by Daniel J. Mahoney and Brian C. Anderson. New Brunswick, NJ: Transaction.

Aron, Raymond (2011) *The Opium of the Intellectuals*. With a new Introduction by Harvey C. Mansfield. Foreword by Daniel J. Mahoney and Brian C. Anderson. New Brunswick, NJ: Transaction.

Baehr, Peter (2010) *Hannah Arendt, Totalitarianism, and the Social Sciences*. Stanford, CA: Stanford University Press.

Baehr, Peter and Walsh, Philip, editors (2017) *The Anthem Companion to Hannah Arendt*. London: Anthem Press.

Bavarez, Nicolas (1993) *Raymond Aron: Un Moraliste au temps des idéologies*. Paris: Flammarion.

Bavarez, Nicolas (2015) " Life and Works: Raymond Aron, Philosopher and Freedom Fighter." In Colen and Dutartre-Michaut (2015), pp. 3–14.

Bell, Daniel (1966) *The End of Ideology: On the Exhaustion of Political Ideals in the Fifties*. New York: Free Press. Revised edition.

Ben-David, Joseph and Clark, Terry Nichols, editors (1977) *Culture and Its Creators: Essays in Honor of Edward Shils*. Chicago: University of Chicago Press.

Bergstraesser, Arnold (1957) "Max Webers Antrittsvorlesung in Zeitgeschichtler Perspektive." *Vierteljahrsheft für Zeitgeschichte*. Vol. 5. No. 3, July, pp. 209–19.

Breiner, Peter (2011) "Raymond Aron's Engagement with Max Weber: Recovery or Retreat?" *Journal of Classical Sociology*. Vol. 11, No. 2, pp. 99–121.

Clausewitz, Carl von (1922) *Politische Schriften und Briefe*. Edited by Dr Hans Rothfels. Munich: Drei Masken.

Clausewitz, Carl von (1973) *Vom Kriege: Hinterlassenes Werk des Generals Carl von Clausewitz*. Eighteenth edition. Complete edition in the original text with a completely revised and expanded historical–critical evaluation by Dr Werner Halweg. Bonn: Ferdinand Dümmlers.

Colen, José and Dutartre-Michaut, Élisabeth, editors (2015) *The Companion to Raymond Aron*. New York: Palgrave-Macmillan.

Colquhoun, Robert (1986a) *Raymond Aron: The Philosopher in History. 1905–1955*. London: Sage.

Colquhoun, Robert (1986b) *Raymond Aron: The Sociologist in Society. 1955–1983*. London: Sage.

Davis, Reed M. (2009) *A Politics of Understanding: The International Thought of Raymond Aron*. Baton Rouge: Louisiana State University Press.

De Tocqueville, Alexis (2000) *Democracy in America: The Complete and Unabridged Volumes I and II*. Translated by Henry Reeve. New York: Bantam Classics.

Delbrück, Hans (1920) *Ludendorff Tirpitz Falkenhayn*. Berlin: Karl Curtius.

Delbrück, Hans (1922) *Ludendorffs Selbstporträt: Mit einer Widerlegung der Foerster'schen Gegenschrift*. Berlin: Verlag für Politik und Wirtschaft.

Frost, Bryan-Paul (1996) "Raymond Aron's *Peace and War*, Thirty Years Later." *International Journal*. Vol. LI, Spring, pp. 339–61.

Frost, Bryan-Paul and Mahoney, Daniel J., editors (2007) *Political Reason in the Age of Ideology: Essays in Honor of Raymond Aron*. New Brunswick, NJ: Transaction.

Hahlweg, Werner (1969) *Clausewitz: Soldat–Politiker–Denker*. Göttingen: Musterschmidt.

Hayek, F. A. (2007) *The Road to Serfdom: Text and Documents. The Definitive Edition*. Edited by Bruce Caldwell. Chicago: University of Chicago Press.

Hayek, F. A. (2011) *The Constitution of Liberty: The Definitive Edition*. Edited by Ronald Hamowy. Chicago: University of Chicago Press.

Herberg-Rothe, Andreas (2001) *Das Rätsel Clausewitz: Politische Theorie des Krieges im Widerstreit*. Munich: Wilhelm Fink.

Käsler, Dirk (1984) *Die frühe deutsche Soziologie 1909–1934 und ihre Entstehungs-Milieus: Eine wissenschaftssoziologische Untersuchung*. Opladen: Westdeutscher Verlag.

Lassmann, Peter (2000) "The Rule of Man over Man: Power, Politics, and Legitimation." In Turner 2000, pp. 83–98.

Lepsius, M. Rainer (1981) "Die Soziologie der Zwischenkriegszeit: Entwicklungstendenzen und Beurteilungskriterien." In *Soziologie in Deutschland und Österreich 1918–1945: Materialen zur Entwicklung und Wirkundsgeschichte*. Opladen: Westdeutscher Verlag, pp. 7–23.

Lipset, Seymour Martin (1977) "The End of Ideology and the Ideology of Intellectuals." In Ben-David and Clark 1977, pp. 15–42.

Ludendorff, General (Erich) (1935) *Der totale Krieg*. Munich: Ludendorffs Verlag.

Mahoney, Daniel J. (1992) *The Liberal Political Science of Raymond Aron: A Critical Introduction*. Lanham, MD: Rowman & Littlefield.

Manent, Pierre (2007) "Raymond Aron – Political Educator." In Frost and Mahoney (2007), pp. 11–30.

Manet, Pierre (2015) "Preface." In Colen and Dutartre-Michaut (2015), pp. ix-x.

Mommsen, Wolfgang J. (1959) *Max Weber und die deutsche Politik: 1890–1920*. Tübingen: J. C. B. Mohr (Paul Siebeck).

Mommsen, Wolfgang J. (1974) *Max Weber und die deutsche Politik: 1890–1920*. Tübingen: J. C. B. Mohr (Paul Siebeck). Second revised and enlarged edition.

Nelson, Scott and Colen, José (2015) "Statesmanship and Ethics: Aron, Max Weber, and Politics as Vocation." In Colen and Dutartre-Michaut 2015, pp. 205–16.

Oppermann, Matthias (2008) *Raymond Aron und Deutschland: Die Verteidigung der Freiheit und das Problem des Totalitarianismus*. Ostfildern: Jan Thorbecke.

Rosinski, Herbert (1935) "Die Entwicklung von Clausewitz' Werke *Vom Kriege*, im Lichte seine 'Vorreden' und 'Nachrichten.'" *Historische Zeitschrift*. No. 151.

Rothfels, Hans (1920) *Carl von Clausewitz: Politik und Krieg. Eine ideengeschichtliche Studie*. Berlin: Ferdinand Dümmler.

Rothfels, Hans (1980) "Clausewitz." In *Clausewitz in Perspektive. Materialen zu Carl von Clausewitz: Vom Kriege*. Edited and with an Introduction by Günter Dill. Frankfurt am Main: Ullstein, pp. 261–90.

Schering, Walther Malmsten (1935) *Die Kriegsphilosophie von Clausewitz: Eine Untersuchung über ihren systematischen Aufbau*. Hamburg: Hanseatische Verlagsanstalt.

Schering, Walther Malmsten, editor (1942) *Geist und Tat: Das Vermächtnis des Soldaten und Denkers. In Auswahl aus seinen Werken, Briefen und unveröffentlichen Schriften*. Stuttgart: Alfred Kröner.

Schlieffen, Count Alfred von (1933) *Gneisenau*. Leipzig: im Insel.

Schmitt, Olivier, editor (2018) *Raymond Aron and International Relations*. London: Routledge.

Schwartz, K. (1878) *Leben des Generals Carl von Clausewitz und der Frau Marie von Clausewitz geboren Gräfin von Brühl: Briefen, Aufsätzen, Tagebüchern und anderen Schriftstücken*. Berlin: Ferdinand Dümmler (Harrwitz & Goffmann).

Shils, Edward (1968) [1955] "The End of Ideology?" In Waxman 1968, pp. 49–63.

Shils, Edward (1972a) *The Intellectuals and the Powers and Other Essays*. Chicago: University of Chicago Press.

Shils, Edward (1972b) "Ideology." In Shils 1972a, pp. 23–41.

Shils, Edward (1972c) "Ideology and Civility." In Shils 1972a, pp. 42–70.

Shils, Edward (1985) "Raymond Aron: A Memoir." In Aron 1985, pp. 1–19.

Shils, Edward (1997) *Portraits: A Gallery of Intellectuals*. Edited and with an Introduction by Joseph Epstein. Chicago: University of Chicago Press.

Shils, Edward (2006) *A Fragment of a Sociological Autobiography: The History of My Pursuit of a Few Ideas*. Edited by Steven Grosby. New Brunswick, NJ: Transaction.

Simon-Nahum, Perrine (2015) "Raymond Aron and the Notion of History: Taking Part in History." In Colen and Dutartre-Michaut 2015, pp. 105–18.

Stammer, Otto (1965) "Ansprache zur Eröffnung des 15. Deutschen Soziologentages." In *Verhandlungen* 1965, pp. 1–13.

Stark, Joachim (1986) *Das unvollendete Abenteuer: Geschichte, Gesellschaft und Politik im Werk Raymond Arons*. Würzburg: Könighausen & Neumann.

Treitschke, Heinrich von (1899) *Politik: Vorlesungen gehalten an der Universität zu Berlin*. Edited by Max Cornicelius. Leipzig: G. Hirzel. Second revised edition.

Turner, Charles (2017) "Arendt and Totalitarianism." In Baehr and Walsh 2017, pp. 25–46.

Turner, Stephen P., editor (2000) *The Cambridge Companion to Weber*. Cambridge: Cambridge University Press.

Turner, Stephen P. and Factor, Regis A. (1981) "Objective Possibility and Adequate Causation in Weber's Methodological Writings." *Sociological Review*. Vol. 29, No. 1, pp. 5–28.

Vad, Erich (1984) *Carl von Clausewitz: Seine Bedeutung Heute*. Herford: E. S. Mitler.

*Verhandlungen* (1923) *Verhandlungen des Dritten Deutschen Soziologentages*. Tübingen: J. C. B. Mohr (Paul Siebeck).

*Verhandlungen* (1965) *Verhandlungen des Fünfzehter Deutschen Soziologentages Tages*. Tübingen: J. C. B. Mohr (Paul Siebeck).

Waxman, Chaim I., editor (1968) *The End of Ideology Debate*. New York: Simon & Schuster.

Weber, Max (2009) *Allgemeine Staatslehre und Politik (Staatssoziologie)*. Edited by Gangolf Hübinger in collaboration with Andreas Terwey. Tübingen: J. C. B. Mohr (Paul Siebeck). *Max Weber Gesamtausgabe*. III/7.

Weber, Max (1921a) "Der Nationalstaat und die Volkswirtschaftspolitik." In Weber 1921b, pp. 7–30.

Weber, Max (1921b) *Gesammelte Politische Schriften*. Munich: Drei Masken.

Weber, Max (1992) *Wissenschaft als Beruf 1917/1919* and *Politik als Beruf 1919*. Edited by Wolfgang J. Mommsen and Wolfgang Schluchter in collaboration with Birgitt Morgenbrod. Tübingen: J. C. B. Mohr (Paul Siebeck). *Max Weber Gesamtausgabe*. Vol. I/17.

Weber, Max (1993a) "Der Nationalstaat und die Volkswirtschaftspolitik: Akademische Antrittsrede." In Weber 1993b, pp. 543–74.

Weber, Max (1993b) *Landarbeiterfrage, Nationalstaat und Volkswirtschaftspolitik: Schriften und Reden 1892–1899*. Tübingen: J. C. B. Mohr (Paul Siebeck). *Max Weber Gesamtausgabe*. Vol. I/4.

Weber, Max (2001) *Wirtschaft und Gesellschaft*. Part vol. 1: *Gemeinschaften*. Edited by Wolfgang J. Mommsen in collaboration with Michael Meyer. Tübingen: J. C. B. Mohr (Paul Siebeck). *Max Weber Gesamtausgabe*. Vol. I/22-1.

Weber, Max (2012) *Collected Methodological Writings*. Edited by Hans Henrik Bruun and Sam Whimster. Translated by Hans Henrik Bruun. London: Routledge.

Young-Bruehl, Elisabeth (1982) *Hannah Arendt: For Love of the World*. New Haven, CT: Princeton University Press.

# *Index*



182

Nazis, 12–13, 76, 135
necessity, 30, 70, 88, 115, 117, 129, 153, 165, 175
Neo-Kantian, 10, 19–20, 24, 33, 40, 50, 138,
New York, 135, 176–9, 181
Nietzsche, Friedrich, 17–18, 24–5, 33, 44, 48, 53
notion, 2, 10, 15, 17–19, 21–2, 25, 28, 35–7, 40–1, 43, 56, 66–8, 70, 72–3, 76–7, 81, 84, 89, 97, 100, 102, 107–9, 115–18, 121–2, 126, 129, 147, 150, 152–3, 157–9, 161, 164, 180
numbers, 22, 55, 65, 69, 87, 108, 113

objectivity, 19–20, 25, 41, 145, 177
Oppermann, Matthias, 46, 180
optimists, 28, 35, 91, 95
organization, 21, 88, 110, 133, 158
outlook, 2, 13, 110

Pareto, Vilfredo, 86, 126, 177
Paris, 3, 7, 28, 134–5, 170–1, 176–8
Parsons, Talcott, 31, 45, 125, 170
passion, 13, 56, 58, 62, 71, 82, 136
peace, v, 3, 9, 11–12, 26, 29, 43, 49, 63, 65, 80–1, 88–9, 92–3, 95, 98, 100–3, 105, 107–11, 113, 115–23, 161, 169, 173, 178–9
Peloponnesian War, 27–9, 81, 83–5, 92, 102–3, 105
people, 2, 4–5, 9, 12–13, 23, 26, 45–6, 48, 50, 55, 57, 60, 63, 75, 84, 86–7, 90–2, 95–6, 106–7, 110, 112–13, 116–17, 119–21, 128–9, 131, 133, 136, 140, 147, 149, 152–3, 155–62, 164–6, 168, 171, 174
Pericles, 83, 98, 176
Persians, 21, 102
pessimists, 28, 35, 91, 95, 135
philosopher, 1, 3–4, 10, 16, 18, 26, 54, 62, 102, 128–9, 139, 143, 175
philosophers, 10, 73, 79, 107, 168–9, 173
philosophy, iii, 2–4, 9–13, 15–19, 23–6, 30–2, 34, 36–41, 46, 62, 73, 76–7, 98, 101, 124, 126–7, 134, 137–8, 148, 157, 160–1, 170–1, 174–5, 177–80
philosophy of history, 3–4, 9–10, 15–16, 18–19, 23–6, 30–1, 36, 126–7, 171, 177
Poland, 49, 87, 112, 137, 169
policy, 2, 29, 84, 87, 96, 101, 104, 106, 113, 117, 136–7, 147–8, 166, 177
politics, 2–4, 9–13, 15–16, 24, 26, 29–30, 32–6, 38–44, 46–8, 51, 53, 54–6, 58–9, 62–5, 74, 81, 84–5, 90, 93, 96, 101, 104, 110, 115–17, 119–20, 122, 127, 130, 137, 144, 147–8, 150, 165–6, 169–79
population, 22, 54, 66, 85, 87, 108, 113, 122, 137, 162–3,
power, 4, 12, 23, 27, 29, 32, 42–4, 46, 48–55, 57, 64, 67, 72, 93, 96–7, 102–5, 108, 110–11, 116–21, 123, 127, 134, 137–8, 146, 154–9, 162–7, 172–3, 179
principles, 23, 38, 71–2, 107, 114–15, 157–8
probability, 22, 30, 66, 70, 84, 94, 97, 126, 150
problem, 1, 17–18, 24–5, 73, 84, 89, 93, 96, 105, 107, 125–8, 132, 134, 136, 141, 151, 154–5, 162–4, 173, 180

process, 13, 18, 20–1, 24–5, 27, 65, 67, 69, 75, 92, 141, 154
production, 88, 91–2, 110, 128, 148, 153, 158, 165
progressive, 17, 26, 34, 127, 131, 159, 161
proletariat, 127–8, 153–4
propaganda, 5, 51, 87
prosecution, 68, 141
prudence, 1, 10, 13, 84, 104, 115–17, 122, 135, 169, 174–5
prudent, 12–13, 104, 133, 175

question, 5, 9–13, 18–20, 22, 25, 30–1, 36–7, 43–4, 46, 48, 50, 63, 67, 69, 71–3, 77, 86, 98, 106–7, 113–15, 119–20, 122, 126, 128, 131–2, 134–8, 141–2, 144–5, 148, 153, 155, 159–60, 170, 174–5

realism, 1, 10–12, 34, 49, 59, 62, 104, 115, 117, 148, 170
realistic, 2, 11, 32, 52, 81, 95, 103–4, 118, 120, 122, 130, 134, 136–7, 166, 169
reality, 10, 24–5, 33–4, 36, 40, 44, 47, 51, 64–5, 69–71, 73, 87, 115, 120–1, 128, 130, 136, 138–9, 151, 158, 165
reason, 7, 13, 17, 23, 29, 32, 35, 47, 65, 68, 95, 98, 102, 127–8, 131, 152, 169, 178–9
reasonable, 13, 19, 29, 90, 92, 95, 103–4, 118–19, 173
reasons, 2, 28, 32–3, 38, 46, 58, 68, 74, 81, 85, 87, 90, 119, 134, 136, 138, 144
regime, 6, 108, 110, 134, 139–42, 148, 150, 154
relativism, 25, 34–5, 129, 138
resources, 89, 108, 148, 159
respect, 2, 7, 12–13, 37, 43–4, 55, 69, 84, 117, 130, 138, 144, 154, 159, 163–4, 166, 168, 170, 175
responsibility, 2–3, 10–11, 13, 15, 22, 34–9, 42–4, 48, 50–2, 54–5, 57, 59, 67, 74–5, 82, 98, 101, 103, 108, 115, 118, 122, 133, 166, 175
results, 1, 23, 51, 80, 101, 104, 113, 139, 151, 159, 163
revolution, 42, 51, 62, 70, 85–6, 127–8, 132, 134, 141, 150, 153–4
Rickert, Heinrich, 10, 17–20, 23, 40–1
Rosinski, Herbert, 59–60, 180
Rothfels, Hans, 77, 79, 178, 180
rule, 30–1, 93, 103, 114–15, 120, 122, 147, 153, 158, 161, 163, 179
rules, 21, 51, 71, 108, 140, 147, 163
Russia, 27, 31, 49, 71, 93, 102–4, 106, 154
Russian Revolution, 85–6

salvation, 43, 128, 133, 151
Sartre, Jean-Paul, 4, 7–8
Scharnhorst, Gerhard von, 79–80
Schering, Walther Malmsten, 63, 70, 74–5, 78–9, 180
Schlieffen, Alfred von, 76, 80, 98, 180
Schmitt, Carl , 53, 58–9, 74, 76–7, 79
Schmitt, Oliver, 175, 180
science, 10, 18, 20–1, 24, 40–1, 135, 144, 177–8

EU Authorised Representative:

Easy Access System Europe Mustamäe tee 50, 10621 Tallinn, Estonia

gpsr.requests@easproject.com

Printed and bound by CPI Group (UK) Ltd, Croydon, CR0 4YY

19/05/2026

02113403-0003